Futures Markets
200 Questions & Answers

W0010551

Futures Markets
200 Questions & Answers

by
Sunil K. Parameswaran
CEO, Tarheel Consultancy Services
Bangalore, India
and
Shantaram P. Hegde
Professor of Finance
University of Connecticut

John Wiley & Sons (Asia) Pte Ltd

Copyright @ 2007 by John Wiley & Sons (Asia) Pte. Ltd.
Published in 2007 by John Wiley & Sons (Asia) Pte. Ltd.
2 Clementi Loop, #02-01, Singapore 129809

This publication is designed to provide accurate and authoritative information in regard to the subject matter covered. It is sold with the understanding that the publisher is not engaged in rendering professional services. If professional advice or other expert assistance is required, the services of a competent professional person should be sought.

Other Wiley Editorial Offices

John Wiley & Sons, 111 River Street, Hoboken, NJ 07030, USA
John Wiley & Sons, The Atrium Southern Gate, Chichester P019 8SQ, England
John Wiley & Sons (Canada) Ltd., 22 Worcester Road, Rexdale, Ontario M9W 1L1, Canada
John Wiley & Sons Australia Ltd., 33 Park Road (PO Box 1226), Milton, Queensland 4064, Australia Wiley-VCH, Pappelallee 3, 69469 Weinheim, Germany

Library of Congress Cataloging-in-Publication Data

ISBN   978-0-470-82288-3

Typeset in 10/12 points, Sabon by C&M Digitals (P) Ltd.
Printed in Singapore by Markono Print Media Pte. Ltd.
10   9   8   7   6   5   4   3   2   1

To my parents
Savitri Parameswaran
and
(Late) A.S. Parameswaran

S.K.P.

To my family
Lalitha, Aneil and Arun

S.P.H.

CONTENTS

ACKNOWLEDGMENTS

We wish to express our sincere gratitude to Nick Wallwork and Patricia Lee of John Wiley & Sons (Asia) Pte. Ltd., Singapore for their support and encouragement for this project from the outset. We are also grateful to them for making arrangements to have this manuscript typeset in *LATEX*.

Thanks are due to R. Chandrasekhar and Roystan LaPorte of McGraw-Hill, New Delhi, for assigning the global rights to this book, which facilitated the production of this international edition. This book was originally published as an Indian edition by McGraw-Hill, titled *Futures Markets Made Easy With 250 Questions and Answers*.

The first author wishes to express his gratitude to Prof. Banikanta Mishra and Prof. Jayesh Kumar of Xavier Institute of Management, Bhubaneshwar, India, for providing detailed feedback. He also wishes to thank his former students Ms. Aarti Desikan and Ms. Swagata Basu for going through the manuscript and offering valuable suggestions for improving the expositional clarity.

Finally, we wish to thank our families for all their help and moral support.

Sunil K. Parameswaran
Shantaram P. Hegde

PREFACE

Over a period of time, as teachers of courses in financial derivatives at business schools in India, Australia, and the U.S., we have come to realize that there exists a large group of readers who wish to study the derivatives market and develop a feel and flavor for the subject, without having to navigate through an excessively technical presentation. Such readers seem to be of the opinion that the level of mathematical proficiency that is required on their part in order to appreciate a standard textbook in the area is an impediment from the standpoint of facilitating their study of the subject.

While we continue to be of the opinion that finance students at the Masters level ought to have the necessary mathematical proficiency to appreciate the intricacies of the subject, we are conscious of the need to facilitate the study of the subject by interested readers who may not have the required quantitative skillset. Consequently, this book is designed to cater to a wider audience—students at the Bachelors and Masters levels, and lay readers—who are interested in a logical, nontechnical exposition of the concepts. Financial market professionals too should find this book to be a handy reference while keeping abreast of the developments in the field.

Many of the questions that we have answered in this book were raised by our students. In other cases, we have attempted to simulate the mind of an inquisitive student, and provide the necessary answers.

Derivatives, on financial products as well as on commodities, are attracting attention at a feverish pace all over the world. We hope that this book will provide a strong conceptual framework for people wishing to get acquainted with this fascinating field.

Sunil K. Parameswaran
Shantaram P. Hegde

Chapter 1

The Fundamentals

QUESTION 1

What are derivative securities and why are they termed as such?

Derivative securities, more appropriately termed as derivative contracts, are assets which confer upon their owners certain rights or obligations as the case may be. These contracts owe their existence to the presence of markets for an underlying asset or a portfolio of assets, on which such agreements are written. In other words, these assets are derived from the underlying asset.

The three major categories of derivative securities are:

1. *Forward* and *futures* contracts.
2. *Swaps.*
3. *Options* contracts.

QUESTION 2

What are forward contracts and futures contracts, and how do they differ from typical cash or spot transactions?

In a cash or a spot transaction, as soon as a deal is struck between the buyer and the seller, the buyer has to hand over the payment for the asset to the seller, who in turn has to transfer the rights to the asset to the buyer. However, in the case of a forward or a futures contract the actual transaction does not take place when an agreement is reached between a buyer and a seller. In such cases, at the time of negotiating the deal the two parties merely agree on the terms on which they will transact at a future point in time, including the price to be paid per unit of the underlying asset. Thus, the actual transaction per se occurs only at a future date that is decided at the outset. Consequently, unlike in the case of a cash transaction, no money changes hands when two parties enter into a forward or a futures contract. But both of them have an obligation to go ahead with the transaction on the scheduled date. Accordingly, these instruments are known as *commitment* contracts.

Numerical illustration

Mitoken Solutions has entered into a forward contract with Wachovia Bank to buy £100,000 after 90 days at an exchange rate of $1.75 per pound. Ninety days from today, the company will be required to pay $175,000 to the bank and accept the pounds in lieu. The bank, as per the contract, will have to accept the equivalent amount in U.S. dollars, and deliver the British pounds.

QUESTION 3

What are the concepts of long and short positions in forward and futures markets?

In the case of both forward and futures contracts, there obviously has to be a buyer and a seller. The person who agrees to buy the underlying asset in such contracts is known as the *long* and he is said to assume a *long position*. On the other hand, the counterparty who agrees to sell the underlying asset as per the contract is known as the *short* and she is said to assume a *short position*. Thus the long agrees to take delivery and pay for the underlying asset on a future date, while the short agrees to make delivery on that date.

QUESTION 4

What are options contracts, and how do they differ from forward and futures contracts?

An options contract refers to the right to buy or sell the underlying asset on or before an agreed future date. In the case of both forward and futures contracts, both the long and the short have an *obligation*. That is, the long is obliged to take delivery and pay for the underlying asset on the date that is agreed upon at the outset, while the short is obliged to make delivery of the asset on that date and accept cash in lieu. On the other hand, the buyer of an options contract (who incidentally is also known as the long) has the *right* to go ahead with the transaction, subsequent to entering into an agreement with the seller of the option who is also known as the short. Option buyers are also referred to as option *holders*, while option sellers are referred to as option *writers*.

The difference between a right and an obligation is that a right need be exercised only if it is in the interest of its holder, and if he deems it appropriate. Consequently, the long in the case of an options contract is under no compulsion to go through with the transaction once he enters into a contract. However, it must be remembered that the short, or the writer, in the case of an options contract always has an obligation. That is, were the long to decide to exercise his right as per the agreement, the short would have no choice but to carry out his part of the deal. Therefore, options contracts are called *contingent* contracts, because the writer's liability is contingent upon the exercise of the right by the buyer of the option.

QUESTION 5

What are call and put options, and how do they differ from each other?

When a person is given a right to transact in the underlying asset, the right can obviously take on one of two forms. That is, he may either have the right to buy the underlying asset, or else he may have the right to sell the underlying asset.

An options contract that gives the long the right to acquire the underlying asset is known as a *call* option. In such cases, if and when the long exercises his right, the short is under an obligation to deliver the asset.

On the other hand, an options contract that gives the long the right to sell the underlying asset is known as a *put* option. If and when the put holder decides to exercise her option, the put writer is obliged to take delivery of the asset, and make payment.

The difference between forward and futures contracts and the two types of options contracts can be illustrated with the help of a simple table (Table 1.1).

Table 1.1 Comparison of futures and forwards, and options

Instrument	Nature of commitment of the long	Nature of commitment of the short
Forward/futures contract	Obligation to acquire the underlying asset	Obligation to sell the underlying asset
Call options	Right to acquire the underlying asset	Contingent obligation to deliver the underlying asset
Put options	Right to sell the underlying asset	Contingent obligation to accept delivery of the underlying asset

QUESTION 6

What are European and American options, and how do they differ from each other?

As discussed above, a holder of an option acquires the right to transact in the underlying asset. If the option were to be European in nature, then the right can be exercised only on a fixed date in the future, which is known as the *expiration date* of the option. Quite obviously, if an option is not exercised on that day, then the contract itself will expire.

In the case of an American option, however, the option holder has the right to transact at any point in time, between the time of acquisition of the right and the expiration date of the contract. The expiration date is the *only* point in time at which a European option can be exercised, and the *last* point in time at which an American option can be exercised.

The terms American and European have nothing to do with geographical locations. Most options contracts that are traded on organized options exchanges, like the Chicago Board Options Exchange (CBOE) in the United States, are American in nature. However, while introducing the concept of options, textbooks tend to focus more on European options. This is because, since such options can be exercised only at a single point in time, one needs to consider possible cash flows only at that instant, which makes the valuation of such instruments relatively simple compared to American options.

QUESTION 7

We keep hearing about option prices and exercise prices in the context of options trading. Do they mean the same thing?

No, the two terms differ in their meaning. The term *option price* or *option premium* refers to the amount paid by the buyer of an option to the writer of the option, for permitting him to acquire the right to transact on a future date.

The term *exercise price*, also known as the *strike price*, represents the amount payable by the option holder per unit of the underlying asset, in the case of call options, if he were to choose to exercise his option on a subsequent date. Equivalently, it is the amount receivable by the option holder per unit of the underlying asset, were she to exercise a put option.

As can be seen, the option premium is a *sunk cost*. Even if the transaction were not to take place subsequently, the premium cannot be recovered. The exercise price, however, enters the picture only if the option holder chooses to go ahead with the transaction. Since he has a right, he may or may not wish to transact, which means that the exercise price may or may not be paid/received subsequently.

Options are essentially insurance contracts. An owner of an asset can protect herself from a price decline by buying a put option. Similarly, a firm that plans to buy an asset in the future can insure itself against a price rise by buying a call option. Consequently, option premiums are comparable to insurance premiums. Option buyers buy protection against a financial loss, while option writers sell insurance.

Numerical illustration

Kevin Smith has taken a long position in call options on IBM, with an exercise price of $75, and three months to maturity. Assume that the options have been written by Kathy Miller, who consequently has a short position.

If the spot price at the time of expiration of the contract were to be greater than $75 per share, it would make sense for Kevin to exercise the option and buy the shares at $75 each. Otherwise, he could simply forget the option, and buy the shares in the spot market at a price which, by assumption, is lower than the exercise price. He is under no compulsion to exercise the option, for it confers a right on the holder, and does not impose an obligation. On the other hand, if Kevin were to decide to exercise his right, Kathy would have no option but to deliver the shares at a price of $75 per share. Thus, options contracts always impose a performance obligation on the writer of the option, in the event of the option holder choosing to exercise his right.

QUESTION 8

Does the person who goes long in a futures contract have to pay an amount to the investor who goes short, at the outset? Why or why not?

In the case of an options contract the buyer is required to pay an option premium to the writer. This is because the buyer is acquiring a right, whereas the writer is taking on an obligation to perform if the buyer were to exercise his right. Rights, it must be understood, are never cost-less in financial markets. In other words, one has to pay to acquire them. Consequently, option holders have to pay option writers for acquiring the right to transact at a fixed price at a future date.

Futures and forward contracts are clearly different, for they impose an equivalent obligation on both the long and the short. As we will see subsequently, the futures price, which is the price at which the long will acquire the asset on a future date, will be set in such a way that the value of the futures contract at inception is zero, from the standpoint of both the long and the short. In other words, the two equivalent and opposite obligations ensure that neither party has to pay the other at the outset.

QUESTION 9

What are swaps?

A swap is a contractual agreement between two parties to exchange cash flows calculated on the basis of pre-specified criteria at predefined points in time.

In a simple interest rate swap, the cash flows being exchanged represent interest payments on a specified principal amount, which are computed using two different yardsticks. For instance, one interest payment may be computed using a fixed rate of interest, while the other may be based on a variable benchmark such as the London Inter Bank Offer Rate (LIBOR).

QUESTION 10

What is LIBOR and how is it computed?

LIBOR is an acronym for the London Inter Bank Offer Rate, which is the rate at which a bank in London is willing to lend to another bank. It is a common benchmark for floating or variable rate loans in international markets.

The most widely used measure of LIBOR is the value computed by the British Bankers' Association (BBA). The BBA computes the LIBOR for the 10 currencies shown in Table 1.2.

Table 1.2 Currencies for which BBA LIBOR is reported

Currency name	Symbol
Pound Sterling	GBP
US Dollar	USD
Japanese Yen	JPY
Swiss Franc	CHF
Canadian Dollar	CAD
Australian Dollar	AUD
Euro	EUR
Danish Krona	DKK
Swedish Krona	SEK
New Zealand Dollar	NZD

The LIBOR is compiled in conjunction with Reuters and is released shortly after 11 a.m. London time every day. The BBA obtains quotes from a panel consisting of a minimum of eight banks for each currency. While calculating the LIBOR, to eliminate possible outliers the quotes in the top quartile and the bottom quartile are disregarded and the remaining rates are averaged.

QUESTION 11

Do all swaps have to be on a fixed rate–floating rate basis?

In the case of simple interest rate swaps where both the cash flows are denominated in terms of the same currency, it would obviously make no sense to have a fixed rate–fixed rate swap. However, we can have floating rate–floating rate swaps, where each of the rates is based on a different benchmark. For instance, one leg of the swap could be based on LIBOR, while the other could be based on the U.S. T-bill rate. Such swaps are called *basis swaps*.

However, there do exist swaps where the two cash flows are denominated in two different currencies. These are called *currency swaps*. In such cases, in addition to fixed–floating and floating–floating arrangements, we could also have a fixed–fixed deal.

QUESTION 12

We keep hearing the term "notional principal," in the case of swap transactions. What does it mean?

In the case of a pure interest rate swap there is obviously no need to exchange the principal amount since both interest streams are computed in the same currency. However, we need to specify a principal amount at the outset, to facilitate the computation of interest. Hence, the underlying principal, which is never exchanged, is called a notional principal.

However, in the case of a currency swap, there are two different currencies that are involved. Consequently, in these cases, the principal amounts are actually exchanged at the beginning as well as at the end of the swap.

QUESTION 13

We have been referring to forward contracts and futures contracts, as if they are essentially the same type of contracts. Is there any fundamental difference between them?

Forward contracts and futures contracts are similar in the sense that both require the long to acquire and pay for the asset on a future date, and the short to deliver the asset on that date. Both types of contracts thus impose an obligation on the long as well as the short.

However, there is one major difference between the two types of contracts. Futures contracts are *standardized*, whereas forward contracts are *customized*.

What do we mean by the terms "standardization" and "customization?"

In any contract of this nature, certain terms and conditions need to be clearly defined. The major terms which should be made explicit are the following:

1. How many units of the underlying asset is the long required to acquire, or put differently, how many units of the asset does the short have to deliver?
2. What is the acceptable grade, or in certain cases, what are the acceptable grades of the underlying asset that is/are allowable for delivery?
3. Where should delivery be made? Can delivery be made only at a particular location, or do one or both parties have a choice of locations?
4. When can delivery be made? Is it possible only on a particular day, or is there a specified period during which it can occur?

In a customized contract, the above terms and conditions have to be negotiated between the buyer and the seller of the contract. Consequently, the two parties are free to incorporate any features which they can mutually agree upon. In a standardized contract, there is a third party which will specify the allowable terms and conditions. The long and the short have the freedom to design a contract within the boundaries specified by such a party. However, they cannot incorporate features other than those that are specifically allowed. The third party in the case of futures contracts is the *futures exchange*. A futures exchange is essentially similar to a stock exchange, and is an arena where trading in futures contracts takes place.

We will illustrate the difference between customization and standardization with the help of an example.

Consider the wheat futures contract that is listed for trading on the Kansas City Board of Trade. According to the terms specified by the exchange, each futures contract requires the delivery of 5,000 bushels of wheat. The allowable grades are No. 1, No. 2, and No. 3. The allowable locations for delivery are Kansas City and Hutchinson. The specifications state that delivery can be made at any time during the expiration month.

Now take the case of Jacob Paret, a wholesale dealer who wants to acquire 5,000 bushels of No. 1 wheat in Kansas City during the last week of the month. Assume that there is another party, Victor Kolb, a farmer who is interested in delivering 5,000 bushels of No. 1 wheat in Kansas City during the last week of the month. In this case, the futures contracts that are listed on the exchange are obviously suitable for both the parties. Consequently, if they were to meet on the floor of the exchange at the same time, a trade could be executed for one futures contract, at a price of say $3.60 per bushel. Notice that the price that is agreed upon for the underlying asset is one feature that is not specified by the exchange. This has to be negotiated between the two parties who are entering into the contract, and is a function of demand and supply conditions.

Let us now consider a slightly different scenario. Assume that Jacob wants to acquire 4,750 bushels of No. 1 quality wheat in Topeka during the last week of the month, and that Victor is looking to sell the same quantity of wheat in Topeka during that period. The terms of the contract that are being sought by the two parties are not within the framework that has been specified by the futures exchange in Kansas City. Consequently, neither party can enter into a futures contract to fulfill its objectives. However, nothing prevents the two men from getting together to negotiate an agreement which incorporates the features that they desire. Such an agreement would be a customized agreement, that is tailor made to their needs. This kind of agreement is called a forward contract.

Thus futures contracts are exchange-traded products just like common stocks and bonds, while forward contracts are private contracts.

One of the key issues in the case of futures contracts that permit delivery of more than one specified grade, and/or at multiple locations, is who gets to decide as to where, and what to deliver. Traditionally, the right to choose the location and the grade has always been given to the short.

Also, the right to initiate the process of delivery has traditionally been given to the short. A person with a long position, therefore, cannot demand delivery. What this also means is that, in practice, investors with a long position who have no desire to take delivery will exit the market prior to the commencement of the delivery period, by taking an opposite or offsetting position. Once the delivery period commences, they can always be called upon to take delivery, without having the right to refuse.

QUESTION 14

What is a clearinghouse and how does it function?

A clearinghouse is an entity that is associated with a futures exchange. It may be a wing of the exchange or else it may be a separate corporation. The clearinghouse essentially guarantees both the long as well as the short that they need not worry about the possibility of the other party defaulting. It does so by positioning itself as the effective counterparty for each of the two original parties to the trade, once a futures deal is struck. That is, the clearinghouse becomes the effective buyer for every seller, and the effective seller for every buyer. Thus, each party to a transaction needs to worry only about the financial strength and integrity of the clearinghouse, and not of the other party with whom it has traded. It must be remembered that neither the long nor the short trades with the clearinghouse. The clearinghouse enters the picture only after an agreement is reached between the two parties.

QUESTION 15

Why is there a need for a clearinghouse?

A futures contract imposes an obligation on both the parties. On the expiration date of the contract, depending on the movement of prices in the interim, it will be in the interest of one of the two parties to the agreement, either the long or the short, to go through with the transaction. However, a price move in favor of one party would clearly translate into a loss for the other. Consequently, given an opportunity, one of the two parties would like to default on the expiration date. We will illustrate this with the help of an example.

Consider two people, Peter and Clara. Assume that Peter has gone long in a futures contract to buy an asset five days hence at a price of $40, and that Clara has taken the opposite side of the transaction. Let us first take the case where the spot price of the asset five days later is $42.50.

If Clara already has the asset, she is obliged to deliver it for $40, thereby foregoing an opportunity to sell it in the spot market at $42.50. Otherwise, if she does not have the asset, she is required to acquire it by paying $42.50, and then subsequently deliver it to Peter for $40. Quite obviously, Clara will choose to default unless she has an impeccable conscience and character.

Now let us consider a second situation where the price of the asset five days hence is $37.50.

If Clara already has the asset, she would be delighted to deliver it for $40, for the alternative is to sell it in the spot market for $37.50. Even if she were not to have the asset, she will be more than happy to acquire it for $37.50 in the spot market, and deliver it to Peter.

The problem here is that Peter will refuse to pay $40 for the asset, if he can get away with it. There are two ways of looking at it. If he does not want the asset, taking delivery at $40 would entail a subsequent sale at $37.50, and therefore a loss of $2.50. On the other hand, even if he were to require the asset, he would be better off buying it in the spot market for $37.50.

The purpose of having a clearinghouse is to ensure that such defaults do not occur. A clearinghouse ensures protection for both the parties to the trade by requiring them to post a performance bond or collateral called a margin. The amount of collateral is adjusted daily to reflect any profit or loss for each party, as compared to the previous day, based on the price movement during the day. By doing so, the clearinghouse effectively takes away the incentive for a party to default, as you shall shortly see.

QUESTION 16

What are margins?

As we have just seen, whenever two parties enter into an agreement to trade at a future date, there is always an element of default risk. In other words, there is always a possibility that one of the parties may not carry out his part of the deal as required by the contract.

In the case of futures contracts, compliance is ensured by requiring both the long and the short to deposit collateral with their broker, in an account known as the *margin account*. This margin deposit is therefore a performance guarantee.

The amount of collateral is related to the potential loss that each party is likely to incur. In the case of a futures contract, since both the parties have an obligation, it is necessary to collect collateral from both the parties. Once such potential losses are collected, the incentive to default is effectively taken away. For even if the party that ends up on the losing side were to fail to perform its obligation, the collateral collected from it would be adequate to take care of the interests of the other party.

QUESTION 17

It is said that once a deal is made between the buyer and the seller, the clearinghouse becomes the effective buyer for every seller and the effective seller for every buyer. How does the clearinghouse ensure that the other party does not default? Does it also collect margin money?

Yes, the clearinghouse also requires that margin money be deposited with it. This margin is known as a clearing margin. What happens is that both the long as well as the short deposit margins with their respective brokers, who in turn deposit margins with the clearinghouse.

QUESTION 18

What is the meaning of offsetting? How are forward and futures contracts offset?

Offsetting essentially means taking a counterposition. It means that if a party has originally gone long, it should subsequently go short, and vice versa. The effect of offsetting is to cancel an existing long or short position in a contract.

Remember that a forward contract is a customized private contract between two parties. Thus, if a party to a forward contract wants to cancel the original agreement, he must seek out the counterparty with whom he had entered into a deal and have the agreement canceled.

However, canceling a futures contract is a lot simpler. A futures contract between two parties, say Jacob and Victor, to transact in wheat at the end of a particular month will be identical to a similar contract between two other parties, say Kimberly and Patricia. This is because both the contracts would have been designed according to the features specified by the exchange. In addition, once Jacob enters into a contract with Victor, he effectively enters into a contract with the clearinghouse, and the link between him and Victor is broken. So if Jacob, who had entered into a long position, wants to get out of his position, he need not seek out Victor, the party with whom he had originally traded. All he has to do is to go back to the floor of the exchange and offer to take a short position in a similar contract. This time the opposite position may be taken by a new party, say Robert. Thus, by taking a long position initially with Victor, and a short position subsequently with Robert, Jacob can ensure that he is effectively out of the market, and that he has no further obligations. As far as the clearinghouse is concerned, its records will show that Jacob has bought and sold an identical contract, and that his net position is zero. This is the meaning of offsetting.

The profit or loss for an investor who takes a position in a futures contract and subsequently offsets it will be equal to the difference between the futures price that was prevailing at the time the original position was taken and the price at the time the position is offset.

QUESTION 19

What exactly is this concept of "marking to market?"

The reason for collecting margins is to protect both the parties against default by the other. The potential for default, to reiterate once again, arises because a position, once opened, can and will invariably lead to a loss for one of the two parties, if it were to comply with the terms of the contract.

This loss, however, will not arise all of a sudden, at the time of expiration of the futures contract. As the futures price fluctuates in the market from trade to trade, one of the two parties to an existing futures position will experience a gain, while the other will experience a loss. Thus, the total loss or gain from the time of getting into a futures position till the time the contract expires or is offset by taking a counterposition, whichever were to happen first, is the sum of these small losses/profits corresponding to each observed price in the interim.

The term *marking to market* refers to the process of calculating the loss for one party, or equivalently the corresponding gain for the other, at specified points in time, with reference to the futures price that was prevailing at the time the contract was previously marked to market. In practice, when a futures contract is entered into, it will be marked to market for the first time at the end of the day. Subsequently, it will be marked to market every day until the position is either offset or else the contract itself expires. The party who has incurred a profit will have the amount credited to his margin account, while the other party, who would have incurred an identical loss, will have his margin account debited.

We will now illustrate how profits and losses arise in the process of marking to market, and will highlight the corresponding changes to the margin accounts of the respective parties.

Let us take the case of Peter, who has gone long in a futures contract with Clara, expiring who has gone long in a futures contracts with Clara, expiring five days hence, at a futures price of $40. Assume that the price at the end of five days is $42.50, and that the prices at the end of each day prior to expiration are as shown in Table 1.3.

Table 1.3   End of the day futures prices

Day	Futures price
0	40.00
1	40.50
2	39.50
3	38.00
4	40.50
5	42.50

Day "0" denotes the time the contract was entered into, and the corresponding price is the futures price at which the deal was struck. Day "t" represents the end of that particular day, and the corresponding price is the prevailing futures price at that instant.

Let us assume that, as per the contract, Peter is committed to buying 100 units of the asset, and that at the time of entering into the contract both the parties had to deposit $500 as collateral in their margin accounts. The amount of collateral that is deposited when a contract is first entered into is called the *initial margin*.

At the end of the first day the futures price is $40.50. This means that the price per unit of the underlying asset for a futures contract being entered into at the end of the day is $40.50. If Peter were to offset the position that he had entered into in the morning, he would have to do so by agreeing to sell 100 units at $40.50 per unit. If so, he would earn a profit of $0.50 per unit, or $50 in all. While marking Peter's position to market, the broker will behave as though he were offsetting. That is, he would calculate his profit as $50, and credit it to his margin account. However, since Peter has not expressed a desire to actually offset, the broker would act as if he were re-entering into a long position at the prevailing futures price of $40.50.

At the end of the second day, the prevailing futures price is $39.50. When the contract is marked to market, Peter will make a loss of $100. Remember that his contract was re-established the previous evening at a price of $40.50, and if the broker were to now behave as if he were offsetting at $39.50, the loss is $1 per unit, or $100 in all. Once again a new long position would be automatically established, this time at a price of $39.50.

This process will continue either until the delivery date, when Peter will actually take possession of the asset, or until the day that he chooses to offset his position, if that were to happen earlier. As you can see from this illustration, rising futures prices lead to profits for the long, whereas falling futures prices lead to losses.

Now let us consider the situation from Clara's perspective. At the end of the first day, when the futures price is $40.50, marking to market would mean a loss of $50 for her. That is, her earlier contract to sell at

$40 will be effectively offset by making her buy at $40.50, and a new short position would be established for her at $40.50. Similarly, by the same logic, at the end of the second day, her margin account will be credited with a profit of $100. As you can see, shorts lose when futures prices rise, and gain when the prices fall.

Thus, the profit/loss for the long is identical to the loss/profit for the short. It is for this reason that futures contracts are called *zero sum games*. One man's gain is another man's loss.

As you can see, by the time the contract expires, the loss incurred by one of the two parties, in this case the short, has been totally recovered. In our illustration, Peter's account would have been credited with $250, by the time the contract expires. This amount represents the difference between the terminal futures price and the initial futures price, multiplied by the number of units of the underlying asset. These funds will have come from Clara's account which would have been debited. Now, if Clara were to refuse to deliver the asset at expiration, Peter would not be at a disadvantage. Since he has already realized a profit of $250, he can take delivery in the spot market at the terminal spot price of $42.50 per unit, in lieu of taking delivery under the futures contract.[1] Thus, effectively, he will get the asset at a price of $40 per unit, which is what he had contracted for in the first place.

QUESTION 20

What role does the clearinghouse play in marking to market?

The clearinghouse essentially plays the role of a banker. Its task is to debit the margin account of the broker whose client has suffered a loss, and simultaneously credit the margin account of the broker whose client has made a profit. Thus the margin accounts maintained with the clearinghouse are adjusted daily for profits and losses depending on the movement of the futures price, in exactly the same way that a client's margin account with his broker is dealt with.

QUESTION 21

Are forward contracts marked to market too? If not, what are the implications?

No, forward contracts are not marked to market. Consequently, both the parties to the contract are exposed to credit risk, which is the

---

1. You will see shortly that at the time of expiration of the contract the spot and futures prices must be equal.

risk that the other party may default. Thus, in practice, the parties to a forward contract tend to be large and well-known, such as banks, financial institutions, corporate houses, and brokerage firms. Such parties find it easier to enter into forward contracts as compared to individuals, because their credit worthiness is easier to appraise. Alternatively, counterparties to a forward contract are asked to offer adequate collateral in order to ensure the integrity of the contract.

QUESTION 22

What are the meanings of the terms maintenance margin and variation margin?

As we have seen, both longs and shorts have to deposit a performance bond with their brokers known as the initial margin, as soon as they enter into a futures contract. If the market were to subsequently move in favor of a party to a futures contract, the balance in his margin account will increase, or if the market were to move against him, the balance will be depleted.

Now, the broker has to ensure that a client always has adequate funds in his margin account. Otherwise the entire purpose of requiring clients to maintain margins can be defeated. Consequently, he will specify a threshold balance called the *maintenance margin*, which will be less than the *initial margin*. If, due to adverse price movements, the balance in the margin account were to decline below the level of the maintenance margin, the client will be immediately asked to deposit additional funds, to take the balance in his account back to the level of the initial margin. In futures market parlance, we would say that the broker has issued a *margin call* to the client. A margin call is always bad news, for it is an indication that a client has suffered major losses since the time he opened the margin account. The additional funds deposited by a client when a margin call is complied with are referred to as a *variation margin*.

These concepts can best be explained with the help of an example. Let us reconsider the case of Peter, who went long in a contract for 100 units of the asset at a price of $40 per bushel, and deposited $500 as collateral for the same. Assume that the broker fixes a maintenance margin of $400. If the contract lasts for a period of five days, and the futures prices on the subsequent days are as shown previously in Table 1.3, then the impact on the margin account will be as summarized in Table 1.4.

Table 1.4 Changes in the margin account over the course of time

Day	Futures price	Daily gain/loss	Cumulative gain/loss	Account balance	Margin call
0	40.00			500	
1	40.50	50	50	550	
2	39.50	(100)	(50)	450	
3	38.00	(150)	(200)	300	200
4	40.50	250	50	750	
5	42.50	200	250	950	

Numbers in parentheses denote losses.

Let us analyze in detail a few of the entries in Table 1.4. Consider the second row. As compared to the time the contract was entered into, the price has increased by $0.50 per unit or $50 for 100 units. Consequently, Peter, who has entered into a long position, has gained $50, which is to be credited to his margin account. Thus, the balance in the margin account has increased to $550 at the end of the first day.

The futures price at the end of the second day is $39.50. Thus, Peter has suffered a loss of $1 per unit or $100 for 100 units. When this loss is debited to his margin account, the balance in the account becomes $450. The price at the end of the next day is $38.00, which implies that Peter has suffered a further loss of $150. When this loss is debited to his margin account, the balance in the account becomes $300, which is less than the maintenance margin of $400. Hence a margin call is issued for $200, which is the amount required to take the balance back to the initial margin level. Peter has to pay a variation margin of $200.

QUESTION 23

Does the initial margin necessarily have to be deposited in cash? What about variation margins?

Initial margins need not always be deposited in the form of cash. Brokers often accept securities like Treasury bills and equity shares as collateral. However, the value assigned to these assets will be less than their current market values. This is because the broker would like to protect himself against a sudden sharp decline in the value of the collateral. For instance, if the required initial margin is $90, the broker may ask you to deposit securities with a market value of $100. Technically speaking, we say that the broker has applied a *haircut* of 10%.

Variation margins, however, must always be paid in cash. The reason for this is that, unlike initial margins which represent performance guarantees, variation margins are a manifestation of actual losses suffered by the client.

QUESTION 24

What is this concept of "value at risk?"

As we have explained, once the potential loss for a party to a futures contract is estimated and collected in advance, then the incentive to default diminishes considerably. If the amount of margin that is collected is adequately high, then the potential for default will be virtually insignificant. In practice, therefore, the margins specified by the exchange would depend on the estimate of the potential loss. Value at risk, or VaR, is a statistical technique for estimating this potential loss.

A priori, we cannot be sure as to the quantum of loss for either the long or the short from one day to the next. At best we can say that with a given level of probability, the loss cannot exceed a specified amount. This is precisely the concept of VaR.

Value at risk may be defined as a summary statistical measure of the possible loss of a portfolio of assets over a pre-specified time horizon.[2] Thus, for instance, if we were to say that the 99% VaR of an asset for a one-day horizon is $1,000, what we would mean is that the loss in terms of the value of the asset over a one-day holding period is expected to exceed $1,000 with a probability of 1% only. In order to interpret a VaR number, it is very important to take cognizance of both the probability level and the holding period that have been specified. For a given asset, changing one or both parameters can lead to significantly different estimates of VaR. It must also be remembered that the calculated VaR is not the maximum possible loss that a portfolio can suffer. For, in principle, the value of a portfolio can always go to zero, and consequently the maximum loss that a portfolio can potentially suffer is its entire current value.

QUESTION 25

Some clearinghouses are said to collect margins on a gross basis, while others are said to do so on a net basis. What is the difference between the two methods?

Let us assume that a broker has three clients A, B, and C. A has a long position in 100 futures contracts, B has a long position in 50 futures

2. See Linsmeier and Pearson (2000).

contracts, while C has a short position in 70 futures contracts. We will assume that the initial margin is $1 per contract.

The broker will obviously collect $100 from A, $50 from B, and $70 from C. That is, in all he will collect $220. If the clearinghouse were to collect margins on a gross basis, then the broker will have to deposit the entire $220 with the clearinghouse. This is the meaning of gross margining.

On the other hand, if a net margining system were to be used, the clearinghouse would calculate the broker's position as net 80 long contracts. This is because he has 150 long contracts as well as 70 short contracts routed through him. Thus, in this case, the broker need deposit only $80 with the clearinghouse.

What are the relative merits and demerits of the two systems? Let us assume that the futures price goes up by $1. The broker will need $150 to pay parties A and B. Of this, $70 should come from party C, while the balance should come through the clearinghouse since the broker has a net long position with it. Assume that party C defaults, that is, it refuses to pay, and that the broker too has become insolvent. In such a case, if a gross margining system were to be in use, the clearinghouse would have the resources to pay both A and B, since the broker would have deposited $220 with it.

However, if net margining had been used and a similar situation were to arise, the clearinghouse would only guarantee payment for 80 contracts, since the broker has only deposited $80 with it. Thus in the case of net margining, clients need to be more concerned with the financial strength and integrity of the broker through whom they route their transactions. They cannot bank on the clearinghouse to bail them out under all circumstances. But gross margining comes with an economic price tag. Firstly, clients may not pay adequate attention to the credit worthiness of their brokers. Secondly, the cost of operations of the clearinghouse will increase, since it now has to provide guarantees on a much larger scale.[3]

QUESTION 26

What happens if a party defaults; that is, he fails to respond to a margin call?

Default can occur at two possible points in time, either before the maturity of the futures contract, or at the time of maturity. Let us first consider the case where a client defaults before maturity. We will illustrate it using the data in Table 1.4.

---

3. See Edwards and Ma (1992).

At the end of day 3, when the balance in the margin account falls to $300, a margin call will be issued for $200. If the client fails to pay the variation margin, the broker will actually offset his position. In this case, since the client has originally gone long, the broker will offset his contract by going short at the market price. In our case, the price at the time the margin call was issued was $38.00. Assume that by the time the broker is able to offset the contract, the price has fallen further to $37.70. If so, the investor would have incurred a further loss of $0.30 per unit or $30 per 100 units. This loss, along with the transaction costs incurred by the broker, will be deducted from the balance of $300 that is available in the margin account. The remaining amount will be refunded to the client. Similarly, if a broker fails to respond to a margin call from the clearinghouse, the futures exchange will close his account at the prevailing market price.

In the case of default at the time of expiration, the broker will act as follows. If the default is on the part of a short, that is, the short fails to deliver the asset, then the broker will acquire the good in the spot market and deliver it to the long. On the other hand, if a long were to default then the broker will acquire the good from the short and sell it in the cash market. In either case, he will deduct his costs and losses from the balance in the defaulting party's margin account.

QUESTION 27

Futures and forward contracts are said to have linear profit diagrams, whereas options contracts are said to have nonlinear profit diagrams. Why is this so?

As we have seen, investors with long positions in futures contracts will gain if the futures price were to rise subsequently, whereas they would lose if the price were to decline. For the shorts it is the opposite. That is, they will lose if the futures price were to rise, and gain if it were to decline.

Thus the profit for a long futures position may be expressed as $F_T - F_0$, where 0 represents the point of time at which the contract is initiated, and T is the point of time at which the contract either expires or is offset. Therefore, for every dollar increase in the terminal futures price the profit is one dollar more, while for every dollar decrease in the terminal futures price, the profit is one dollar less.

Hence if we plot the profit from the position versus the terminal futures price, the graph will be linear, as can be seen from the depiction in Figure 1.1.

Figure 1.1   Profit profile: Long futures

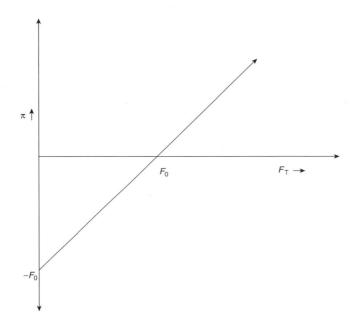

Let us interpret the above diagram. π represents the profit, which is shown along the Y-axis. F_T is the terminal futures price which is shown along the X-axis. The maximum loss occurs when $F_T = 0$, and is equal to F_0 in magnitude. The maximum profit is unlimited since F_T has no upper bound. The position breaks even if the terminal futures price is equal to the initial futures price, or in other words the price remains unchanged.

For an investor with a short position in a futures contract, the profit may be depicted as $F_0 - F_T$. The profit diagram for a short futures position (Figure 1.2) is therefore also linear. In this case, the maximum profit occurs when $F_T = 0$, and is equal to F_0 in magnitude. The maximum loss is obviously unlimited.

Numerical illustration

Nigel Peck has gone long in a futures contract at a price of $40, and the opposite short position has been taken by Maya Solow.

Assume that the futures price at the time of expiration of the contract is $42.10. By then, due to marking to market, Nigel's margin account

Figure 1.2 Profit profile: Short futures

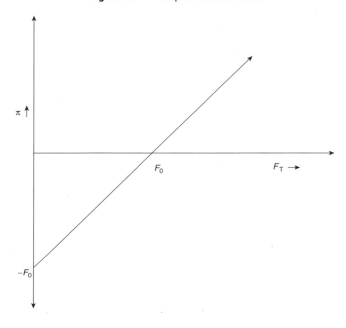

would have been credited with $2.10 per unit of the underlying asset, whereas Maya's account would have been debited by $2.10.

Options contracts are different from futures contracts. Let us look at an options contract at the time of expiration of the contract. In the case of call options, if the price of the asset in the spot market at that point in time is greater than the exercise price, then it will obviously make sense for the call holder to exercise his right and acquire the asset at the exercise price. Or else he will choose not to exercise. If so, his loss will be equal to the premium paid at the outset. Thus, in the case of call options, the maximum loss for the holder is limited to the premium paid at the beginning. The maximum gain is however unlimited, since the spot price of the asset at the time of the expiration of the contract has no upper bound.

The profit for a call holder may therefore be expressed as $-C_0 + \text{Max}$ $[0, S_T - X]$. The maximum loss is equal to $-C_0$, the premium that was paid at the outset. As long as the terminal spot price S_T remains below the exercise price, the option will not be exercised and the holder will lose the initial premium. As the stock price goes above this value, the profit will increase dollar for dollar. The position will break even when the terminal stock price is equal to the exercise price plus the premium paid at the outset. The maximum profit is obviously unbounded.

Figure 1.3 Profit profile: Long call

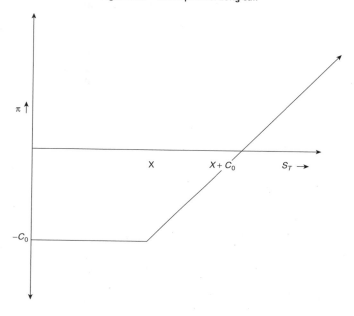

The profit diagram for a call holder may therefore be depicted as shown in Figure 1.3. As you can see, the diagram is certainly not linear. Rather, it resembles a *hockey stick*.

For a call writer the profit can be expressed as $C_0 - \text{Max}[0, S_T - X]$. His maximum gain will be equal to the initial premium, which will be the case if the option is not exercised. Once the spot price at expiration crosses the exercise price, his profit will decline dollar for dollar. The maximum loss is obviously unbounded, and the position will break even at a terminal spot price of $X + C_0$. The profit diagram is as depicted in Figure 1.4.

Numerical illustration

Assume that Nigel has acquired a European call option on a stock, from Maya, with an exercise price of $100. Let the option premium per underlying share be $7.50. Maya, who is the writer of the option, will consequently get a cash inflow of $7.50 per share, at the outset.

If the stock price at the time of expiration of the option were to be less than $100, then Nigel will simply allow the option to expire. He will lose $7.50 per share, while Maya will walk away with $7.50 per share.

Figure 1.4   Profit profile: Short call

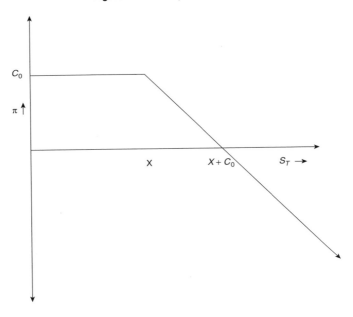

However, if the share price at expiration were to be greater than $100, say $120, then Nigel will exercise his option. His profit per share will be:

$$-7.50 + (120 - 100) = \$12.50$$

Maya will in this case incur a loss of $12.50, for her net cash flow will be:

$$7.50 - (120 - 100) = -\$12.50$$

Notice that it is not necessary that S_T, the stock price at expiration, be greater than the sum of the exercise price and the premium, $X + C_0$, in order for the exercise decision to be worthwhile. For instance, assume that the terminal stock price is $105. If Nigel does not exercise his option, he will lose $7.50. But if he were to exercise, his cash flow would be:

$$-7.50 + (105 - 100) = -\$2.50$$

Clearly it is better to lose $2.50 than $7.50. This illustration is a manifestation of the principle that sunk costs are irrelevant while taking subsequent investment decisions.

Figure 1.5 Profit profile: Long put

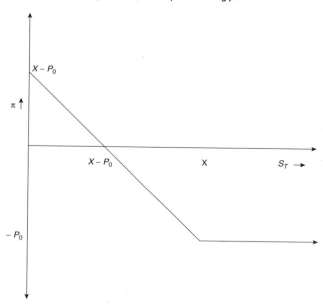

The maximum gain for Nigel, or equivalently the maximum loss for Maya, is unlimited. The breakeven stock price for both of them is $107.50. The maximum loss for Nigel or equivalently the maximum gain for Maya is $7.50.

Now let us look at put options. A holder of a put would like to exercise his right to sell at the exercise price only if the spot price of the asset is lower than the exercise price. Otherwise he will simply let the option expire. Thus the profit expression for a put holder may be written as $-P_0 + \text{Max}[0, X - S_T]$. The maximum loss is once again equal to the premium paid at the outset, and will occur if the option is not exercised subsequently. As the terminal spot price dips below the exercise price, the profit will increase dollar for dollar. The position will break even when $S_T = X - P_0$. The maximum profit will also be equal to $X - P_0$, since the price of the asset cannot dip below zero. The profit diagram will be as depicted in Figure 1.5.

The profit diagram for a put writer will be as depicted in Figure 1.6. The maximum gain for him is equal to the premium received at the outset. The maximum loss will be equal to $X - P_0$, which will be the case when the terminal spot price is zero. The breakeven point is the same as for a put holder.

Figure 1.6   Profit profile: Short put

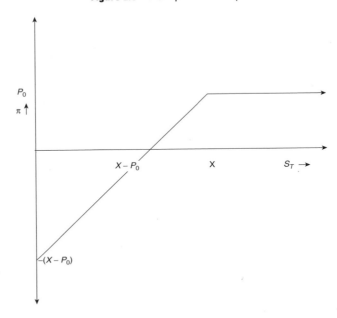

Numerical illustration

Assume that Nigel has taken a long position in a European put option with an exercise price of $100, by paying a premium of $4.50 to Maya.

If the terminal stock price is greater than $100, then Nigel will let the option expire worthless. His outflow under these circumstances will be $4.50 per underlying share. Quite obviously, Maya will have a corresponding inflow of $4.50 per share.

However, if the share price at expiration were to be less than $100, say $85, then Nigel will exercise his option. His inflow in this case will be:

$$-4.50 + (100 - 85) = \$10.50$$

Maya's cash flow will be:

$$4.50 - (100 - 85) = -\$10.50$$

The maximum profit for Nigel, or equivalently the maximum loss for Maya, will occur when $S_T = 0$, and will be equal to $95.50. The breakeven stock price for both of them is $95.50. The maximum loss for Nigel, or equivalently the maximum gain for Maya, is $4.50. Once again, the premium, which is a sunk cost, ought not to be factored in while taking a decision to exercise.

Notice also that the magnitude of the profit/loss for a call/put holder is equal to the magnitude of the loss/profit for a call/put writer. Thus, both call and put options, like futures contracts, represent *zero sum games.*

QUESTION 28

Who is a futures commission merchant? Are all futures commission merchants authorized to clear transactions with the clearinghouse?

A futures commission merchant (FCM) is a broker who is authorized to open an account on behalf of a client who wishes to trade. Opening and maintenance of an account on behalf of a client entails the collection of margin money, the maintenance of balances in the margin accounts, and the recording and reporting of all trading activities. It must be remembered that not all brokers are FCMs. There is a category of brokers called *introducing brokers*, who as the name suggests perform the function of getting a client acquainted with an FCM. In other words, they will accept an order and route it through an FCM. It is important to note that introducing brokers cannot maintain margin accounts.

Not every FCM is a member of the clearinghouse, or in other words is not a *clearing member*. Only clearing members are authorized to maintain clearing margins with the clearinghouse and clear transactions through it. Consequently, if your FCM is not a clearing member, he must route the order through a clearing member.

QUESTION 29

Futures and options are said to provide leverage. What is leverage, and how does it manifest itself in the case of futures and options?

A strategy is said to be *levered* or *geared* if a fairly small market movement tends to have a disproportionately large impact on the funds deposited. We will first illustrate the principle of leverage in the context of companies.

Consider two firms A and B. Company A has a paid up capital of $100,000 with no debt, whereas company B has a paid up capital of

$50,000, with debt of $50,000 at an annual interest rate of 10%. We will consider two cases, the first where the two companies make an operating profit of $25,000, and the second where they make a loss of $25,000. To keep matters simple, we will assume that there are no taxes. Consider the situation as depicted in Table 1.5.

Table 1.5 An illustration of leverage

	Case I		Case II	
	Firm A	**Firm B**	**Firm A**	**Firm B**
Equity capital	100,000	50,000	100,000	50,000
Debt	–	50,000	–	50,000
Profit before interest	25,000	25,000	(25,000)	(25,000)
Profit after interest	25,000	20,000	(25,000)	(30,000)
Return on equity	25%	40%	−25%	−60%

Company A is unlevered whereas company B is a levered firm. As you can see, from the standpoint of the shareholders of company B, leverage is a double-edged sword. In a booming market, a 25% rate of return gets magnified to 40%, but in a market downturn, a loss of 25% gets translated to a loss of 60%. Futures and options similarly provide leverage.

Consider a person who has gone long in a wheat futures contract at a price of $4 per bushel, by depositing a margin of $100. Assume that each contract is for 100 bushels. If the price were to move up to $4.25, the investor would make a profit of $25, which is 25% of the initial deposit. Had he chosen to go long in the spot market at a price of $4 a bushel, he would have procured 100 bushels by paying $400, and a profit of $25 would have meant a return of only 6.25%. However, as always, leverage is a double-edged sword. If the futures price were to fall to $3.75 at the end of the day, the investor would make a loss of $25, which is equivalent to a 25% erosion of his margin deposit. However, had he chosen to buy the wheat in the spot market, a loss of $25 would be a loss of only 6.25% of his initial investment.

Options also similarly provide leverage. Consider a share which is selling for $100. Assume that European call options with an exercise price of $100 are available for $8. We will first consider the case where the share price at the time of expiration of the option is $110. If the investor were to have bought a share, he could sell it for a profit of $10, which is equivalent to a 10% return on investment. If he had chosen to buy a call option, he would get a payoff of $10 by exercising, which represents a 25% return on an investment of $8. However, if the stock price at the time of expiration of the options contract were to be $90, the option holder would have to forego the entire premium, amounting to a loss of 100%, since he will not exercise. Had he chosen to acquire the share at the outset, he would now incur a loss of only 10%.

QUESTION 30

What is the meaning of arbitrage?

Arbitrage refers to the ability to make a cost-less, risk-less profit, by simultaneously transacting in two or more markets. The key phrase here is "cost-less and risk-less." Arbitrage opportunities, if perceived, will be exploited till they vanish. The rationale is as follows. If one has to invest in a risky asset, he will do so only if the expected return is commensurate with the level of risk. Even if the investment is risk-less, a person will invest only if he is assured of a risk-less rate of return. However, if a person is assured of an opportunity to earn a risk-less return without making an investment of his own, he would be irrational not to exploit it. Such opportunities are referred to as arbitrage opportunities.

The concept can best be explained with the help of an example. Consider a share that trades on both the New York Stock Exchange (NYSE) and the Chicago Stock Exchange (CSE). Let the price be $100 on the NYSE and $102 on the CSE. Consider a person who is in a position to borrow $1,000,000 for an infinitesimal period of time. He can then acquire 10,000 shares on the NYSE and immediately sell them for $1,020,000 on the CSE. After repaying his loan, he will be left with a profit of $20,000 which was made without his having to invest any money, and without taking any risk.

Such opportunities obviously cannot persist for long. As people perceive this opportunity and rush to buy shares on the NYSE, the price there will rise. At the same time, when the arbitrageurs start unloading their shares on the CSE, the price there will fall. Together, these two factors will quickly eliminate any opportunity for such profits.

Our illustration has assumed that there are no transaction costs like bid–ask spreads and brokerage fees. For small investors, such costs will be significant in practice, and may preclude them from exploiting perceived arbitrage opportunities. However, large financial institutions will face much lower costs, and will exploit such opportunities so as to maximize their profits.

QUESTION 31

Is it true that the futures price at the time of expiration of the contract should be the same as the price of a cash transaction at that point in time? What would happen if this were not to be the case?

Yes, at the time of expiration of the futures contract, the futures price must be the same as the cash or spot market price. After all, what is a futures contract? It is a contract to transact at a future point in time. At the expiration date of the contract, any futures contract that is entered into must lead to an immediate transaction because the contract is scheduled to expire immediately and hence is valid only for an instant. Thus a person who enters into a futures contract at the time of expiration is effectively entering into a spot market transaction. Consequently, if the futures price at expiration were to be different from the spot price, there would be arbitrage opportunities.

Let us denote the futures price at expiration by F_T and the spot price at that point in time by S_T. It must be the case that $F_T = S_T$. We will examine the consequences if F_T were to be greater than S_T or if F_T were to be less than S_T.

1. $F_T > S_T$

This situation can be exploited by an arbitrageur as follows. He can acquire the asset in the spot market at a price of S_T and simultaneously go short in a futures contract. Since the contract is scheduled to expire immediately, he can at once deliver for a price of F_T. Thus $F_T - S_T$, which by assumption is positive, represents an arbitrage profit for such an individual.

Numerical illustration

Assume that the futures price of an asset at the time of expiration is $425, whereas the spot price is $422. An arbitrageur will immediately acquire the asset in the spot market at $422 per unit, and simultaneously go short in a futures contract. Since the contract is expiring he will immediately deliver at $425, thereby making a cost-less, risk-less profit of $3 per unit.

2. $F_T < S_T$

An arbitrageur will exploit this condition by going long in a futures contract. Since it is about to expire, he can take immediate delivery by paying F_T, and can then sell the asset in the spot market for S_T. In this case, $S_T - F_T$, which by assumption is positive, represents an arbitrage profit.

Numerical illustration

Assume that the futures price of an asset at the time of expiration is $422, whereas the spot price is $425. An arbitrageur will immediately take a long position in a futures contract, which will entail taking immediate delivery at $422 per unit. The asset can then be immediately sold in the spot market for $425 per unit. Thus, once again, the arbitrageur will be able to lock in a cost-less, risk-less profit.

QUESTION 32

If a futures contract permits the short to deliver more than one grade or variety at expiration, which spot price will the futures price converge to? Obviously each grade will have its own spot price.

In order to answer this question, we must first examine the system of price adjustment when multiple grades are permitted for delivery. In such cases, one grade will be designated as the *par* grade. If the short delivers the par grade, he will receive the prevailing futures price at expiration, F_T. If he were to deliver a more valuable grade, he will receive a premium, whereas if he were to deliver a less valuable grade, he would have to do so at a discount. The process by which the futures price is adjusted to take into account the delivery of grades other than the par grade may be either multiplicative or additive. We will examine each method in turn.

1. Multiplicative adjustment

Under this procedure, if the short delivers a particular grade i, he will receive $a_i F_T$. For premium grades, a_i will be greater than 1.0, whereas for discount grades, it will be less than 1.0.

Let us denote the spot price of grade i at expiration by profit for the short if he were to deliver grade i is:

$$a_i F_T - S_{i,T}$$

Grade i will be preferred to another grade j if:

$$a_i F_T - S_{i,T} > a_j F_T - S_{j,T}$$

At expiration, in order to preclude arbitrage, the profit from delivering the most preferred grade must be zero. If we denote this grade as grade i, it must be the case that:

$$a_i F_T - S_{i,T} = 0$$

$$\Rightarrow F_T = \frac{S_{i,T}}{a_i}$$

For all other grades, it must be the case that:

$$a_j F_T - S_{j,T} < 0$$

$$\Rightarrow F_T < \frac{S_{j,T}}{a_j}$$

Thus, the grade that will be chosen for delivery will obviously be the one for which $\frac{S}{a}$ is the lowest. Such a grade is called the *cheapest to deliver grade,* and $\frac{S}{a}$ is called the *delivery adjusted spot price.* Thus, the cheapest to deliver grade is the one with the lowest delivery adjusted spot price. At expiration, therefore, the futures price must converge to the delivery adjusted spot price of the cheapest to deliver grade.

2. Additive adjustment

In the case of contracts where the additive method of price adjustment is used, the short will receive $F_T + a_i$, if he were to deliver grade i. For a premium grade, a_i will be positive, whereas for a discount grade, it will be negative.

The profit from delivering grade i will be:

$$F_T + a_i - S_{i,T}$$

And grade i will be preferred to another grade j if:

$$F_T + a_i - S_{i,T} > F_T + a_j - S_{j,T}$$

$$\Rightarrow S_{i,T} - a_i < S_{j,T} - a_j$$

Hence, the cheapest to deliver grade is the one for which $S - a$ is the lowest. That is, grade i will be the cheapest to deliver grade if:

$$S_{i,T} - a_i < S_{j,T} - a_j \forall j$$

To rule out arbitrage, the profit from delivering the cheapest to deliver grade must be zero. That is:

$$F_T + a_i - S_{i,T} = 0$$
$$\Rightarrow F_T = S_{i,T} - a_i$$

In this case $S - a$ is the delivery adjusted spot price, and once again, the futures price will converge to the delivery adjusted spot price of the cheapest to deliver grade.

It must be noted that irrespective of whether the multiplicative or the additive system is used, the cheapest to deliver grade need not be the one with the lowest spot price. For example, consider the data for wheat shown in Table 1.6.

Table 1.6 An illustration of additive price adjustment

Grade	Spot price	Conversion factor	Delivery adjusted spot price
No.1	4.29	0.015	4.275
No.2	4.28	0	4.280
No.3	4.25	−0.05	4.300

The par grade is obviously No.2. But the cheapest to deliver grade is No.1, which incidentally has the highest spot price.

QUESTION 33

We keep hearing about a term called the "settlement price." What is it, and how is it calculated?

The settlement price is the price that is used to compute the daily gains and losses for the longs and the shorts, when the futures contracts are marked to market at the end of each day.

In many cases, futures exchanges adopt the practice of setting the settlement price equal to the observed closing price for the day. Sometimes, if there is heavy trading towards the close of the day, the exchange may set the settlement price equal to the average of the observed futures prices, in the last half hour or hour of trading. At the other extreme, if there were to be no trades at the end of the day, the exchange may set the settlement price equal to the average of the observed "bid" and "ask" quotes.

What do we mean by the terms "bid" and "ask?" Any market maker or dealer, who is essentially a broker who stands ready to buy and sell on his own account, will offer a two-way quote at any point in time. That is, he will quote a price for buying from a customer, and another price for selling to a customer. The "bid" is the price at which a market maker is willing to buy from a client, while the "ask" is the price at which he is willing to sell to a client.

The bid will always be less than the ask[4]; that is, the market maker will buy low and sell high in order to make a profit.

In the context of futures markets, the "bid" represents the futures price at which a customer can take a short position, while the "ask" is the price at which he can take a long position.

QUESTION 34

Forward and futures contracts call for delivery at the time of expiration of the contract. Are there any differences between the two types of contracts from the standpoint of delivery?

Although both forward and futures contracts call for delivery at the time of expiration, there are fundamental differences between them in this context.

Firstly, in practice, most forward contracts are settled by delivery. However, only a small fraction of the futures contracts that are entered into (in some markets the figure is as low as 2%) result in actual delivery. The remainder are offset prior to expiration by taking a counterposition.

Secondly, since a forward contract is a customized agreement between two parties, unless the contract is canceled subsequently, it will result in the short delivering to the original party who had gone long. In the case of futures, however, the link between the long and the short is broken by the clearinghouse, once a contract is entered into. Subsequently, one or both parties may offset and exit the market. Hence, when a short expresses his desire to deliver, it is not necessary that the person with whom he had originally traded be in a position to take delivery of the asset, for this person may no longer have an open long position. Thus, in the case of futures contracts, the exchange will decide as to who the short should deliver to. In practice, the person with the oldest outstanding long position is usually called upon to take delivery.

Finally, the price that is paid by the long at the time of taking delivery under a forward contract would be different from what he would

---

4. We will discuss an exception when we study the principle of "indirect quotes" in foreign exchange markets.

have to pay to take delivery under a futures contract with the same features and on the same underlying asset. A forward contract, it must be remembered, is not marked to market at intermediate points in time. Consequently, at expiration the long has to pay the price that was agreed upon at the outset, in order to take delivery. However, in the case of a futures contract, the contract would have been marked to market on every business day during its lifetime. Hence, in order to ensure that the long gets to acquire the asset at the price that was agreed upon at the outset, he has to be asked to pay the prevailing futures price at expiration, which, as you have seen earlier, will be the same as the prevailing spot price at expiration. We will illustrate the above arguments using symbols, as well as with the help of a numerical example.

Consider a futures contract that was entered into on *day 0* at a price F_0, and which expires on *day T*. We will denote the price at expiration by F_T. Such a contract will be marked to market on days 1, 2, 3 . . . . up to day T. The cumulative profit for the long due to marking to market is:

$$(F_T - F_{T-1}) + (F_{T-1} - F_{T-2}) + (F_{T-2} - F_{T-3}) + \cdots +$$
$$(F_2 - F_1) + (F_1 - F_0) = (F_T - F_0)$$

In order to ensure that the long is able to acquire the asset at the original price of F_0, he must be asked to pay a price P at the time of delivery, such that:

$$P - (F_T - F_0) \equiv F_0$$
$$\Rightarrow P = F_T = S_T$$

Thus the price paid by the long at the time of delivery must equal the prevailing futures price at expiration, or equivalently, the prevailing spot price at expiration.

In the case of a forward contract, however, there will be no marking to market, and hence there will be no intermediate cash flows. Consequently, at the time of delivery, the price paid by the long, P, must be the same as the price that was agreed upon originally. That is:

$$P = F_0$$

We will now illustrate these arguments using a numerical example. Consider a futures contract on wheat, that was entered into at a price of $3.50 per bushel. We will assume that the contract lasts for a period of five days, and that the movement in the futures price on subsequent days is as depicted in Table 1.7.

Table 1.7 Marking a contract to market

Day	Futures price	Profit from marking to market
0	3.5	
1	3.4	(0.10)
2	3.2	(0.20)
3	3.5	0.30
4	3.8	0.30
5	4.0	0.20
	Total	0.50

In this case, $F_0 = 3.5$ and $F_T = 4.0$. A person who had gone long in a futures contract at a time when the futures price was $3.50 would have to pay $4.00 at the time of delivery. Taking into account the profit of $0.50 due to marking to market, he will effectively get the asset for $3.50, which is nothing but the initial futures price.

On the other hand, a person who had gone long in a forward contract at a price of $3.50 would have to pay $3.50 at the time of taking delivery.

QUESTION 35

What is the process involved when a futures contract is settled by delivery? Does trading in the contract have to cease as soon as delivery commences?

Once a short declares his intention to deliver, the actual process takes three days. On the day of announcement by the short, called the *position day*, the short's broker will convey his intention to the clearinghouse. The notice will state how many contracts are being delivered, the location of delivery in case the contract permits delivery at multiple locations, and the grade of the underlying asset being delivered, which is important for contracts that give the short the freedom to deliver one of many acceptable grades. On the next business day, called the *notice day*, the exchange will select the person with the oldest outstanding long position to accept delivery, for reasons which have been explained earlier. On the following day, called the *delivery day*, the long will pay the short, and in return will get a warehouse receipt granting him title to the goods.

Trading need not stop as soon as delivery commences. In the case of most assets, the first day on which a short can declare his intention to deliver is before the last day of trading, whereas the last delivery day is on or after the day on which trading ceases. Given in Table 1.8 are the details for the corn futures contract on the Chicago Board of Trade.

Table 1.8   Delivery schedule for corn futures on the CBOT

First notice day	Last notice day	Last trading day
Last business day prior to the delivery month	Business day following the last trading day	Business day prior to the 15th calendar day of the delivery month

QUESTION 36

What are the meanings of the terms "exchange for physicals" and "alternative delivery procedure?"

Under normal circumstances delivery can be made only during the period specified by the exchange, and as per the terms and conditions specified in the contract. At times, however, two parties with opposite positions can transact prior to the time when delivery is called for under exchange rules. Such an arrangement is called *exchange for physicals* or EFP. It permits a long and a short to get together and agree on a transaction that would close out their respective positions prior to the commencement of the delivery period. An EFP is an *off-the-exchange* transaction. It offers the two parties greater flexibility, and makes physical delivery a more attractive option. We will illustrate it with the help of an example.

Kurt Norris has a short position in wheat futures, while Max Kilburn has an equivalent long position. Max is prepared to take delivery from Kurt. However, the wheat that Kurt has is different from the grade specified in the contract. Under normal circumstances, Kurt will be unable to deliver this wheat. However, under an EFP, once he and Max mutually agree on a price, the two can transact after reporting it to the exchange. The exchange will treat such a transaction as though each party had offset his position with the other.

An *alternative delivery procedure* or ADP also permits transactions under conditions that are different from those specified by the exchange. However, there is a critical difference. An ADP is possible only after the exchange has matched a long and a short, in response to a short's declaration of his intent to deliver. In an ADP transaction, the two parties can agree to transact on terms different from those specified in the contract, provided they notify the clearinghouse of the same.

QUESTION 37

What is "cash settlement" in futures contracts? Why is it adopted in practice?

There are certain futures contracts which do not allow for physical delivery of the underlying asset. In such cases, the contract is marked to market till the last day, and subsequently all positions are declared closed. Under such circumstances, both the long and the short will exit the market, with their cumulative profit (which could also be a loss) since the inception of the contract. However, the short will not deliver the underlying asset at the end.

Cash settlement is the prescribed mode of settlement for Stock Index Futures, which, as the name suggests, are contracts on stock indices like the Dow Jones and the S&P 500. In order to form a portfolio that mimics an index, one is required to buy all the stocks that are included in the index, and in exactly the same proportions as they are present in it. Quite obviously, physical delivery under such circumstances will be extremely cumbersome.[5]

Cash delivery may also be specified as a mechanism to control manipulation of prices by traders by creating artificial shortages in the underlying asset.

QUESTION 38

What are the meanings of the terms "trading volume" and "open interest?" How do they differ from each other?

The trading volume in a futures contract on a given day is the number of contracts that were traded on that particular underlying asset, during the course of the day. The open interest at any point in time is the total number of outstanding contracts at that point in time. The open interest is a measure of the number of open positions at any instant of time. Since every long position must be matched by a corresponding short position, open interest may be measured either as the number of open

---

5. If you think it is difficult for an index like the Dow Jones which contains 30 stocks, contemplate delivery in the case of the Standard & Poor's 500, which includes 500 companies!

long positions at a point in time, or equivalently, as the number of open short positions at the same point in time.

The relationship between the trading volume for a day and the change in the open interest from the close of trading on the previous day depends on the nature of the transaction, and can best be illustrated with the help of an example.

Let us assume that a new contract in silver futures has just opened for trading and that three trades have taken place on the first day as depicted in Table 1.9.

Table 1.9 Trade details for the first day

Time	Trade	No. of contracts
10 a.m.	Maureen goes long and Anthony goes short	50
1 p.m.	Rachel goes long and Victor goes short	100
4 p.m.	Peter goes long and Robert goes short	50

The trading volume for the day is obviously 200 contracts. Since nobody has offset any contracts after entering into a trade, the number of open positions or the open interest is also 200 contracts.

Now consider the following scenarios for the next day.

1. Case A

Maureen goes long in 50 contracts and Anthony goes short.

Both these parties are entering into a trade that increases their open positions. The trading volume for the second day is obviously 50 contracts. The number of open positions at the end of the day is 250 contracts. Hence, the change in the open interest as compared to the previous day is 50 contracts. Thus, if a trade involves two parties who are establishing new positions by entering into a contract with each other, the open interest will rise.

2. Case B

Maureen goes long in 50 contracts and Rachel goes short.

The trading volume for the day is once again 50 contracts. But what about the open interest? In this case, no new positions have been opened. All that has happened is that Rachel, who had a long position in 100 contracts, has partially offset by taking a counterposition in 50 contracts, and her place has been taken by Maureen. The number of open positions at the end of the day continues to remain at 200 contracts. Here the change in the open interest as compared to the previous day is zero. Hence, if a trade involves one party taking a counterposition by trading with another party who is opening a position, then the open interest will remain unchanged.

3. Case C

Anthony goes long in 50 contracts and Rachel goes short.

As before, the trading volume for the day is 50 contracts. The change in the open interest can be analyzed as follows. Rachel has partially offset her long position by going short, and at the same time the trade has also resulted in Anthony offsetting his short position by going long. Thus, the overall result is that the number of open contracts has reduced by 50 and the change in the open interest as compared to the previous day is therefore −50 contracts. Consequently the open interest at the end of the second day is only 150 contracts in this case. Therefore, if a trade involves one party taking a counterposition by trading with another party who is also taking a counterposition, then the open interest will fall.

If the trading volume is high on a given day, then it signifies greater liquidity. On the other hand, high open interest at the end of a day indicates more scope for counterpositions on subsequent days, and consequently is a signal that futures volumes are likely to be high.

QUESTION 39

What is the primary economic role of derivative contracts? In other words, why do we need them?

Futures, forwards and options help investors in a number of ways. We will analyze some of the major benefits of derivatives trading.

1. Re-allocation of risk

Quite obviously, not all investors have an identical propensity to take risk. On one hand we have "hedgers," who seek to avoid risk, while on the other hand we have "speculators," who consciously seek to take calculated risks. Derivative contracts can be used to transfer or re-allocate risk from those who seek to avoid it to those who are willing to bear it.

Their efficiency in risk management has resulted in a phenomenal growth of such instruments and markets all over the globe.

2. Price discovery

In a free market economy, prices are the most fundamental variables of interest. Fair and accurate prices are imperative for ensuring the correct allocation of resources.

Supply and demand information tends to percolate in derivative markets more easily, and consequently such markets help facilitate the dissemination of such information. Why is this so?

Taking a long derivatives position entails the depositing of a small margin, whereas in a spot position the investor is required to pay the full price. Similarly, an investor who anticipates a bear market can more easily take a short position in derivatives than sell the asset short. Short selling is not freely possible in the case of all assets. Even in those cases where it is permitted, the investor is required to deposit the entire proceeds with the broker who will pay a low or nil rate of interest. Thus, from the standpoints of both the longs and the shorts, trading in derivatives is attractive. This has two major consequences which further fuel the level of activity in such markets.

Firstly, transaction costs tend to be lower as compared to spot markets. Secondly, derivatives markets are characterized by a high degree of liquidity.

What is liquidity, and why is it important?

Liquidity refers to the ability of market participants to transact quickly at prices which are close to the true or fair value of the asset. It refers to the ability of buyers and sellers to discover each other quickly and without having to induce a transaction by offering a large premium or discount. Quite obviously, an investor would like to trade without having to make major price concessions, irrespective of the size of the trade.

3. Market efficiency

Since derivatives trading is relatively easier and cheaper, perceived inefficiencies in the market can be quickly arbitraged away. Thus, the presence of a derivatives market helps ensure an effcient asset market.

4. Ease of speculation

Speculation is a sine qua non for the efficient functioning of a capital market. Derivatives markets enable speculators to take positions by depositing small amounts of collateral.

QUESTION 40

Derivative assets have been around for more than a century. Why is it that we hear so much about them these days?

Until the late 1960s, most of the activity in derivatives trading was restricted to commodities. Financial derivatives as a concept became significant only in the 1970s and 1980s. The explosion of trading in financial futures and options has not only manifested itself by way of higher observed trading volumes, but has also served to inject more glamour and controversy into the world of finance. The primary reasons for the rapid growth of derivatives trading over the past few decades are:

1. After the collapse of the Bretton Woods system, the major economies of the world switched from fixed exchange rate regimes to floating rate mechanisms. Consequently, currency risk and its management became very important, leading to growth and innovations in the market for Forex derivatives.

2. After the 1973 war in the Middle East, petroleum prices became highly volatile and unpredictable. This had far-reaching effects on the prices of all commodities, since the transportation costs of goods is directly linked to the price of crude oil. This gave a further impetus to the commodity derivatives markets.

3. Beginning with the U.S. Federal Reserve, led by Paul Volcker, major central banks began to abandon their policies of keeping interest rates stable. The focus shifted to the levels of money supply, and interest rates became market determined. Consequently, the market for interest rate derivatives developed and grew rapidly.

4. Many countries began to liberalize their economies. With the removal of restrictions, capital began to move freely across borders, and markets became more integrated. Not surprisingly, risks multiplied and became a common matter of concern.

5. In October 1986 the London Stock Exchange (LSE) eliminated fixed brokerage commissions. This event came to be known as the *big bang*. From February of the same year, the LSE had started admitting foreign brokerage firms as full members. These changes were intended to make London an attractive international financial market.[6] London is ideally located geographically, and serves as a middle link between markets in the U.S. and those in the Far East, thereby facilitating 24-hour trading.

---

6. See Resnick (1996).

Similar changes were effected in the United States in 1975 and in Japan in 1999. Today, in most countries commissions are negotiable between the broker and the client. There are however countries where government or exchange regulations specify fixed commission rates that ought to be charged by a broker. For instance, until early 2003 the minimum commission in Hong Kong was mandated to be 0.25% of the trade value.[7]

In a deregulated brokerage industry, commissions will vary substantially from broker to broker depending on the extent and quality of services provided. On one hand, we have *full-service* brokers who charge the maximum commissions, but offer value-added services and investment advice. On the other hand, there exist *discount* and *deep discount* brokers who charge the least by way of commissions, but whose only function is to execute trades. In other words they do not provide research reports or other investment advice to their clients.

6. The rapid growth in *information technology* has been a key factor in the development of derivatives exchanges. From streamlining back-end operations to facilitating Stock Index Arbitrage, computers have played a pivotal role in the growth of these markets.

Test your concepts

The answers are provided on page 241.

1. Which of these aspects of a futures contract is not decided by the exchange?
   (a) The number of units of the underlying asset per contract
   (b) The grade(s) of the underlying asset that may be delivered
   (c) The location(s) where delivery may be made
   (d) The transaction price.

2. The price that is paid to acquire an option is known as:
   (a) The option price
   (b) The exercise price
   (c) The strike price
   (d) (a) and (c).

---

7. See Harris (2003).

3. Which of these positions can lead to unlimited losses?
   (a) A short call position
   (b) A short put position
   (c) A short futures position
   (d) (a) and (c).

4. An investor who anticipates a bull market may take:
   (a) A long position in a futures contract
   (b) A long position in a call option
   (c) A short position in a put option
   (d) All of the above.

5. While marking a futures contract to market, the profit/loss between one day and the previous day is calculated by:
   (a) Comparing that day's closing spot price with the previous day's closing spot price
   (b) Comparing that day's futures settlement price with the previous day's futures settlement price
   (c) Comparing that day's futures settlement price with the previous day's closing spot price
   (d) None of the above.

6. Gross level margining:
   (a) Is inferior to net level margining from the standpoint of reducing the economic costs
   (b) Provides greater safety to traders
   (c) Reduces the incentive for brokers to handle their financial affairs prudently
   (d) All of the above.

7. If two investors who already have open positions in the futures maket enter into a fresh trade with each other:
   (a) Open interest will rise
   (b) Open interest will fall
   (c) Open interest will remain unchanged
   (d) Cannot say.

8. When a short delivers the asset under a futures contract, he will receive:
   (a) The spot price that was prevailing at the inception of the contract
   (b) The futures price that was prevailing at the inception of the contract
   (c) The spot price that is prevailing at the time of delivery
   (d) None of the above.

9. If the 99% value at risk of a portfolio over a one-day horizon is $5,000, it means that:
   (a) 99% of the maximum possible loss over a one-day horizon is $5,000
   (b) The maximum possible loss in a one-day period is 99% of $5,000
   (c) The portfolio will suffer a loss of $5,000 with a 99% probability
   (d) The portfolio will suffer a loss exceeding $5,000, over a one-day period, with a probability of only 1%.

10. Which of these instruments gives the short the right to deliver the underlying asset?
   (a) A European put option
   (b) A European call option
   (c) An American call option
   (d) None of the Above.

CHAPTER 2

VALUATION

QUESTION 41

How are forward contracts priced?

A forward contract entails an obligation on the part of the short to make delivery of the asset on a future date, and an equivalent obligation on the part of the long to take delivery.

From the perspective of the short, if the difference between the forward price and the prevailing spot price were to exceed the cost of carrying the asset until delivery, then clearly there would exist an arbitrage opportunity. For instance, in the case of an asset that pays no income before the maturity of the forward contract, the cost of carrying the asset will be rS, where r is the risk-less rate of interest and S is the prevailing spot price. Consequently, if:

$$F - S > rS$$

then a person could exploit the situation by borrowing and buying the asset, and simultaneously going short in a forward contract to deliver on a future date.

Such an arbitrage strategy is called *cash and carry arbitrage*. Hence, to rule it out, we require that:

$$F - S \leq rS \Rightarrow F \leq S(1 + r)$$

Numerical illustration

Cash and carry arbitrage can be illustrated with the help of an example.

Assume that IBM is currently selling for $100 per share, and is not expected to pay any dividends for the next six months. The price of a forward contract for one share of IBM to be delivered after six months is $106.

Consider the case of an investor who can borrow funds at the rate of 5% per six-monthly period. Such an individual can borrow $100 and acquire one share of IBM, and simultaneously go short in a forward contract to deliver the share after six months for $106. Thus the rate of return on his investment is:

$$\frac{(106 - 100)}{100} = 0.06 \equiv 6\%$$

whereas his borrowing cost is only 5%.

Consequently, cash and carry arbitrage is a profitable proposition under such circumstances. This is because:

$$F > S(1 + r)$$

or, in other words, the forward contract is overpriced.

The rate of return obtained from a cash and carry strategy is called the *implied repo rate*. Thus, a cash and carry strategy is profitable if the implied repo rate exceeds the borrowing rate.

By engaging in a cash and carry strategy, the investor has ensured a payoff of $106 after six months for an initial investment of $100. Thus, it is as if he has bought a *zero coupon* or *deep discount* debt instrument with a face value of $106, for a price of $100. Hence, a combination of a long position in the stock and a short position in a forward contract is equivalent to a long position in a zero coupon instrument. Such a deep discount instrument is referred to as a *synthetic T-bill*. Hence we can express the relationship as:

$$\text{Spot} - \text{Forward} = \text{Synthetic T-bill}$$

A negative sign indicates a short position in that particular asset. Thus, if we own any two of the three assets, we can artificially create the third. Notice that even though the spot and forward positions are exposed to price risk when held separately, their long–short combination results in a risk-less position.

QUESTION 42

The potential for arbitrage has been demonstrated from a short's perspective. What about the potential for arbitrage on the part of a long?

Cash and carry arbitrage requires a short position in a forward contract and arises if:

$$F > S(1 + r)$$

However, if F were to be less than $S(1 + r)$, then such a situation too would represent an arbitrage opportunity, this time for the long. Under such circumstances, an investor could short sell the asset and invest the proceeds at the risk-less rate, and simultaneously go long in a forward contract to reacquire the asset at a future date.

This kind of an arbitrage strategy is called *reverse cash and carry arbitrage*. In order to rule out such profit opportunities, we require that:

$$F \geq S(1 + r)$$

QUESTION 43

What is short selling and why would an investor wish to avail of a facility to short sell?

Let us look at asset markets from the standpoint of an investor who is bullish about the market, or in other words expects the price of a certain asset(s) to increase in value. Such a person will obviously seek to acquire the asset in the hope of being able to sell it subsequently at a higher price. Thus the ability to take a long position in an asset facilitates speculation on the part of bullish traders. The principle being followed here is *buy low and sell high*.

However, every trader need not be bullish about the market. There will always be those who expect the price of an asset(s) to decline in value. The issue is, how can these traders take a speculative position?

Short selling is a technique that permits such traders, who are said to be bearish about the market, to speculate. This mechanism entails the borrowing of an asset from another party in order to sell it. The borrower or short-seller is responsible for eventually returning the asset to the lender. He must also compensate the lender for any payouts that the asset may make during this time. This is because if the lender had not parted with the asset he would have received these payouts from it, and since he continues to be the owner of the asset, as he has merely lent it and not sold it, it is the responsibility of the short-seller to compensate him for this lost income.

Similarly, if there were to be any corporate action such as a stock split during the interim, then the short-seller has to make the necessary adjustment while returning the shares. For instance, an *n:1* stock split would imply that *1* old share is equivalent to *n* new shares post split. Thus, a short-seller who has borrowed one share prior to the split will be responsible for returning *n* shares if he were to return the shares after the split.

Short selling is a desirable feature in a free market, in as much as it provides liquidity, and helps drive down the prices of overvalued assets to realistic levels. However, there are economists who view short sales as a root cause of market downturns.

A short-seller obviously anticipates that he will be able to re-acquire the asset subsequently at a price that is lower than what was prevailing at the time of the short sale. The principle being followed here is therefore *sell high and buy low*.

The process of acquisition of shares to close out an existing short position is called *covering the short position*.

QUESTION 44

Is a short position inherently more risky than a long position?

From an economic standpoint, short selling entails betting against the general direction of the market. This is because in the medium to long term, we would expect asset prices to rise to compensate investors for the effects of inflation, if for no other reason.

The problem with short sales is that profits are finite, whereas losses in principle are infinite. This is because a stock has limited liability and consequently the lowest possible share price is zero. Hence, the maximum possible profit for a short-seller is the price received at the time of the short sale. However, since share prices do not have a theoretical upper limit, the cost of re-acquiring the share can be infinitely high. Thus losses are unbounded.

As opposed to this, a long position entails finite losses and unbounded profits.

QUESTION 45

What is a "short squeeze?"

Consider a situation where the price of a share suddenly begins to rise. It could induce a lot of short-sellers to cover their positions at the same time. This in turn can cause prices to rapidly rise further, translating into major losses for investors with a short position. This phenomenon is known as a *short squeeze*.

A short squeeze can be a consequence of positive news filtering into the market. However, it can also be artificially induced. A trader who observes that the number of short positions in a stock is high can create a short squeeze by placing a large buy order.

QUESTION 46

Lending a share for the purpose of a short sale appears to be a risky proposition, for there is always the possibility of the short-seller refusing to return the share. How does the lender protect himself in practice?

When a trader borrows a share from a broker and sells it, the sale proceeds will not be released by the broker. The broker will retain the proceeds with him, and will in fact require that the trader deposit additional collateral. The additional collateral as well as the sale proceeds will show up as a credit balance in the trader's account.

Numerical illustration

Natalie decides to short sell 100 shares of IBM, which is currently quoting at $130. Thus the proceeds from the sale will be $13,000. Regulation T, which is the regulation governing margin trading and short selling in the United States, requires the short-seller to deposit additional collateral equivalent to at least 50% of the proceeds from the short sale. Let us assume that Natalie therefore deposits an additional $6,500 with the broker. Her account position may be represented as shown in Figure 2.1.

Figure 2.1

Liabilities	Assets
100 Shares $130 = $13,000	Credit balance = $19,500
Owner's equity = $6,500	

Now there is always a risk that the share price could increase and that the owner's equity could get rapidly depleted. In the above account, the credit balance will remain at $19,500 irrespective of the share price. Consequently, any increase in the share price will manifest itself as a reduction in the owner's equity.

The broker will therefore set up a maintenance margin level, which in the United States is typically 30%. Corresponding to this level, we will have a trigger point for the stock price. If the price were to breach the trigger, a margin call will be issued.

The trigger point in Natalie's case may be computed as follows. The trigger obviously corresponds to a price that will make the owner's equity exactly equal to 30%. Therefore:

$$\frac{19,500 - 100P}{100P} = 0.30$$
$$\Rightarrow 19,500 - 100P = 30P \Rightarrow P = \$150$$

So if the price were to hit $150 or above, Natalie will receive a call asking her to deposit additional collateral. If she were to disregard it, the broker will automatically cover her short position and recover the costs of doing so.

QUESTION 47

There is always a possibility that a share price will fall after a short sale. In this case the owner's equity will obviously rise. What are the implications for the short-seller?

There are two possibilities. The short-seller can either withdraw the surplus equity in his account, or else he can use it to short additional shares. Let us take Natalie's case. Assume that the share price falls from $130 to $100. If so, Natalie's equity will increase to $9,500. Since the shares are worth $10,000 at this point in time, her equity must be a minimum of $5,000. Consequently she can withdraw up to $4,500. If she were to do so, her account position would look as shown in Figure 2.2.

Otherwise, if Natalie desires, she can use the amount to short additional shares worth $9,000 (0.5 × $9,000 = $4,500). Hence, she can short 90 more shares. If she were to do so, her account position would look as shown in Figure 2.3.

Figure 2.2

Liabilities	Assets
100 Shares $100 = $10,000	Credit balance = $15,000
Owner's equity = $5,000	

Figure 2.3

Liabilities	Assets
190 Shares $100 = $19,000	Credit balance = $28,500 ($19,500 + $9,000)
Owner's equity = $9,500	

QUESTION 48

We keep hearing about a term called the "uptick rule," in the context of short selling in the U.S. markets. What does this rule signify?

We will answer this question by first defining a tick. The *tick* or *tick size* in a market is the smallest amount by which two prices can differ. In the U.S. until the year 2000, the tick size for stocks was one-sixteenth of a dollar or 6.25 cents. Now the system has been decimalized, and the tick size is 0.01 dollars or 1 cent. The tick size could also vary along with the share price. For instance, on the Tokyo Stock Exchange (TSE) the tick size varies with the stock price as shown in Table 2.1.

Table 2.1   Tick sizes on the TSE

Price range	Tick size
$0 \leq P \leq 2,000$ yen	1 yen
$2,000 < P \leq 3,000$ yen	5 yen
$3,000 < P \leq 30,000$ yen	10 yen
$30,000 < P \leq 50,000$ yen	50 yen
$50,000 < P \leq 100,000$ yen	100 yen
$100,000 < P \leq 1,000,000$ yen	1,000 yen
$P > 1,000,000$ yen	10,000 yen

Source: www.tse.or.jp

Prices are classified with respect to previous prices. The price is said to be on an *uptick* if it is higher than the last observed price, on a *downtick* if it is lower, and on a *zero tick* if it is the same. Zero tick prices are further classified depending on the last different price that was observed. If the last different price was higher, then the price is said to be on a *zero downtick*, whereas if the last different price was lower, then it is said to be on a *zero uptick*. We will illustrate these concepts with the help of Table 2.2.

Table 2.2   Illustration of price moves corresponding to upticks, downticks, and zero ticks

Previous to last price	Last price	Current price	Term
72.00	72.00	72.10	Uptick
72.00	72.00	71.90	Downtick
72.10	72.00	72.00	Zero downtick
71.90	72.00	72.00	Zero uptick

In the U.S. the Securities Exchange Commission (SEC), the New York Stock Exchange (NYSE) and the National Association of Securities Dealers (NASD) have rules that prevent short selling, unless the sale is at a price that is higher than the last different price. That is, the trade must be on an uptick or on a zero uptick. The objective is to prevent short sales from sending the market on a downward spiral, for sustained short selling in a declining market can cause the market to crash.

QUESTION 49

We have seen that cash and carry arbitrage is ruled out if the implied repo rate is less than the borrowing rate. Is there an equivalent condition to preclude reverse cash and carry arbitrage?

We will first illustrate reverse cash and carry arbitrage with the help of a numerical example.

Assume once again that IBM is selling for \$100 per share, and that the company is not expected to pay any dividends for the next six months. Let the price of a forward contract for one share of IBM to be delivered after six months be \$104.

Consider the case of an arbitrageur who can lend money at the rate of 5% per six-monthly period. Such an individual can short sell a share of IBM and invest the proceeds at 5% interest for six months, and simultaneously go long in a forward contract to acquire the share after six months for \$104.

We are assuming that the arbitrageur can lend the proceeds from the short sale. In practice, the amount has to be deposited with the broker who, of course, can invest it to earn interest. In a competitive market, brokers will pass on a part of the interest income to the client who is short selling. This is called a *short interest rebate*. However, the effective rate of return earned by the short-seller will be lower than the prevailing market rate.

His effective borrowing cost is:

$$\frac{(104 - 100)}{100} = 0.04 \equiv 4\%$$

which is less than the lending rate of 5%.

Consequently there is a profit to be made by employing a reverse cash and carry strategy under such circumstances. This is because:

$$F < S(1 + r)$$

or, in other words, the forward contract is underpriced.

The cost of borrowing funds under a reverse cash and carry strategy is called the *implied reverse repo rate*. Thus reverse cash and carry arbitrage is profitable only if the implied reverse repo rate is less than the lending rate.

By engaging in a reverse cash and carry strategy, the investor has ensured the sale of a zero coupon instrument with a face value of $104, for a price of $100. Hence a combination of a short position in the stock and a long position in a forward contract is equivalent to a short position in a zero coupon instrument. Hence we can express the relationship as:

$$-\text{Spot} + \text{Forward} = -\text{Synthetic T-bill}$$

Cash and carry arbitrage is ruled out if $F \leq S(1 + r)$, while reverse cash and carry arbitrage is ruled out if $F \geq S(1 + r)$. Thus, in order to rule out both forms of arbitrage, we require that $F = S(1 + r)$.

QUESTION 50

The above no-arbitrage condition is obviously valid for assets that do not make any payouts during the life of the forward contract. What will be the no-arbitrage condition if the asset were to make payouts?

If a person who is holding an asset in his inventory were to receive income from it, then such an inflow would obviously reduce the carrying cost. The carrying cost can now be defined as $rS - I$ where I is the future value of the income as calculated at the time of expiration of the forward contract. Consequently, in order to rule out cash and carry arbitrage we require that:

$$F - S \leq rS - I \Rightarrow F \leq S(1 + r) - I$$

Similarly, from a short-seller's perspective, the effective income obtained by investing the proceeds from the short sale will be reduced by the amount of payouts from the asset, since the short-seller is required to compensate the lender of the asset for the payouts. Hence, reverse cash and carry arbitrage is profitable only if:

$$F - S < rS - I$$

Thus to rule out reverse cash and carry arbitrage we require that:

$$F - S \geq rS - I \Rightarrow F \geq S(1 + r) - I$$

Therefore, to preclude both forms of arbitrage it must be the case that:

$$F = S(1 + r) - I$$

We will illustrate cash and carry arbitrage in the case of assets making payouts, with the help of a numerical example. The extension to reverse cash and carry arbitrage is straight forward.

Numerical illustration

Let us go back to the case of the IBM share. Assume that the share is selling for $100, and that the stock is expected to pay a dividend of $5 after three months and another $5 after six months. Forward contracts with a time to expiration of six months are available at a price of $96 per share. We will assume that the second dividend payment will occur just an instant before the forward contract matures.

Consider the case of an investor who can borrow at the rate of 10% per annum. Such an individual can borrow $100 and buy a share of IBM, and simultaneously go short in a forward contract to sell the share after six months for $96. After three months he will get a dividend of $5 which can be invested for the remaining three months at a rate of 10% per annum. And finally, just prior to delivering the share under the forward contract, he will receive a second dividend of $5.

Thus, at the time of delivery of the share, the total cash inflow for the investor will be:

$$96 + 5 \times \left[1 + \frac{0.10}{4}\right] + 5 = 106.125$$

Hence the rate of return on the synthetic T-bill is:

$$\frac{(106.125 - 100)}{100} = 0.06125 \equiv 6.125\%$$

This is greater than the borrowing rate of 5% for six months.

Consequently cash and carry arbitrage is profitable. This is because:

$$F + I > S(1 + r)$$

where I is the future value of the payouts from the asset as calculated at the point of expiration of the forward contract.

QUESTION 51

While financial assets generate cash inflows for the investor, physical assets require the payment of storage costs and related expenses like insurance premia. How will this affect the no-arbitrage condition?

A cost is nothing but a negative income. Hence, if the future value of all storage-related costs were to be Z, as calculated at the time of expiration of the forward contract, then $I = -Z$. Thus the no-arbitrage pricing relationship can be expressed as:

$$F = S(1 + r) - (-Z) = S(1 + r) + Z$$

If this relationship were to be violated, then arbitrage profits can be made. We will demonstrate this in the case of an overpriced gold forward contract.

Numerical illustration

Assume that the spot price of gold is $500 per ounce and that storage costs are $5 per ounce for a period of six months, payable at the end of the period. Forward contracts are available with a time to expiration of six months and the price per ounce of gold is $535.

Consider the case of an investor who can borrow at the rate of 10% per annum. Such a person can borrow $500 and buy one ounce of gold, and simultaneously go short in one forward contract. At the end of six months, he will get $535 when he delivers the asset. His interest cost for six months is $25 and the storage cost of gold is $5. Thus the effective carrying cost is $30.

In this case, the rate of return on the investment, which is:

$$\frac{(535 - 500)}{500} = 0.07 \equiv 7\%$$

is greater than the effective carrying cost, which is:

$$\frac{(530 - 500)}{500} = 0.06 \equiv 6\%$$

Hence cash and carry arbitrage is profitable. Such a strategy yields a profit because:

$$F > S(1 + r) + Z$$

where Z is the storage cost. In order to rule out both cash and carry as well as reverse cash and carry arbitrage, we therefore require that:

$$F = S(1 + r) + Z$$

QUESTION 52

The facility for short selling of assets seems to be imperative for ensuring that the no-arbitrage condition holds in practice. Is short selling of assets always feasible? If not, what are the consequences?

Short selling need not always be feasible for an asset. Consequently, assets can be divided into two categories, *pure* or *investment* assets, and *convenience* or *consumption* assets.

An investment asset, as the name suggests, is one that is held by the investor as an investment. Hence, as long as the owner receives the asset intact at the end of the period during which he wishes to hold it as an investment, and is compensated for any payments that he would have received in the interim had he not parted with the asset, he will not mind parting with it. In other words, he will be amenable to lending the asset to facilitate short selling on the part of another investor. All financial assets fall into this category. A precious metal like gold is also an investment asset.

However, an agricultural commodity like wheat is often held for reasons other than potential returns. Consider the situation from the perspective of a person who chooses to hoard wheat before a harvest. Prices of commodities normally rise before the harvesting is completed, and fall thereafter. Consequently, such an investor not only has to incur storage costs, but also faces the specter of a capital loss. Therefore, from an investment angle, it makes little sense to hoard wheat prior to a harvest. The fact that the investor nevertheless chooses to do so implies that he is getting some intangible benefits from hoarding the commodity. For instance, he may wish to ensure that he does not have to close his wheat mill during an unanticipated shortage due to a cyclone or a rainfall failure. The value of such intangible benefits is called the *convenience value*.

If the holder of an asset is getting a convenience value from it, he will not part with it to facilitate short sales.

The question that one may ask is, isn't the convenience value a form of implicit dividend? Therefore, can we not compensate the holder of the convenience asset and induce him to part with it?

There are two key differences between such implicit dividends and explicit payouts like dividends from shares. Firstly, the convenience value cannot be quantified. Secondly, the perception of such value will differ from holder to holder.

Therefore in the case of those assets which are being held for consumption purposes, we can only state that:

$$F \leq S(1 + r) + Z$$

The possibility of earning profits through a cash and carry strategy will help ensure that:

$$F \not> S(1 + r) + Z$$

However, F may be less than $S(1 + r) + Z$ without giving rise to arbitrage, because facilities for short sales may not exist.

QUESTION 53

It has been mentioned that while borrowing an asset for short sales, the lender of the asset has to be compensated for any payouts that he would have received, had he not parted with it. However, in the case of physical commodities, a person who lends an asset will actually save on storage costs. What consequences does this have for reverse cash and carry arbitrage?

In the case of reverse cash and carry arbitrage involving financial assets, the arbitrageur, who is also the short seller, has to compensate the lender for any income which he foregoes by parting with the asset.

However, in the case of physical assets, the lender would not have received any payouts had he chosen to hold on to the asset. On the contrary, he would have incurred storage costs had he held on to the asset rather than lending it for a short sale. Under such circumstances, it turns out that reverse cash and carry arbitrage is often profitable only if the arbitrageur receives the cost savings experienced by the lender of the asset.

We will illustrate the situation using our earlier example of a forward contract on gold.

Assume that gold is currently selling for $500 per ounce, and that the price of a six-month forward contract is $525. The cost of storage is $5 per ounce per six months, payable at the end of the period, and the borrowing/lending rate is 10% per annum.

$$F = 525 < S(1 + r) + Z = 500(1 + 0.05) + 5 = 530$$

An investor engaging in reverse cash and carry arbitrage will short sell the asset and will receive $500. This amount will be lent at the rate of 10% per annum. Simultaneously, he will go long in a forward contract to acquire the asset after six months for $525. Thus, at the end of six months his cash inflow will be $525, which will be the same as his cash outflow. Therefore, in order for him to make a profit on this strategy, he ought to be compensated by the lender of the asset with an amount equal to the storage cost saved by him, which in this case is $5.

In practice, however, such an arrangement may not be feasible. Does this therefore mean that such a mispriced contract cannot be exploited? The answer is no.

Consider the situation from the perspective of an investor who owns one ounce of gold. He can sell the gold in the spot market and lend the proceeds for six months. Simultaneously, he can go long in a forward contract to reacquire the gold six months later at $525. Six months hence, he will receive a cash inflow of $525, which will be just adequate to repurchase the gold. On top of it, he will have $5 cash in his possession, which represents the storage cost saved.

Such an individual is not an arbitrageur in the conventional sense, although he has clearly exploited an arbitrage opportunity. Consequently, such activities are referred to as *quasi-arbitrage*. In derivatives parlance, we say that the investor has replaced an actual spot position in gold with a synthetic spot position. Such quasi-arbitrage will help ensure that:

$$F = S(1 + r) + Z$$

for a physical commodity that is perceived as an investment asset. For consumption assets, however, even a quasi-arbitrage strategy may not be able to ensure that $F = S(1 + r) + Z$. This is because an asset holder who is receiving a convenience value may not be willing to substitute his natural spot position with a synthetic spot position.

QUESTION 54

We have used the terms "repo" and "reverse repo" repeatedly in the context of arbitrage. What exactly do these terms signify?

Repo is a short form for a *repurchase transaction*. An investor who needs funds, and is in a position to offer securities as collateral, can undertake a repurchase transaction. In such a deal, he will sell the securities to the lender of funds at a price, with a promise to buy it back subsequently, usually a day later, at a higher price. The difference between the purchase and sale prices of the securities constitutes the interest on the loan. Sometimes both the purchase and subsequent sale transactions are done at the same price, in which case the interest is separately calculated and paid. Thus a repo is nothing but a collateralized loan arrangement. From the perspective of the borrower, such a transaction is termed a repo, whereas from the perspective of the lender it is termed a reverse repo. Thus a reverse repo is nothing but a repo looked at from a lender's perspective. In practice there are money market dealers who will do a repo with one party and a reverse repo with another. In the process they will make a spread.

Most repos are done on an overnight basis. In practice a dealer will locate a corporation or a money market mutual fund which has funds to invest overnight, and will borrow from it. The funds will then be lent out to a party which has an overnight shortfall. There are also repos undertaken for longer periods, which are called term repos. The rate of interest on such transactions is higher.

Most repo transactions in global markets are done on the strength of government securities. In the U.S. other money market securities such as commercial paper may also be used as collateral for repo transactions.

QUESTION 55

Does a forward contract have any value? If so, how does the value of a contract change over time? What about an open futures position, does it too have value?

When a forward contract is first entered into, its value to both the parties is zero. That is, neither the long nor the short has to pay any money to take a position in a forward contract. It may be argued that both of them need to post margins. But a margin, remember, is a performance bond and not a cost.

Before we proceed to discuss the evolution of a forward contract's value over time, let us first understand the difference between the *forward price* and the *delivery price*.

The delivery price is the price that is specified in the forward contract. That is, it is the price at which the short agrees to deliver, and the long agrees to accept delivery, as per the contract.

What then is the forward price? At any point in time, the forward price is the delivery price of a contract that is being negotiated at that particular instant. Once a contract is entered into, its delivery price will remain unchanged. However, the forward price will keep changing as new trades are negotiated.

To put things in perspective, if one were to come and say that he had entered into a forward contract a week ago, we would ask "what was the delivery price?" and not "what was the forward price then?", although both would mean the same thing. However if we were to negotiate a contract at the current point in time, we would ask "what is the forward price?". If the contract were to be sealed, the prevailing forward price would become the delivery price of the contract.

At the time a contract is entered into, its value will be zero. However as time passes, a pre-existing contract will acquire value. Let us consider a long forward position that was taken at some point of time in the past and which has a delivery price of K. In order to offset this position, the investor will have to take a short position, which will obviously be executed at the prevailing forward price, F. Thus, after taking a counter-position, the investor will have a payoff of $(F - K)$ awaiting him at the time of expiration of the contract. The value of the contract is nothing but the present value of this payoff.

Assume that a forward contract exists that expires at time T, and has a delivery price of K. Let F be the forward price that is currently prevailing for a contract expiring at T, and let r be the risk-less rate of interest for the period between now and T. Then the value of the long forward position is:

$$\frac{F - K}{1 + r}$$

Quite obviously, the value of a short forward position with a delivery price of K will be:

$$-\frac{F - K}{1 + r} = \frac{K - F}{1 + r}$$

We will now give a numerical illustration.

Numerical illustration

Assume that a forward contract with nine months to expiration was entered into three months ago at a delivery price of $100. Let today's forward price for a six-month contract be $120. The risk-less rate of interest for six months is 10%. The value of a long forward position with a delivery price of $100 will therefore be:

$$\frac{120 - 100}{1.10} = 18.18$$

The value of a short forward position with a delivery price of $100 will be −18.18. Thus, once a forward contract is sealed, a subsequent increase in the forward price will lead to an increase in value for holders of a long position, while a subsequent decrease in the forward price will lead to an increase in value for holders of a short position.

Now let us turn to futures contracts. When a trade is executed, neither the long nor the short have to pay to get into a position. However, as the futures price changes subsequently, an open futures position will acquire value. But the difference, as compared to a forward contract, is that at the end of every day, the profit/loss is calculated and credited/debited to the margin account. The position is then re-initialized at the settlement price. This process of marking to market is nothing but a settlement of built-up value. Once the contract is re-initialized, the value will once again revert back to zero. Thus futures contracts accumulate value in the period between two successive settlement price calculations. Once the marking to market procedure is undertaken, the value of both long and short positions will be zero.

QUESTION 56

Is the price of a forward contract on an asset the same as the price of a futures contract on the same asset, if the contracts expire at the same time?

Under certain conditions, the price of a forward contract on an asset will be the same as the price of a futures contract, on the same asset, with the same expiration date. More specifically, if the risk-less rate of interest is a constant, and is the same for all maturities, then forward and futures prices will be identical. Thus, under such circumstances, all the no-arbitrage conditions that we have derived for forward contracts will be equally valid for futures contracts.

QUESTION 57

In real life, interest rates are random and not constant. What will be the impact of this on the relationship between forward and futures prices, for contracts with the same time to expiration?

The fundamental difference between forward and futures contracts is that the latter are marked to market, and consequently lead to cash flows on a daily basis, whereas the former are not marked to market, and hence give rise to a cash flow only at the time of expiration.

Let us first consider a situation where interest rates and futures prices are positively correlated. If the futures price were to rise, then the corresponding interest rate will also be high. Rising futures prices lead to cash inflows for investors with long futures positions. Thus, the longs will be able to invest their profits at high rates of interest. At the same time, rising futures prices will lead to cash outflows for investors with short futures positions, who will consequently have to finance these losses at high rates of interest. On the contrary, if futures prices were to decline, the corresponding interest rates will be low. Declining futures prices will lead to losses for the longs and profits for the shorts. Thus the longs can finance their losses at low rates of interest while the shorts will have to invest their profits at low rates.

Compared to an investor with a long position in a forward contract, who will not be affected by interest rate movements in the interim, an investor with a long futures position will be better off. By the same logic, a person with a short futures position will be worse off as compared to an investor with a short forward position. Therefore, as compared to a forward contract, a person taking a long futures position should be required to pay a higher price for this relative advantage. Or, as viewed from the short's angle, a person taking a short futures position should receive a higher price for this relative disadvantage. Hence, if interest rates and futures prices are positively correlated, futures prices will exceed forward prices.

A similar argument will demonstrate that if interest rates and futures prices are negatively correlated, then futures prices will be less than the corresponding forward prices.

QUESTION 58

What do we mean when we say that a market is at "full carry?"

Let us first define the term "net carry." It refers to the net carrying cost of the underlying asset, expressed as a fraction of its current spot price. Therefore, if the risk-less rate of interest is r, and the future value of payouts from the asset is I, then:

$$\text{Net carry} = \frac{rS - I}{S} = r - \frac{I}{S}$$

For physical assets which entail the payment of storage costs:

$$\text{Net carry} = r + \frac{Z}{S}$$

We know that for investment assets:

$$F = S(1 + r) - I$$

or

$$F = S(1 + r) + Z$$

as the case may be. Therefore, in either case:

$$F = S + (\text{Net carry})S$$

In the case of convenience assets:

$$F \leq S(1 + r) + Z$$
$$\Rightarrow F = S(1 + r) + Z - Y = S + (\text{Net carry})S - Y$$

where the variable Y, which equates the two sides of the relationship, is the *marginal convenience value*.

If $Y = 0$, then we say that the market is at *full carry*. Thus investment asset markets will always be at full carry, whereas convenience asset markets will not.

QUESTION 59

What do the terms "backwardation" and "contango" mean?

If the futures price for an asset exceeds its spot price or if the price of a near-month contract is less than the price of a far-month contract, then we say that there is a *contango* market.

However, if the futures price is less than the spot price or if the price of the near-month contract is more than the price of a far-month contract, then the market is said to be in *backwardation*.

We will illustrate these situations with the help of an example. Consider the following spot and futures prices for wheat. Table 2.3 depicts a backwardation market, whereas Table 2.4 depicts a contango market.

Table 2.3 Backwardation market

Contract	Price
Spot	4.50
March futures	4.42
May futures	4.35
July futures	4.30
September futures	4.20

Table 2.4 Contango market

Contract	Price
Spot	4.50
March futures	4.55
May futures	4.62
July futures	4.70
September futures	4.80

For financial assets, the net carry can either be positive or negative, depending on the relationship between the financing cost, rS, and the future value of the payouts from the asset, I. A positive net carry will manifest itself as a contango market, whereas a negative net carry will reveal itself as a market in backwardation.

In the case of physical commodities, if the market is at full carry, then we will have a contango market. However, if the market is not at full carry, then we may either have a backwardation or a contango market, depending on the relative magnitudes of the net carry and the convenience yield.

QUESTION 60

Arbitrage refers to the ability to make a cost-less, risk-less profit. Are cash and carry and reverse cash and carry strategies really devoid of risk in practice?

In our discussion, we have presented cash and carry arbitrage and reverse cash and carry arbitrage as if the outcomes of the two strategies are virtually certain. However, in practice, both the strategies are characterized by an element of risk for a variety of reasons.

Let us recapitulate the cash and carry arbitrage strategy. It requires the arbitrageur to borrow and finance the purchase of the asset and simultaneously go short in a futures contract. In our discussion we have assumed that he is able to borrow at an interest rate that remains constant for the entire period. In practice, he may have to borrow for a shorter period and roll over the loan. In such cases, there is a risk that interest rates may rise subsequently. This is called *financing risk*.

Also in the case of assets which make payouts, the decision to engage in cash and carry arbitrage is taken after forecasting the payouts that the asset is likely to make during the life of the contract. If the asset does not make payouts as forecasted, the expected profit may not materialize. This risk is called *payout risk* or *dividend risk*.

What about reverse cash and carry arbitrage? This strategy requires the arbitrageur to short sell the asset and lend the proceeds, and simultaneously go long in the futures contract. As should be obvious, both interest rate risk and dividend risk are factors in this case as well.

QUESTION 61

We often hear of a term called "risk arbitrage." What exactly does it mean?

We have already discussed the financing risk and payout risk inherent in arbitrage strategies. However, there is a third element of risk as well. In the case of contracts which specify more than one acceptable grade of the asset for delivery, the option as to which grade to deliver is always given to the short. As we have seen earlier, the short will choose the cheapest to deliver grade at the time of delivery. This grade, however, need not be the same as the one which was originally sold short by the arbitrageur in a reverse cash and carry operation. Therefore, in the event of the short delivering a different grade, the arbitrageur will have to acquire the asset which he had originally sold short, at the prevailing market price, and deliver it. The net result could be an ex-post implied reverse repo rate that is higher than the lending rate. Consequently, reverse cash and carry arbitrage under such circumstances is fraught with danger, and is more appropriately termed as *risk arbitrage.*

To understand this issue, let us first examine cash and carry arbitrage in a situation where multiple grades are permitted for delivery. Assume that the arbitrageur goes long in one unit of grade i of the asset. Normally, when only one grade is permissible for delivery, cash and carry arbitrage and reverse cash and carry arbitrage entail spot–futures positions in the ratio of 1:1. That is, if the cash and carry arbitrageur goes long in one unit of the asset, he will short one futures contract. Similarly, when a reverse cash and carry arbitrageur short sells one unit of the underlying asset, he will go long in one futures contract.

The situation is different when multiple grades are specified for delivery, and a multiplicative system of price adjustment is used. Assume that a cash and carry arbitrageur goes long in one unit of grade i of the underlying asset and takes a short position in h futures contracts. At expiration when he delivers the asset, he will receive $ha_iF_T = hS_T$, assuming that *grade i* is the cheapest to deliver grade. If h is less than 1.0, then he will sell the remaining quantity in the spot market so as to realize $(1 - h)S_T$. However, if h is more than 1.0, he will have to incur additional expenditure in order to acquire the necessary units to satisfy his delivery obligation, and $(1 - h)S_T$ will represent an outflow. His profit from marking to market will be $h(F_0 - F_T)$. For the strategy to be risk-less, we require that:

$$ha_iF_T + (1 - h)S_T + h(F_0 - F_T) = a_iF_0$$
$$\Rightarrow ha_iF_T + (1 - h)a_iF_T + h(F_0 - F_T) = a_iF_0$$
$$\Rightarrow h = a_i$$

Thus the appropriate number of futures contracts is equal to the price adjustment factor of the grade in which the arbitrageur takes a long position.

The very fact that a cash and carry arbitrage strategy was initiated signifies that the ex-ante implied repo rate was greater than the borrowing rate. That is:

$$\frac{a_i F_0 - S_{i,0}}{S_{i,0}} > r$$

At expiration, there are two possibilities. Grade i may be the cheapest to deliver, in which case the arbitrageur will deliver it. Or else some other grade, grade j, may have become the cheapest to deliver. If so, the arbitrageur can sell the unit of grade i in his possession at its prevailing spot price, and acquire a_i units of grade j to deliver under the futures contract.[1]

The inflow will be:

$$S_{i,T} + a_i \times (a_j F_T) + a_i(F_0 - F_T)$$

The outflow will be:

$$a_i S_{j,T}$$

The net inflow will therefore be:

$$S_{i,T} + a_i \times (a_j F_T) + a_i(F_0 - F_T) - a_i S_{j,T}$$
$$= S_{i,T} + a_i S_{j,T} + a_i(F_0 - F_T) - a_i S_{j,T}$$
$$= a_i F_0 + a_i \left[\frac{S_{i,T}}{a_i} - \frac{S_{j,T}}{a_j} \right]$$
$$> a_i F_0$$

because if grade j is the cheapest to deliver by assumption, then its delivery adjusted spot price $\dfrac{S_{j,T}}{a_j}$ will be lower than that of grade i, and will be equal to the futures price, F_T. Thus if a cash and carry arbitrage strategy is initiated because it looks profitable at the outset, it can only lead to a greater profit, if not the anticipated profit. In other words, the ex-post implied repo rate will be greater than or equal to the ex-ante implied repo rate, which by assumption was greater than the borrowing rate. Consequently, there is no risk as such.

---

1. We have used the symbol $S_{i,0}$ to denote the spot price of ith asset at time 0, $S_{i,T}$ to denote its spot price at time T. Similarly, F_0 and F_T denote the futures prices at times 0 and T respectively.

However, what if a reverse cash and carry strategy is initiated? The very fact that such a strategy is being initiated implies that:

$$\frac{a_i F_0 - S_{i,0}}{S_{i,0}} < r$$

If the short were to deliver grade i at the end, then the anticipated arbitrage profit will be realized. However, consider a situation where the arbitrageur who has gone long is forced to take delivery of another grade, j, because the short finds that it is the cheapest to deliver. If so, the arbitrageur would have to sell this grade in the spot market and acquire grade i at its prevailing spot price to cover his short position.

The outflow is:

$$a_i(a_j F_T) + S_{i,T}$$

The inflow is:

$$a_i S_{j,T} + a_i (F_T - F_0)$$

The net outflow is:

$$a_i(a_j F_T) + S_{i,T} - a_i S_{j,T} - a_i(F_T - F_0)$$
$$= a_i S_{j,T} + S_{i,T} - a_i S_{j,T} - a_i(F_T - F_0)$$
$$= a_i F_0 + a_i \left[\frac{S_{i,T}}{a_i} - \frac{S_{j,T}}{a_j} \right]$$
$$> a_i F_0$$

Consequently, the ex-post implied repo rate could be greater than the ex-ante implied repo rate, and perhaps even greater than the lending rate. Thus, what looked like a profitable reverse cash and carry arbitrage opportunity may end up as a reduced arbitrage profit or perhaps even as a loss. Consequently, reverse cash and carry arbitrage is more appropriately termed as *risk arbitrage* under such circumstances.

QUESTION 62

It has been demonstrated that a cash and carry arbitrage strategy tantamounts to making an investment in a synthetic T-bill. Is it possible to create a forward contract itself synthetically?

From our understanding of cash and carry arbitrage, we know that:

Spot – Forward = Synthetic T-bill

Expressed in words, it means that a long position in the underlying asset, coupled with a short position in a forward contract, is equivalent to an investment in a zero coupon asset. Thus if we have natural positions in two assets, the third position can be created artificially. Rewriting the above equation, we can see that:

$$\text{Spot} - \text{T-bill} = \text{Synthetic forward}$$

Thus, by taking a long position in the underlying asset and borrowing at the risk-less rate, we can create a synthetic long position in a forward contract. Similarly:

$$\text{T-bill} + \text{Forward} = \text{Synthetic spot}$$

That is, a long position in the underlying asset can be replicated by taking a long position in a forward contract and investing in T-bills.

Short positions in forward contracts and spot contracts can be similarly created.

QUESTION 63

What is quasi-arbitrage? And can quasi-arbitrage opportunities exist in the absence of the potential for pure arbitrage?

As we have just seen, if we have two natural positions, we can synthetically create a position in the third asset. For instance, if we go long in the spot commodity and short in forward contracts, then we can effectively create a long position in a synthetic T-bill. Consequently, a person who is contemplating a risk-less investment has two alternatives. He can either buy T-bills in the market, or else he can invest in synthetic T-bills by buying the asset underlying the forward contract and taking a short forward position. This is akin to cash and carry arbitrage, except that the investor is not an arbitrageur in the conventional sense. Unlike an arbitrageur who is looking to make a cost-less, risk-less profit, this kind of an investor is seeking avenues to earn an additional return on investment. Such strategies which entail the use of traded assets to create synthetic investments are referred to as quasi-arbitrage, and the investors who employ them are referred to as *quasi-arbitrageurs*. In this case, unlike a pure arbitrageur who will compare the implied repo rate with his borrowing rate, a quasi-arbitrageur will compare it with his alternative lending rate, which in this case is the rate of return that can be earned by investing in natural T-bills.

As to whether quasi-arbitrage opportunities can exist even if there is no potential for pure arbitrage, the answer is yes, they can. As we have seen, a pure arbitrageur will compare the implied repo rate from a cash and carry strategy with his borrowing rate, whereas a quasi-arbitrageur will compare it with the rate of return on natural T-bills. There could be situations, therefore, where the implied repo rate, although not high enough to make pure arbitrage profitable, is greater than the rate of return that can be earned by investing in natural T-bills. Under such circumstances, an investor who is contemplating an investment in T-bills will choose to undertake an investment in synthetic T-bills. This is but one example of a case where it may be more profitable to take a synthetic rather than a natural position. Consequently, quasi-arbitrage may be profitable in situations where pure arbitrage is not.

QUESTION 64

While deriving the no-arbitrage pricing relationships, we assume that arbitrageurs will exploit perceived opportunities for profit till they are eliminated, and that consequently, such opportunities are ephemeral. Is this true for quasi-arbitrage as well?

While deriving the pricing relationships for forward and futures contracts, it was assumed that arbitrageurs could borrow and lend unlimited amounts of money at the market rate of interest. Under such conditions, arbitrage opportunities are unlikely to persist for significant periods.

However, there is a crucial difference between arbitrage and quasi-arbitrage. Unlike a pure arbitrageur, a quasi-arbitrageur faces a funds constraint. Let us go back to the case of the quasi-arbitrageur who is contemplating an investment in synthetic T-bills. His ability to take a long position in the asset underlying the forward contracts, which is an integral part of the strategy, is constrained by the funds at his disposal. That is, he cannot invest more in the spot position than what he could otherwise invest in T-bills. Thus, the quasi-arbitrage strategy can be employed only until his resources are exhausted. It may be argued that he can always borrow additional amounts and invest in synthetic T-bills. But remember that this will be tantamount to pure arbitrage. And pure arbitrage may not always be profitable in a situation where quasi-arbitrage is attractive.

Thus each quasi-arbitrageur faces his own budget constraint, and as a consequence, such opportunities persist for relatively longer periods of time as compared to pure arbitrage opportunities.

QUESTION 65

We hear of terms like "normal backwardation" and "normal contango" in the context of futures prices. Do they mean the same as the terms "backwardation" and "contango" respectively?

There is a fundamental difference between the concepts of backwardation and contango on one hand, and normal backwardation and normal contango on the other.

The terms backwardation and contango are used to describe the relationship between the current futures price of an underlying asset and its prevailing spot price. If the futures price exceeds the spot price, we say that the market is in contango. However, if the futures price is less than the spot price, then we say that the market is in backwardation.

The terms normal backwardation and normal contango on the other hand are used while making a comparison between the current futures price and the current expectation of the futures price that is likely to prevail at the time of expiration of the contract.

What do we mean by expectation of the terminal futures price?

Remember that the futures price at expiration will not be revealed until that point in time. Consequently, at any prior instant, this price is a random variable. As with all random variables, we can have only an expectation of the value that it is likely to take, where the term expectation refers to a probability weighted average of all the possible values that the variable can take.

In the case of futures contracts, the terminal futures price will also be equal to the terminal spot price. Hence, if we denote the current point in time by t and the point of contract expiration by T, the terms normal backwardation and normal contango refer to the relationship between F_t and $E[F_T]$ or equivalently $E[S_T]$. The terms backwardation and contango, however, are used in the context of a comparison between F_t and S_t.

QUESTION 66

What is the significance of normal backwardation and normal contango?

The theory of normal contango states that $F_t > E[F_T]$. This would imply that investors with a short futures position can expect to earn a profit on the average, since the futures price is expected to decline.

On the other hand, the theory of normal backwardation states that $F_t < E[F_T]$. This theory therefore implies that investors with long futures positions can expect to earn a profit on the average.

QUESTION 67

What is the "unbiased expectations hypothesis" of futures prices?

This is another hypothesis regarding the relationship between the current futures price and the current expectation of the terminal futures price. It argues that the current futures price is nothing but an expectation of the terminal futures price. In symbolic terms:

$$F_t = E[F_T] = E[S_T]$$

Thus according to this theory neither the longs nor the shorts can hope to make a profit on the average.

QUESTION 68

Why would we expect either normal backwardation or normal contango to prevail?

One of the explanations advanced to explain these theories is based on the requirements of hedgers. This is called the *hedging pressure hypothesis*, and has been advanced by eminent economists like Keynes and Hicks.

We will study hedging in detail in the next chapter. For the moment we will merely define a hedger. A hedger is an investor who seeks to minimize if not totally eliminate the risk of an adverse price movement in the spot market of a commodity in which he has either a long or a short position. Futures contracts can be used for hedging. If an investor has a long position in the spot market, he will seek to take a short position in the futures market, and vice versa. A hedger's sole motivation is to mitigate risk. He does not hedge because he anticipates the outcome with hedging to be superior to the outcome without hedging.

There is another kind of actor in futures markets called a speculator. Such an investor will take a calculated risk in the hope of realizing a profit. In other words, such a trader will choose to take a futures position only if he expects the profit to be commensurate with the risk that he is taking.

Keynes and Hicks argued that hedgers are net short in futures markets. This would then imply that speculators are net long. If so, these long positions must yield an expected profit which is consistent with the theory of normal backwardation.

Can hedging be used as an explanation for normal contango? Yes, it can, if we reverse the argument and assume that hedgers are net long in futures contracts. This would imply that speculators are net short and that therefore short positions must yield an expected profit on an average.

QUESTION 69

Finance theory postulates a relationship between the risk of an asset's returns and the expected return from the asset. Can this framework be used for futures contracts as well?

The risk–return framework can certainly be used for futures contracts. Remember that:

$$\text{Spot} - \text{T-bill} = \text{Synthetic futures}$$

T-bills are risk-less. Therefore the risk of a futures position is equal to the risk of the underlying asset.

The expected return from a futures position is equal to the expected return on the asset minus the risk-less rate of return or the return on the T-bill.

Why is it that futures have the same inherent risk as the underlying commodity, but a lower expected rate of return? The answer is that to take a position in an asset one has to invest an amount equal to its spot price. This investment must earn the risk-less rate of return plus a premium for the risk being taken. Futures contracts, however, do not require any up front investment. Consequently the expected return is equal to the risk premium on the underlying asset.

From the capital asset pricing model, we know that the rate of return on asset i, $E(r_i)$ is given by:

$$E(r_i) = r_f + \beta_i[E(r_M) - r_f]$$

where r_f is the risk-less rate of return, r_M is the rate of return on the market portfolio, and β_i is a measure of the systematic risk of asset i.

Thus the expected rate of return on a long futures position on the asset should be:

$$\beta_i[E(r_M) - r_f]$$

If the underlying asset has a beta greater than zero, then a long futures position will have a positive expected return. For a short futures position the relationship is just the opposite. If the underlying asset has a positive beta, then a short futures position will have a negative expected return.

We can draw one more conclusion from this relationship. The unbiased expectations hypothesis will be valid only if the underlying asset has a zero systematic risk, or in other words, its beta is zero.

QUESTION 70

Backwardation and contango are related to the cost of carry of an asset, and the convenience value from it, if any. Does this have any implications for when an asset should optimally be delivered during a prescribed delivery period? After all, the short does have a choice.

Take the case of a futures contract on a commodity with T periods to expiration. Let r be the continuously compounded rate of interest. Assume that storage costs are continuously compounded at a rate z.

If interest rates and storage costs are assumed to be continuously compounded, then the equivalent no-arbitrage condition for a futures contract on a commodity is $F \leq Se^{(r+z)T}$ which implies that:

$$Fe^{yT} = Se^{(r+z)T}$$

where y is the convenience value.[1]

We have modeled the convenience yield as a continuously compounded variable. It is legitimate, since the convenience yield is nothing but a measure of an implicit dividend, that will equate the LHS and the RHS.

Therefore $F = Se^{(r+z-y)T} = Se^{[r-(y-z)]T}$. From the perspective of a short, $(y - z)$ represents the benefit from holding the asset by way of a convenience yield, net of the storage cost involved. r represents the cost of financing the asset, which is either an actual interest outflow or an opportunity cost.

In a contango market, $F > S$. This implies that $r > (y - z)$. In other words, it is costing the short more by way of financing costs to keep the asset in his possession as compared to what he is gaining from holding on to it. It is therefore obvious that the short would like to deliver the asset as early as possible under these circumstances. Thus, in a contango market, it is optimal for the short to deliver at the commencement of the delivery period.

In a backwardation market however, $F < S$. This implies that $r < (y-z)$. In other words, the cost of financing the asset is less than the net benefit

1. See Hull (2004).

received by holding on to it. Under such circumstances, the short would like to delay delivery as much as possible. Consequently, in a backwardation market, it will be optimal for the short to deliver at the end of the prescribed delivery period.

This analysis has a significant implication for the pricing of futures contracts. We denote the time to expiration of a futures contract, in general, by T. In a case where a time interval is prescribed for delivery, the value of T to be used for computing the no-arbitrage price would obviously depend on whether the short is expected to deliver right at the outset of the delivery period or at the end of it. From the above arguments, it is obvious that futures prices in a contango market ought to be calculated under the assumption that delivery will take place right at the outset, whereas in a backwardation market, the logical assumption is that delivery will take place at the end of the stated period.

Test your concepts

The answers are provided on page 241.

1. If cash and carry arbitrage is possible:
   (a) The implied repo rate is greater than the borrowing rate.
   (b) The futures contract is overpriced.
   (c) The implied reverse repo rate is less than the lending rate.
   (d) (a) and (b).

2. Consider the following price sequences. At the terminal value of which sequence could a short sale order have been placed?
   (a) 92, 91, 91
   (b) 92, 92, 91
   (c) 90, 91, 91
   (d) None of the above.

3. If a market is at full carry:
   (a) Cash and carry arbitrage is infeasible.
   (b) Reverse cash and carry arbitrage is infeasible.
   (c) The asset is pure.
   (d) All of the above.

4. Which of these price sequences is a manifestation of backwardation?
   (a) Spot = 100; 1 month futures = 105; 2 month futures = 108
   (b) Spot = 100; 1 month futures = 108; 2 month futures = 112

(c) Spot = 100; 1 month futures = 98; 2 month futures = 95
(d) None of the above.

5. If an asset is in contango:
(a) The net carry is positive
(b) The marginal convenience value is zero
(c) The market is at full carry
(d) None of the above.

6. Financing risk and payout risk are faced by:
(a) Cash and carry arbitrageurs
(b) Reverse cash and carry arbitrageurs
(c) Both (a) and (b)
(d) Neither (a) nor (b)

7. In the case of arbitrage using contracts with multiple deliverable grades:
(a) The implied repo rate may be lower than anticipated
(b) The implied reverse repo rate may be higher than anticipated
(c) The implied reverse repo rate may be lower than anticipated
(d) (a) and (c).

8. From the capital asset pricing model, we can deduce that the unbiased expectations hypothesis is valid only if:
(a) The asset has zero risk
(b) The asset has zero systematic risk
(c) The asset has a rate of return equal to the risk-less rate
(d) (b) and (c).

9. As per Keynes and Hicks:
(a) Hedgers as a group are net short in futures
(b) Speculators as a group are net long in futures
(c) Hedgers as a group are net long in futures
(d) (a) and (b).

10. It is optimal for the short to deliver at the beginning of the delivery period if:
(a) The market is in backwardation
(b) The market is in contango
(c) The market is in normal contango
(d) None of the above.

CHAPTER 3

HEDGING AND SPECULATION

QUESTION 71

What is hedging?

A hedger, by definition, is a person who wants to protect himself against an unfavorable movement in the price of the underlying asset. Quite obviously, a person who seeks to hedge has already assumed a position in the underlying asset. If he already owns the asset, or in other words has a long position, his worry will be that the price of the asset may fall subsequently. On the other hand, if he has made a commitment to buy, or in other words has taken a short position, his worry will be that the price of the asset may rise subsequently. In either case, his desire to hedge is a manifestation of his wish to avoid risk.

Notice that we have defined a short position in a broader sense than in the case of a short sale involving an asset. In the case of a short sale, the short seller borrows an asset from a broker in order to sell, and therefore has a commitment to buy it back at a future date and return it. Now take the case of a company which has imported goods from the U.S. and has been given 90 days credit by the American supplier. The company therefore has a commitment to buy dollars after 90 days. Just like in the case of the short-seller, this company too would be worried that the price of the asset, in this case the U.S. dollar, may go up by the time it is procured. Thus in a more general sense, a short position connotes a commitment to buy an asset at a future date. An example in the case of physical commodities would be the case of a wheat mill which knows that it will have to procure wheat after the harvest, which we will assume is one month away. Its worry consequently would be that the harvest may be less plentiful than anticipated, and that consequently the price of the wheat in the spot market may turn out to be higher than what is currently expected. Such an entity may too exhibit a desire to hedge.

In general, investors and corporations possess special talents and knowledge in certain economic activities, and consequently take on concentrated risky positions in related securities and ventures. Let us call this *good risk*. At the same time they may be uncomfortable with other sources of risk to which they are exposed. Let us term this *bad risk*. The goal of hedging is to allow investors and firms to concentrate on "good risk," while reducing if not eliminating their exposure to "bad risk."

QUESTION 72

How do futures contracts help investors to hedge their positions?

Futures contracts can help people to hedge, irrespective of whether they have a long or a short position in the underlying asset. Consider a person who owns an asset. His fear is that he may have to subsequently sell it at a lower price. Such a person can hedge, by taking a short position in a futures contract. If the price of the underlying asset were to fall subsequently, he can still sell at the original futures price, since the other party is under an obligation to buy at this price. We will illustrate this with the help of an example.

Numerical illustration

Greg knows that he will have 500,000 bushels of wheat to sell after three months. His worry is that the spot price of the wheat may decline substantially by then.

Futures contracts on wheat are available with a time to maturity of three months, and each contract is for 5,000 bushels. If the current futures price is $4 per bushel, then by going short in 100 futures contracts, Greg can ensure that he can sell the wheat three months hence for $2,000,000.

This amount of $2,000,000 is guaranteed irrespective of what the actual spot price at the end of three months turns out to be. Thus, by locking in this amount, Greg can protect himself against a decline in the price below the contracted value of $4 per bushel. However, the flip side is that he will be unable to benefit if the spot price at expiration were to be greater than $4, for he is obliged to deliver at this price.

Now consider the issue from the perspective of a person who has a short position in the underlying asset. His worry is that the price may rise by the time he acquires it in the cash market. Such a person can hedge by taking a long position in the futures market. If the spot price were to rise subsequently, he can still buy at the original futures price since the other party is under an obligation to sell at this price.

Numerical illustration

Vicky has imported goods worth £312,500 from London, and is required to pay after one month. She is worried the dollar may depreciate by then, or in other words, that the dollar price of the pound may go up by then. A futures contract expiring after one month is available, and the contract size is 62,500 pounds. Let the futures price be $1.75 per pound.

So if Vicky takes a long position in five futures contracts, she can lock in a dollar value of $546,875 for the pounds. Once again this would be true irrespective of the spot exchange rate one month later. So while she can protect herself against a depreciating dollar, or in other words an exchange rate greater than $1.75 per pound, she is precluded from taking advantage of an appreciating dollar, which would manifest itself as an exchange rate below $1.75 per pound.

QUESTION 73

What do the terms "selling hedge" and "buying hedge" connote?

A *selling hedge*, also known as a *short hedge*, requires the hedger to take a short position in the futures market to mitigate the risk faced by him in the spot market.

On the other hand, a *buying hedge*, also known as a *long hedge*, requires the hedger to take a long position in the futures market, in order to offset his exposure in the spot market.

QUESTION 74

What is the difference between an "inventory hedge" and an "anticipatory hedge?"

A person who initiates a selling hedge does so because he expects to sell the asset at some point of time in the future. However, at the time of initiating the hedge, he may or may not have the asset in his possession.

For instance, a farmer who is harvesting wheat and plans to sell after three months may go in for a selling hedge. Such a hedger already has the asset in his inventory and can therefore be said to be hedging his inventory. This is an example of an *inventory hedge*.

On the other hand, take the case of a company which has exported goods to Germany and knows that it will be paid in euros after 90 days. It knows that it will have the euros in its possession after three months, and may therefore go short in futures contracts to hedge the amount that it will effectively receive in dollars. This kind of a selling hedge is in anticipation of a future event, for the euros are not currently in stock but are expected to arrive in 90 days. This is an example of an *anticipatory hedge*.

Buying hedges which are used by investors who have a prior commitment to buy on a future date are obviously always *anticipatory hedges*.

QUESTION 75

Can options be used for hedging?

Yes, both call and put options can be used for hedging. Let us consider the case of a call option first. Such an option gives the holder the right to acquire the underlying asset, at a pre-specified price called the *exercise price* or the *strike price*. Thus, a person who has a short position in the underlying asset can protect himself by buying a call option. If the price of the underlying asset at the time of acquisition were to exceed the exercise price of the option, he can always exercise the option and acquire the asset by paying the exercise price. Thus, he can protect himself against upward price movements. However, if the price at expiration is lower than the exercise price, he can let the option expire worthless and simply buy the asset in the spot market.

Numerical illustration

Assume that Vicky has bought 10 call options contracts with an exercise price of $1.75, where each options contract is for 31,250 pounds.

If the spot rate of exchange after one month is greater than $1.75 per pound, she can exercise the option and acquire 312,500 pounds for a consideration of $546,875. If the spot rate after a month is less than

$1.75 per pound, say $1.72 per pound, then she can forget the option and simply buy the pounds in the spot market by paying $537,500.

Similarly, a person who has a long position in the underlying asset can protect himself by buying a put option. A put option gives the holder the right to sell the underlying asset at a pre-specified exercise price. Thus, if the price of the underlying asset were to fall by the time the investor decides to sell it, he can always exercise the put option and sell it at the exercise price. Hence, such an investor can protect himself against downward price movements. However, if the price at expiration is higher than the exercise price, he can allow the option to expire, and sell the asset in the spot market.

Numerical illustration

Assume that Gary has bought 500 put options on IBM with an exercise price of $75, where each options contract is for 100 shares.

If the spot price of IBM after three months is less than $75 per share, then he can exercise the options and deliver the shares for a total consideration of $3,750,000. However, if the spot rate after three months is more than $75 per share, say $77, then he can forget the options and sell the shares in the spot market for $3,850,000.

QUESTION 76

Are futures and options interchangeable instruments from the standpoint of hedging?

No, futures contracts and options contracts both facilitate hedging, but they work differently, and consequently are not substitutes for each other.

Consider the case of a person who has a long position in the underlying asset. One alternative for him would be to hedge by going short in futures contracts. Such a strategy protects him from losses if the price of the asset were to fall subsequently, as you have seen above. However, if the price of the asset were to rise subsequently, he will be unable to profit from the situation since he is under an obligation to sell at the original futures price. The situation would be different if such a person were to use a put option for hedging. If the price of the asset were to fall subsequently and go below the exercise price, he can exercise the put and sell at the exercise price. However, if the price were to rise subsequently, he can forego the option to exercise and simply sell his asset in the cash market at a higher price. He can do this because a put option is a right and not an obligation.

Now, let us consider the case of a person who has a short position in the underlying asset. One option would be for him to hedge by going long in futures contracts. Such a strategy will protect him from losses if the price of the asset were to rise subsequently, as you have seen earlier. But if the price of the asset were to fall subsequently, he will be unable to benefit since he is under an obligation to buy at the original futures price. However, the situation would be different if such a person were to use a call option for hedging. If the price of the asset were to rise subsequently and exceed the exercise price, he could exercise the call and buy at the exercise price. If the price were to fall subsequently, he can forego the option to exercise and simply buy the asset in the cash market at a lower price. Once again, this is possible because a call option is a right and not an obligation.

Thus, futures contracts lock in the price at which the hedger can buy or sell the asset, as the case may be. However, options give protection on one side while permitting the hedger to benefit from favorable price movements on the other side. In other words, a person with a long position who uses a put option for hedging is assured of being able to sell at least at the exercise price. This is because if the price in the cash market at the time of sale were to be higher, he is not precluded from taking advantage of the situation. Similarly, a person with a short position, who uses a call option for hedging, is assured of the fact that he need not pay more than the exercise price. For, if the cash market price were to be lower than the exercise price at the time of purchase, he is in a position to buy at the market price.

QUESTION 77

If options give protection to the hedger on one side, while permitting him to take advantage of favorable price movements in the other direction, why would anyone want to use futures contracts for hedging?

In the case of a futures contract, the futures price that is fixed at the outset is set in such a way that the value of the contract to either party is zero. That is, neither the long nor the short need pay any money to take a position in a futures contract. Of course they have to post margins. But a margin is a performance guarantee and not a cost.

However, the buyer of an option, whether it is a call or a put, has to pay a price to the writer of the option in order to acquire the right. This price, called the *option price or option premium*, is payable at the outset, and cannot be recovered if the option is not exercised subsequently.

Thus a hedger has a choice. He can pay nothing and lock in a price using a futures contract, or else he can pay and acquire an option. If the price moves against him, he can exercise the option and transact at the exercise price, or if the price moves in his favor, he can forego the right to exercise and transact at the prevailing market price. Clearly, the two instruments are not interchangeable, and the choice of the instrument would depend on the individual.

We will now use an example to illustrate as to why one strategy will not dominate the other, where by the word *dominance* we mean having superiority under every conceivable outcome.

Numerical illustration

Xanadu, a software firm based in San Mateo, California, has a receivable of 5,000,000 GBP two months hence.[1]

The exchange rate for a two-month futures contract is 1.50 USD/GBP. Put options with an exercise price of 1.50 USD/GBP are available at a premium of 0.005 USD/GBP or at 0.5 cents.

Let us first consider a futures hedge. If the company goes short in futures contracts written on British pounds, it is guaranteed a dollar inflow of:

$$5,000,000 \times 1.50 = \$7,500,000$$

irrespective of the spot exchange rate prevailing at expiration.

However, if it were to use put options with an exercise price of 1.50 USD/GBP for hedging, it will receive:

$$5,000,000 \times 1.50 - 5,000,000 \times 0.005 =$$
$$7,500,000 - 25,000 = 7,475,000$$

---

1. GBP is the standard symbol for the British pound in foreign currency markets, as is USD for the U.S. dollar.

if S_T, the spot rate at expiration, were to be less than 1.50 USD/GBP, for the options would be exercised under these circumstances.

However, if S_T were to be greater than 1.50 USD/GBP, then the firm will opt to sell the pounds in the spot market. In this case, it will receive:

$$5,000,000 S_T - 25,000$$

We can see that if the exchange rate at expiration were to be 1.505 USD/GBP, then the outcome for the firm will be the same irrespective of whether it had chosen futures or options for hedging. This can be seen by equating the payoffs in both cases:

$$7,500,000 = 5,000,000 \, S^*_T - 25,000 \Rightarrow S^*_T = 1.505$$

If the terminal exchange rate were to be higher, then the options hedge would yield a superior outcome. However, for values of S_T less than 1.505 USD/GBP, the outcome with a futures hedge would be better.

So clearly a futures hedge cannot be said to dominate an options hedge or vice versa. Market participants will have different perceptions about the future spot rate. Consequently, while one party may decide in favor of an options hedge, others may prefer to hedge using futures.

QUESTION 78

It appears that a hedger who uses futures contracts may end up regretting his decision ex-post, for it may be the case that he would have been better off if he had not hedged. Is this true?

Yes, this could indeed be the case. Take the case of Vicky who went long in futures to acquire £312,500 at $1.75 per pound. If the spot exchange rate at the end turns out to be greater than $1.75 per pound, or in other words, if the dollar depreciates, then her decision to hedge would certainly be perceived as wise and sound.

But, if the spot exchange rate at expiration were to be less than $1.75 per pound, or in other words if the dollar appreciates, she would end up looking a little foolish. For she could have bought the pounds at a lower cost in terms of dollars had she decided not to hedge.

The problem is that, *a priori*, Vicky cannot be expected to be certain as to whether the dollar would depreciate or appreciate. So if she is a risk averse individual then she may very well decide to hedge her risk, notwithstanding the possibility that she may end up looking silly ex-post.

Thus, an investor will hedge if she feels that she is uncomfortable leaving her exposure to price risk open, where price risk refers to the risk that the spot price of the asset may end up moving in an adverse direction from her perspective. She cannot however guarantee that ex-post her decision will be vindicated. Hindsight as they say is a *perfect science*. A normal individual cannot be expected to be prescient, and if she were, she certainly would not need derivatives in order to hedge.

It is not just in the case of a futures hedge that an outcome without hedging may appear subsequently superior to the hedged outcome.

Let us take the case of Xanadu and assume that it used put options for hedging.

The payoff in terms of dollars would be:

$$7,475,000 \text{ if } S_T \leq 1.50$$

and:

$$5,000,000 S_T - 25,000 \text{ if } S_T > 1.50$$

On the contrary, had the firm chosen to stay unhedged, its payoff would have been:

$$5,000,000 S_T$$

It can be seen that for values of S_T greater than 1.495 USD/GBP, it would have been better if Xanadu had stayed unhedged. This can be seen by equating the payoffs in the two cases:

$$7,475,000 = 5,000,000 S_T \Rightarrow S_T = 1.495$$

A priori, one would not know for sure whether S_T will be below 1.495 or exceed it. So the potential for ex-post regret exists very much in the case of an options hedge as well.

QUESTION 79

The above illustrations assume that the futures contracts are settled by delivery. Will our conclusions change if the contracts were to be cash settled?

The effective price at which a hedger is able to sell if he takes a short futures position, or buy if he takes a long futures position, will be equal to the futures price prevailing at the time of initiation of the futures position, irrespective of whether the contract is delivery settled or cash settled.

Let us first take the case of a hedger who goes short in futures contracts. If the contract is cash settled, his total profit from marking to market would be $F_0 - F_T$. He will have to sell the asset in the spot market at a price of S_T. His overall cash inflow will be:

$$S_T + (F_0 - F_T) = F_0$$

because by the no-arbitrage condition, $F_T = S_T$. Notice that the profit from the futures position has to be added to determine the effective inflow. If it is a positive number, that is, it actually is a profit, then it will lead to a higher effective inflow. If it is a negative number, that is, it is a loss, then it will lead to a lower effective inflow.

Numerical illustration

Let us take the case of Greg who went short in 100 futures contracts at a price of $4 per bushel. Assume that the futures price or equivalently the spot price at expiration is $4.15 per bushel.

Greg's cumulative profit from marking to market will be:

$$100 \times 5,000 \times (4.00 - 4.15) = -\$75,000$$

He can sell the wheat in the spot market for $4.15 per bushel or $2,075,000 in all. The effective amount received for 500,000 bushels of wheat is:

$$\$2,075,000 - \$75,000 = \$2,000,000$$

which amounts to $4 per bushel.

The same is true for a hedger who goes long in futures. If the contract is cash settled, his cumulative profit from marking to market will be $F_T - F_0$. He will have to then buy the asset in the spot market by paying S_T. His overall cash outflow will be:

$$-S_T + (F_T - F_0) = -F_0$$

Notice that the profit from the futures position is added to the outflow in the spot market to determine the effective outflow. Thus a profit, or inflow from the futures market, will reduce the effective outflow, whereas a loss, or outflow from the futures market, will increase the effective outflow.

Numerical illustration

Take the case of Vicky who went long in a futures contract at a price of $1.75 per pound. Assume that the terminal spot or equivalently the futures price is $1.72 per pound. Her cumulative profit from marking to market will be:

$$312,500 \times (1.72 - 1.75) = -\$9,375$$

She can acquire £312,500 in the spot market by paying $537,500. Her effective outflow is therefore $546,875 which translates into an exchange rate of $1.75 per pound, which is nothing but the initial futures price.

QUESTION 80

What is a "perfect hedge?"

A hedge using futures contracts which can lock in a selling price for an investor with a long position in the spot market, or a buying price for an investor with a short position in the spot market, with absolute certainty, is called a *perfect hedge*. Both the examples given earlier are illustrations of a perfect hedge. In the first case Greg was assured of a selling price of $4 per bushel, while in the second case, Vicky was assured of a buying price of $1.75 per pound. Thus a perfect hedge transforms a risky (unhedged) spot position into a risk-free (hedged) position.

QUESTION 81

What are the necessary conditions for a hedge to be perfect?

The conditions that must hold if we are to ensure that the hedge is perfect are the following:

1. The date on which the hedger wishes to buy or sell the underlying asset must coincide with the date on which the futures contract being used is scheduled to expire.

2. The number of units of the underlying asset, which is sought to be bought or sold by the hedger, must be an integer multiple of the size of the futures contract.
3. Futures contracts must be available on the commodity which the hedger is seeking to buy or to sell.

QUESTION 82

Why is it important that the date on which the asset is bought or sold be the same as the expiration date of the futures contract?

For ease of exposition, let us assume that the futures contract specifies a single delivery date rather than a delivery period.

Take the case of a hedger who has gone short in futures contracts. We will denote the initial futures price by F_0 and the terminal spot and futures prices by S_T and F_T respectively. Now assume that the hedger wishes to sell the goods in his possession on day t^*, where $0 < t^* < T$. That is, he wishes to sell the goods prior to the date of expiration of the futures contract. If he does so, then he will have to offset the futures position on that day by taking a counterposition.

The cumulative profit from the futures market due to marking to market will be $F_0 - F_{t^*}$. The proceeds from the sale of the good in the spot market will be S_{t^*}. Thus the effective sale proceeds will be:

$$S_{t^*} + (F_0 - F_{t^*}) = F_0 + (S_{t^*} - F_{t^*})$$

Now if t^* were to be the same as T, then S_{t^*} would be equal to F_{t^*} and so the effective price received would be F_0. In other words, the hedge would be perfect, for the initial futures price would have been locked in. But in general, when t^* is a date prior to the expiration of the futures contract, F_{t^*} will not be equal to S_{t^*}. Thus, the effective price received ultimately would depend on both F_{t^*} and S_{t^*}. Since these are unknown variables until the end, there will always be uncertainty regarding the effective price that will ultimately be received by the hedger.

A similar argument can be advanced for the case where the hedger takes a long position in the futures contract. If the asset is bought on day t^* and the futures position offset, the effective outflow on account of the asset will be:

$$-S_{t^*} + (F_{t^*} - F_0) = -F_0 - (S_{t^*} - F_{t^*})$$

Once again there will be uncertainty about the effective price at which the asset will be bought.

Thus, since spot–futures convergence is assured only at the time of expiration of the futures contract, it is necessary that the date on which the transaction in the underlying asset takes place be the same as the expiration date of the futures contract, if we are to ensure that the hedge is perfect.

QUESTION 83

Why is it essential that the number of units that the hedger is seeking to buy or sell be an integer multiple of the size of the futures contract, in order to ensure that the hedge is perfect?

Assume that a farmer has 1,050 units of a commodity that he wishes to sell after one month. Futures contracts on the commodity expiring after one month are available, and each contract is for 100 units. So this farmer theoretically needs to go short in 10.5 futures contracts. In practice, he can either go short in 10 contracts or in 11. In either case, the effective price received per unit will be uncertain.

Case A: The farmer uses 10 contracts

The profit from marking to market will be:

$$10 \times 100 \times (F_0 - F_T)$$

The proceeds when the goods are sold in the spot market will be $1,050\, S_T$. The effective price received per unit of the good will be:

$$\frac{1,050 S_T + 1,000(F_0 - F_T)}{1,050}$$
$$= \frac{50 S_T + 1,000 F_0}{1,050}$$

Since S_T is a random variable whose value will be known only at the end, the effective price that will be received per unit will be uncertain.

Case B: The farmer uses 11 contracts

The profit from marking to market will be:

$$11 \times 100 \times (F_0 - F_T)$$

The proceeds from the sale of goods will be $1,050S_T$. The effective price received per unit of the good will be:

$$\frac{1,050S_T + 1,100(F_0 - F_T)}{1,050}$$
$$= \frac{1,100F_0 - 50S_T}{1,050}$$

Once again there will be uncertainty regarding the effective price that will be received.

QUESTION 84

What would be the consequences if the hedger is unable to find a futures contract on the commodity whose price he wishes to hedge?

If a contract is not available on the commodity whose price one wishes to hedge, there is no option but to use a contract on a related commodity, if such a contract is available. The use of a contract on a closely related commodity is called *cross hedging*. When we say closely related, we mean that the prices of the two commodities should move together. The higher the degree of positive correlation, the greater will be the effectiveness of the hedge.

We will now show why a cross hedge will be imperfect, by considering a short hedge.

Let S_T be the spot price of the asset that the hedger is selling on day T. We will assume that day T is the expiration date of a futures contract on a related commodity that is being used for hedging. Let F^*_0 be the initial futures price of this contract and F^*_T the terminal futures price. $S^*_T = F^*_T$ is the terminal spot price of the asset underlying the futures contract.

On day T the hedger will sell his asset at its prevailing spot price and collect his profit/loss from the futures market. The effective price received per unit will be:

$$S_T + (F^*_0 - F^*_T) = F^*_0 + (S_T - F^*_T)$$

In this case, S_T will in general not equal F^*_T because they represent two different commodities. Consequently, there will be uncertainty regarding the effective price.

QUESTION 85

Let us assume that futures contracts are available on the commodity whose price we wish to hedge, and that the transaction size is an integer multiple of the size of the futures contract. However, rarely will the scheduled transaction date coincide with the expiration date of the futures contract. What will we do under these circumstances, and what is the inherent risk?

The only option under such circumstances would be to choose a futures contract that expires after the date on which the hedger wishes to transact. For if we use a futures contract that expires earlier, then subsequently we will have an open or uncovered position, which would mean that we would not be hedged or protected till the transaction date.

If we use a contract that expires after the transaction date, then such a contract would have to be offset on the transaction date. For a short hedger, the effective price received under such circumstances will be:

$$F_0 + (S_{t^*} - F_{t^*})$$

The uncertainty in this case arises because S_{t^*} need not equal F_{t^*}. The same holds true for a hedger who takes a long position in futures contracts.

At any point in time, t, $S_t - F_t$ is called the basis, and is denoted by b_t. At the time of expiration of the futures contract, S_T is guaranteed to equal F_T, and we can be sure that the basis will be zero. However, prior to expiration we cannot make such an assertion. Consequently, a hedger who is forced to offset the futures contract prior to expiration will face uncertainty regarding the basis, or what is called *basis risk*.

We have defined the basis as $S_t - F_t$.[2]

In a contango market the basis, as per our definition, will be negative. If it becomes more negative over time, it is said to widen. Whereas, if it becomes less negative, it is said to narrow.

In a backwardation market, the basis will be positive. If it were to become more positive over time, we would say that it has widened. However, if it were to become less positive, it would be said to have narrowed.

Thus the terms "widening" and "narrowing" connote changes in the absolute value of the basis.

---

2. Some authors prefer to define it as the futures price minus the spot price.

For a short hedger, the effective price received is $F_0 + b_t$. Thus the higher the value of the basis the better it is for him. Thus he will benefit from a rising basis.

However, for a long hedger, the effective outflow is $F_0 + b_t$. Thus the lower the value of the basis, the smaller is the outflow.

Therefore short hedgers benefit from an increasing value of the basis while long hedgers benefit from a declining value. We know that longs benefit from rising prices while shorts benefit from declining prices. Hence if we were to treat the basis itself as a price (for after all it is nothing but a difference of two prices), we can say that a short hedger is *long the basis*, while a long hedger is *short the basis*.

QUESTION 86

How is basis risk measured, and why would a hedger wish to hedge despite knowing that he is exposed to basis risk?

The basis is defined as $S_t - F_t$. In Finance theory we measure risk by the variance of the random variable. So, using this yardstick:

$$\sigma^2(b) = \sigma^2(S) + \sigma^2(F) - 2\rho(S,F)\sigma(S)\sigma(F)$$

where $\sigma(S)$ is the standard deviation of the spot price, $\sigma(F)$ is the standard deviation of the futures price, and $\rho(S,F)$ is the correlation coefficient between the two variables.

Consider a person who is planning to sell an asset at time t^*. He is exposed to uncertainty regarding the price at t^*, namely S_{t^*}. This risk, as measured by the variance of the spot price, is called price risk.

If the investor were to choose to hedge, he would be exposed to uncertainty regarding the basis at time t^*, as measured by the variance of the basis. Thus hedging replaces price risk with basis risk.

An investor would therefore choose to hedge only if he were to be of the opinion that the basis risk is less than the price risk to which he would otherwise be exposed. As you can see from the expression for the variance of the basis, the higher the correlation between the spot and the futures price, the lower will be the variance of the basis or the basis risk.

QUESTION 87

If we decide to terminate the hedge on a date, and wish to choose a futures contract expiring thereafter, which contract month should we select? For, in practice, contracts for a number of delivery months are usually available at any point in time.

In general, we would not use a futures contract that expires in the same month as the month in which we wish to terminate the hedge. For instance, take the case of an investor who has a long position in a commodity that he wishes to unwind on September 15. Assume that futures contracts expiring on September 21 are available.

If the investor takes a short position in such a contract, he would have to offset by going long on September 15. The problem is that futures prices often behave erratically during the delivery month, and the hedger would not like to be exposed to such erratic price movements.

In the case of a long hedger who is planning to acquire the asset on September 15, besides the desire to avoid erratic price movements, there is another reason why the hedger may not like to use the September contract.

Assume that the long hedger is based in St. Louis. His intention is to procure the asset in the local market on September 15. However, there are no futures contracts being traded in St. Louis and the nearest futures exchange offering contracts on the commodity is in Chicago, and the contracts specify that delivery ought to take place in Chicago.

If such a hedger were to take a long position on the Chicago exchange, it will be solely because he wants to mitigate price risk. He obviously will have no intention of taking delivery in Chicago. The problem is that being the holder of a long position, he may be called upon to take delivery on or before September 15 assuming that the delivery period commences before that date. This is because the delivery process is initiated by the shorts, and if a particular long happens to have the oldest outstanding long position, he cannot refuse to accept delivery. For this reason, a long will generally avoid a contract that expires in the month in which he wishes to terminate the hedge.

So if the September contract is ruled out, then we clearly need a contract expiring after that. Assume that contracts expiring in October, November, and December are available. Which one should the hedger select?

It turns out that the further away the expiration month, the greater will be the basis risk. So in our case, the hedger will prefer the October contract. Thus the principle to be followed while choosing a futures contract is, *choose an expiration month after the month in which the hedge is to be terminated, but as close as possible to it.*

QUESTION 88

Why is it that the further away the expiration date of the contract, the greater is the basis risk?

Let t^* denote the point in time at which we wish to terminate the hedge by offsetting our futures position. The issue of concern to us is the basis at that time, which is expressed as:

$$b_{t^*} = (S_{t^*} - F_{t^*})$$

At any point in time, the spot and futures prices are being influenced by virtually the same economic factors. The difference is that the spot market is discovering the price for a trade at that particular instant, whereas the futures market is discovering the price for a trade at a point of time in the future. If the expiration date of the futures contract is very near, then both the spot and the futures markets will be discovering the price for a trade at virtually the same point in time. Thus, the difference between the two prices, which is nothing but the basis, may be expected to converge to a fairly predictable value. However, if the expiration date of the futures contract is far away, then the spot and futures prices are likely to be influenced by different supply and demand factors reflecting different sets of information, as a consequence of which we could expect to observe much greater variability in the basis.[3]

QUESTION 89

Is it true that a trader may deliberately go in for a cross hedge, even though futures contracts are available on the commodity whose price risk he wishes to hedge?

This at times happens, because of thin trading in the contracts on the commodity in which the hedger has a position.

3. See Koontz and Purcell (1999).

In a thin or illiquid market, prices may deviate substantially from the true or fair value of the asset. And every investor, whether he is taking a position or offsetting a position, would like to do so at a price that is perceived to be an accurate measure of economic value.

So, for instance, a cocoa farmer may not be comfortable taking a short position in cocoa futures even though such contracts happen to be available, because of perceived illiquidity. In such a case, assuming that cocoa and coffee prices are highly positively correlated for the sake of argument, he may deliberately choose to cross hedge using coffee futures.

QUESTION 90

Is it true that a hedger may sometimes initiate the hedge with a short-term futures contract expiring before the date on which he wishes to transact, and then subsequently move into a futures contract expiring later?

Yes he may. Such a procedure is called a *rolling hedge*. We will illustrate it with the help of an example. Assume that we are currently in the month of July and that we wish to sell a commodity in January next year. So using the logic developed earlier, we would prefer a contract expiring in February or immediately thereafter.

Assume that February contracts are not currently available, but contracts expiring in September, November and January are. If so, we may first go short in September contracts. As the expiration date approaches, we will offset the September position and go short in November contracts. Once again, as this contract nears expiration, we will offset it and take a position in January contracts. Assuming that the February contract becomes available by the end of December, we will at that point in time offset our January position and move into the February contract. Finally, in January, we will sell our asset in the spot market and offset our February position. Of course, each time we close out a futures position and take a fresh position, we will make a profit or a loss.

Such a procedure may be employed by us in July even if contracts expiring in February of the following year were to be available. This would be the case if we were to feel that February contracts are illiquid in July. Remember, liquidity is a key factor while designing a hedging strategy. In practice, however, we may not roll forward too frequently, because each time we unwind an existing position and take a position afresh, we will incur transactions costs.

QUESTION 91

Assuming that the investor's position in the underlying asset is an integer multiple of the size of the futures contract, is it necessary that he should use a hedge ratio of 1:1? In other words, should he ensure that the number of units of the underlying asset represented by the futures contracts be the same as the number of units of the asset to which he has an exposure in the spot market?

Let Q be the number of units of the underlying asset in which the investor has a long position in the spot market. Assume that each futures contract is for N units, and that C contracts are being used. So the total number of units of the underlying asset being represented by the futures contracts is $Q_f = NC$.

The question being asked is, is it always optimal to set $Q_f = Q$, or in other words should we use a hedge ratio of 1:1?

Let us look at the effective revenue for the hedger. It can be represented as:

$$R = QS_{t^*} + (F_0 - F_{t^*})Q_f$$

If $t^* = T$, that is, the hedge is terminated on the expiration date of the futures contract, then it would obviously make sense to have $Q_f = Q$, so that $R = QF_0$, an amount about which there would be no uncertainty.

However, when $t^* < T$, that is, the futures position is offset prior to expiration, it turns out that a hedge ratio of 1:1 need not be optimal.

If we define the hedge ratio as $h = \dfrac{Q_f}{Q}$ then $Q_f = hQ$. We can then write:

$$R = QS_{t^*} + (F_0 - F_{t^*})hQ$$

The issue is, what is the value of h that will minimize the variance of the revenue? We can determine this optimal hedge ratio by differentiating the variance of the revenue with respect to h, and setting it equal to zero, in order to calculate the minima.

It turns out that the optimal hedge ratio is given by:

$$h^* = \frac{\rho \sigma_s}{\sigma_f}$$

where σ_s is a measure of the variance of $\Delta S = (S_{t^*} - S_0)$ and σ_f is a measure of the variance of $\Delta F = (F_{t^*} - F_0)$ and ρ is a measure of the correlation between the two.

So in general the minimum variance hedge ratio will not be equal to 1.0.

QUESTION 92

?&A

Can we estimate the optimal hedge ratio using historical data?

Yes we can run a linear regression of the form:

$$\Delta S = \alpha + \beta \Delta F + \epsilon$$

The slope coefficient is a measure of the minimum variance hedge ratio.

QUESTION 93

?&A

How can we measure the effectiveness of a hedge?

We can define the hedging effectiveness as:

$$1 - \frac{\sigma^2(b)}{\sigma^2(S)}$$

If the basis risk is equal to the price risk, then the risk reduction is nil, and the hedging effectiveness will be zero. However, if the basis risk is zero, it would mean that we have a perfect hedge, and the hedging effectiveness will be 1.0.

In practice, when we run a linear regression of the form:

$$\Delta S = \alpha + \beta \Delta F + \epsilon$$

the R^2 of the regression is a measure of the hedging effectiveness.

QUESTION 94

?&A

What do we mean by the term "tailing a hedge?"

Assume that we get into a long forward contract at a price of F_0, and that the spot price at expiration is S_T. Our profit is $S_T - F_0$.

Now assume that we get into a futures contract at the same time, with the contract being scheduled to expire on the same date as the forward contract. Also assume that the interest rate is a constant and is the same for all maturities. If so, the initial futures price will be F_0 and the profit from the futures position will be $S_T - F_0$.

The problem is that in the case of the futures contract the profit does not arise all of a sudden at the time of expiration. Rather, it is the sum of profits and losses paid and received on a daily basis due to the process of marking to market. Consequently, if we take into account the fact that any interim profits can be invested while any interim losses have to be financed, then our profit from the futures position will be different from $S_T - F_0$.

Tailing is a procedure which attempts to ensure that the effective profit from a futures contract is equal to what would have been received from an identical forward contract on the same asset.

Let us assume that each forward/futures contract is for one unit of the underlying asset and that we wish to take a position in Q_f contracts. Let r be the daily rate of interest and assume that there are T days to maturity.

Consider a strategy where you start with $\dfrac{Q_f}{(1+r)^{T-1}}$ futures contracts.

The profit/loss from marking to market at the end of the day will be:

$$(F_1 - F_0) \times \frac{Q_f}{(1+r)^{T-1}}$$

This amount can be invested/financed for the remaining $T - 1$ days at a daily rate of r, so as to yield $Q_f (F_1 - F_0)$ at the time of expiration of the contract.

Now at the end of the first day, increase your futures position to $\dfrac{Q_f}{(1+r)^{T-2}}$ futures contracts. By the same logic, the profit/loss at the end of the second day can be invested/financed for the remaining $T - 2$ days to yield $Q_f (F_2 - F_1)$ at the time of expiration.

Continue with this strategy; that is, at the end of day n increase your position to $\dfrac{Q_f}{(1+r)^{T-n-1}}$ futures contracts.

If we sum up all these cash flows at expiration we will get an accumulated value of:

$$Q_f [(F_1 - F_0) + (F_2 - F_1) + (F_3 - F_2) + ------- (F_T - F_{T-1})]$$
$$= Q_f [(F_T - F_0)]$$

which is exactly equal to the amount that we would have got had we used forward contracts instead of futures contracts.

Thus had we started off with Q_f futures contracts from the outset, it would have amounted to overhedging. This could be profitable ex-post if we end up making sustained profits. However, were we to end up with a series of losses we would regret the fact that we had not tailed.

Once again, like rolling, tailing also entails transaction costs. So, in practice, one may not tail everyday. Also, tailing is feasible only if Q_f is large, because when we are dealing with a small number of contracts, we cannot buy and sell fractional contracts in practice.

QUESTION 95

What is speculation?

Unlike a hedger, whose objective is to avoid risk, a speculator is a person who consciously seeks to take on risk, hoping to profit from subsequent price movements. Such a person is either betting that the price will rise, in which case he is said to be bullish, or else he is hoping that it will fall, in which case he is said to be bearish.

QUESTION 96

Is speculation the same as gambling?

From the standpoint of finance theory, speculation and gambling are two different phenomena. A speculator is a person who evaluates the risk of an investment and the anticipated return from it prior to committing himself. Such a trader will therefore take a position only if he feels that the anticipated return is adequate considering the risk that he is taking. In other words, he may be said to be taking a calculated risk.

A gambler on the other hand is someone who takes a risk purely for the thrill of taking it. The expected return from the strategy is of no consequence for such a person while he is taking a decision to gamble.

QUESTION 97

Why are speculators important?

Active speculation adds depth to a market and makes it more liquid. A market characterized solely by hedgers will not have the kind of volume required to make it efficient. In practice, when a hedger seeks to take a position, very often the opposite side of the transaction will be taken by a speculator. Divergence of views, and a desire to take positions based on those views, is a *sine qua non* for making the free market system a success. Thus speculators, along with hedgers and arbitrageurs, play a pivotal role in financial markets.

QUESTION 98

How can futures contracts be used for speculation?

Consider an investor who is of the view that the price of an asset is going to rise. One way that he could take a speculative position is by buying the asset in the spot market and holding on to it, in the hope of offloading it subsequently at a higher price.

However, buying the asset in the spot market would entail incurring substantial costs. In addition, in the case of a physical asset, the investor has to face the hassle of storing and insuring it.

All this can be avoided if futures contracts are used for speculation. If the investor takes a long futures position, then he can lock in a price at which he can acquire the asset subsequently. If his hunch is true and the spot price at the time of expiration of the futures contract is higher, then he can take delivery at the initial futures price as per the contract and sell it at the prevailing spot price, thereby making a profit.

The advantage of using futures is that the entire value of the asset need not be paid at the outset. All that is required is a small margin. In other words, as we have studied before, futures contracts provide leverage.

Numerical illustration

Futures contracts on IBM with three months to expiration are available at a price of $75 per share. Alex is of the opinion that the spot price of IBM three months hence will be at least $78 per share. Therefore, he chooses to speculate by going long in 100 futures contracts, each of which is for 100 shares.

If his hunch is right and the spot price after three months is $80 per share, then Alex will make a profit of:

$$100 \times 100 \times (80 - 75) = \$50,000$$

However there is always a possibility that Alex could have been wrong. Let us assume that he read the market incorrectly and the price at expiration turns out to be $72 per share. If so, he would have to acquire the shares at $75 per share and sell them in the spot market at $72 per share, thereby making a loss of:

$$100 \times 100 \times (72 - 75) = \$30,000$$

Thus speculation using futures can give rise to substantial gains if one is right, but can lead to significant losses if one misjudges the market.

Now let us take the case of a bear, who is of the opinion that the market is going to fall. He too can speculate, but by going short in a futures contract. If his hunch turns out to be right, and the market price at the time of expiration of the futures contract is indeed lower than what the futures price was at the outset, he can buy at the prevailing market price and sell at the contract price, thereby making a profit.

Numerical illustration

Nina, like Alex, observes that the futures price for a three-month contract on IBM is $75 per share. However, unlike Alex, she is of the opinion that in three months time, IBM will be selling for $72 or less per share in the spot market. Assume that she takes a short position in 100 futures contracts.

If her hunch is right and the price of IBM after three months is $70 per share, Nina will make a profit of:

$$100 \times 100 \times (75 - 70) = \$50,000$$

However, if the market were to rise to, say, $78 after three months, Nina would incur a loss of:

$$100 \times 100 \times (75 - 78) = \$30,000$$

So while bears like bulls can use futures to speculate, in their quest for substantial gains there is always a risk that they could make substantial losses.

QUESTION 99

Is it possible to use options for speculation?

Yes, options too can be used for speculation. A trader who believes that the market will rise can buy a call option. If his hunch turns out to be right, he can exercise the option, acquire the asset at the exercise price, and sell it profitably at the prevailing market price.

Numerical illustration

Let us assume that call options on IBM for delivery three months hence are available, with an exercise price of $75 per share. Each contract is for 100 shares. Alex, who is optimistic about the market, buys 100 call option contracts.

Assume that his hunch is right and that the price of IBM after three months is $80 per share. He can then exercise the option, acquire the shares at $75 per share, and immediately dispose of them for $80 per share. In the process he will make a profit of:

$$100 \times 100 \times (80 - 75) = \$50,000$$

If we assume that an option premium of $3.50 per share was paid, then the net profit will be:

$$\$50,000 - 100 \times 100 \times 3.50 = \$15,000$$

But if Alex reads the market wrong and the spot price turns out to be $72 per share, he will simply refrain from exercising the option. The loss will be equal to the premium paid for the options, which is $35,000.

Similarly, a person who believes that the market will fall can speculate by buying a put option. If the market does indeed fall, she can acquire the asset at the market price, and sell it at the exercise price by exercising the option, thereby making a profit.

Numerical illustration

Assume that put options on IBM for delivery three months hence are available with an exercise price of $75 per share, and that each contract is for 100 shares. Nina is pessimistic about the market and therefore decides to go long in 100 put option contracts.

If she is right and the market does decline, say to $72 per share, she can acquire the shares in the spot market and deliver them under the options contract at $75 per share. Thus she would make a profit of:

$$100 \times 100 \times (75 - 72) = \$30,000$$

Assuming an option premium of $2.25 per share, the net profit will be:

$$\$30,000 - 100 \times 100 \times 2.25 = \$7,500$$

However, if it turns out that her prediction was wrong and the spot price after three months turns out to be $78 per share, then she will simply refrain from exercising the option. In this case, the option premium of $22,500 would constitute a loss.

QUESTION 100

Are futures and options similar from the standpoint of speculation?

Once again, the answer is no. Consider the case of the speculator who goes long in a futures contract. If he is right and the market does rise, he makes a profit as you have seen. What if he is wrong and the market actually falls? If so, he will make a loss which may be substantial, because he is under an obligation to buy at the contract price, whereas the price at which he can now sell in the market will be much lower. Similarly, a speculator who goes short in a futures contract can also make substantial losses if his forecast of the market turns out to be wrong. This is because if the price were to rise, he will have to acquire the asset in the market at a price that will be higher than what he will get when he delivers it as per the contract.

Speculation with options is different. A person who speculates by buying a call will benefit if prices rise. However, if he is wrong and prices fall subsequently, he will simply refrain from exercising and let the option expire worthless. In this case, his loss will be limited to the option premium that he paid at the outset. The case of a speculator who buys a put option is similar. If prices fall subsequently, he will obviously benefit. However, if it turns out that he was wrong, and prices subsequently rise, he need not exercise the option and can allow it to expire worthless.

Does this mean that everyone who seeks to speculate will always prefer options to futures? The answer, as before, is no. For one can speculate with futures by just depositing a margin, whereas one has to pay a price to acquire an option, which is irrecoverable if the option were not to be exercised. Options and futures are therefore not interchangeable from the standpoint of speculation. In other words, one strategy cannot be said to dominate the other.

Test your concepts

The answers are provided on page 241.

1. Futures and options are interchangeable from the standpoint of:
   (a) Hedging
   (b) Speculation
   (c) Both (a) and (b)
   (d) Neither (a) nor (b).

2. The ex-post outcome without hedging will always be inferior if:
   (a) Futures are used for hedging
   (b) Options are used for hedging
   (c) Futures or options are used for hedging
   (d) None of the above.

3. A hedger plans to terminate the hedge on 15 September. Futures contracts expiring on the 21st of every month are available. The hedger will choose:
   (a) September futures
   (b) October futures
   (c) November futures
   (d) December futures.

4. The minimum hedge ratio will always be:
   (a) Equal to 1.0
   (b) Greater than 1.0
   (c) Less than 1.0
   (d) None of the above.

5. A calculated risk taker is known as:
   (a) A hedger
   (b) A speculator
   (c) A gambler
   (d) None of the above.

6. An exporter in India who is expecting a payment is U.S. dollars would hedge using:
   (a) A short position in futures
   (b) A long position in futures
   (c) A long position in put options
   (d) (a) and (c).

7. Frequent adjustments of the futures position will lead to greater transaction costs for the following strategy:
   (a) Rolling the hedge
   (b) Tailing the hedge
   (c) Both (a) and (b)
   (d) Neither (a) nor (b).

8. If the standard deviation of the spot price is less than the standard deviation of the futures price, then the minimum variance hedge ratio:
   (a) Will always be greater than 1.0
   (b) Will always be less than 1.0
   (c) Will always be equal to 1.0
   (d) None of the above.

9. The basis will be equal to zero on the expiration date of the futures contract:
   (a) Only if the market is in Contango
   (b) Only if the market is in Backwardation
   (c) Irrespective of whether the market is in contango or Backwardation
   (d) None of the above.

10. The further away the expiration of the futures contract chosen for hedging, the greater is the basis risk for:
    (a) Buying hedges
    (b) Selling hedges
    (c) Both buying as well as selling hedges
    (d) None of the above.

CHAPTER 4

ORDERS AND EXCHANGES

QUESTION 101

What are orders?

An order is a trade instruction given to a broker or to an exchange. In other words, when a trader wishes to buy or to sell an asset, he needs to place an order to indicate what he wishes to accomplish, and the terms and conditions subject to which he wants his instructions to be carried out.

QUESTION 102

What kind of information must an order contain in order to be meaningful?

Firstly, the trader needs to indicate as to whether he wishes to take a long position or a short position. A desire to go long is communicated by placing a *buy order*, while a wish to go short is conveyed by placing a *sell order*. In addition, he needs to clearly identify the security that he wants to be bought or sold on his behalf. For instance, let us assume that we are standing on January 2, 20XX, and wish to go long in IBM futures. We would obviously place a buy order. However, on January 2, we will find that futures contracts expiring in January, February, March, and June are available. Each of these contracts is a different security. Hence we need to clearly specify the security in which we wish to go long. Let us assume that we decide to buy the March futures.

The next issue is how many contracts do we wish to buy. This is called the *order size*, and obviously needs to be specified at the outset.

To continue with our example, let us assume that we place a buy order for 200 March futures contracts.

Then comes the question of price. Are we prepared to accept the best price that is currently available in the market? If not, assuming that we wish to buy, what is the maximum price at which we are willing to buy? Or, if we wish to sell, what is the minimum price that we are prepared to accept?

Traders who are prepared to accept the best terms available in the market place what are called *market orders*. Others who wish to place a price ceiling or a price floor, depending on whether they wish to buy or to sell, place what are called *limit orders*. The corresponding price ceiling or floor is called the *limit price*.

Let us assume that we place a limit buy order with a limit price of $69.50.

Finally we need to specify as to how long we wish our order to remain valid for, in the event of a delay in execution due to the unavailability of a suitable matching order on the other side of the market. For instance, a trader may specify that his order should be either executed on submission or else canceled. Others may specify a period of time for which they are prepared to wait if a suitable match were to be currently unavailable. In practice, an exchange will not allow an order to stay alive indefinitely. In other words, it will specify a maximum validity period, and if an order were to fail to get executed within this period, it would automatically stand canceled.

Let us assume that we place a *day order*. In such a case, if a suitable match is not found by the end of the day on which the order is entered, it will be automatically canceled. We also need to specify as to whether we will accept a partial match. For instance, in our case we have placed a buy order for 200 contracts. It may so happen that a suitable counterparty is found for 100 contracts by the end of the day. If we do not wish to accept such an eventuality, we will place an *all-or-nothing* or *all-or-none* (AON) order. In these cases, an order must either be filled completely by the end of the stipulated time period, or else the trader will refuse to accept it.

QUESTION 103

When a market order is specified, quite obviously no price limit is mentioned. At what price will such an order get executed in practice?

A market buy order will get executed at the best available price from the standpoint of the trader. The best available price in this case will be the lowest of the limit prices specified by all those traders who have placed limit sell orders prior to the placement of the market order in question, and whose orders have not been executed thus far.

Similarly, when a market sell order is placed, it will be executed at the highest of the limit prices specified by all those traders who have placed limit buy orders prior to the placement of the market order in question, and whose orders are still pending.

QUESTION 104

If it has to be ensured that incoming market orders get executed at the best available prices, quite obviously the unexecuted but valid limit orders at any point in time must be sorted according to some priority rules. What are these priority rules?

Yes, there are two priority rules that are used to sort limit orders. The first is called the *price priority rule*. According to this, a limit buy order with a higher limit price ranks higher than all other limit buy orders with lower limit prices. Similarly, a limit sell order with a lower limit price ranks higher than all other limit sell orders with higher limit prices. Thus, an incoming market buy order is guaranteed to get executed at the lowest available price on the sell side of the market, while an incoming market sell order is assured of getting executed at the highest available price on the buy side of the market.

The next obvious question will pertain to the ranking of two or more buy orders, or sell orders, with the same limit price. In such cases the *time priority rule* comes into effect. That is, the order which comes in first is automatically accorded priority.

These priority rules can of course be easily enforced in a modern electronic or screen-based system. We will see later as to how these rules are enforced in the traditional or open-outcry system of trading, where traders crowd around a trading ring or pit and attempt to have their orders executed.

QUESTION 105

What is a Limit Order Book, and how do orders build up in a book?

A Limit Order Book (LOB) at any point in time contains the details of those limit orders which are currently valid, but which have not been executed thus far due to the unavailability of a suitable match.

In the earlier days, the LOB was physically maintained in the form of a book of orders, hence the name. These days, of course, everything is maintained in an electronic form.

We will illustrate a Limit Order Book and changes in its composition over time with the help of an example. This elaborate example should be helpful in comprehending how orders are arranged based on the priority rules, and how matching between orders on the opposite sides of the market takes place.

Illustration

Assume that today is January 2, 20XX, and that February futures contracts on IBM have just commenced trading.[1] Assume that in the first half-hour of trading, the following nine orders are placed (Table 4.1).

Table 4.1 Chronological sequence of incoming orders

Time	Trader	Order side	Order size	Limit price
10:01	Amy	Buy	100	70.00
10:03	Brian	Buy	200	70.20
10:07	Chip	Sell	200	70.10
10:10	Dana	Sell	500	70.25
10:15	Elaine	Buy	200	70.00
10:18	Francis	Buy	400	Market
10:20	Greg	Sell	500	70.00
10:25	Harry	Sell	200	69.90
10:30	Laura	Buy	500	69.75

Now let us see how the Limit Order Book will build up, and examine the changes in it over a period of time.

At 10:01, Amy's order will enter the system. Since it is the very first order, it obviously cannot be matched with an existing order on the other side of the market. Being a buy order, it will go to the top of the buy side of the LOB (Table 4.2).

At 10:03, Brian's buy order will enter the system. It, too, cannot be matched, for at that point in time there are no sell orders in the book. So, the order will queue up on the buy side of the LOB. And since Brian has specified a limit price of $70.20, which is higher than the price of $70.00 specified by Amy, his order will get priority based on the price priority rule (Table 4.3).

---

1. The symbol 20XX denotes a general year in the 21st century.

Table 4.2 Snapshot of the LOB at 10:01

	Buyers			Sellers	
Trader	Order size	Limit price	Limit price	Order size	Trader
Amy	100	70.00			

Table 4.3 Snapshot of the LOB at 10:03

	Buyers			Sellers	
Trader	Order size	Limit price	Limit price	Order size	Trader
Brian	200	70.20			
Amy	100	70.00			

At 10:07, Chip's sell order will enter the system. It has a limit price of $70.10 which indicates that he is prepared to sell provided he can do so at a price of $70.10 or more. The system will try and match it with the best buy order in the LOB, which is Brian's. Brian has given a limit price of $70.20, indicating that he is prepared to pay up to $70.20. Quite obviously, a trade is feasible under these circumstances.

Chip has sought to sell 200 contracts while Brian has sought to buy 200 contracts. So in the process of execution both the orders will be completely filled.

One question remains however. At what price will the trade get executed? On most exchanges, an incoming or *active* order will get executed at the price of the existing or *passive* order with which it is matched. So, in this case, the trade will be executed at the price of $70.20 specified by Brian. This leaves us with the situation shown in Table 4.4.

At 10:10, Dana's sell order will enter the system with a limit price of $70.25. The system will try and match it with the best, in this case the only, buy order, which has a limit price of $70.00. Quite obviously, a trade is infeasible. Consequently, Dana's order will take its place on the top of the sell side of the book (Table 4.5).

Table 4.4 Snapshot of the LOB following the trade

	Buyers			Sellers	
Trader	Order size	Limit price	Limit price	Order size	Trader
Amy	100	70.00			

Table 4.5 Snapshot of the LOB at 10:10

	Buyers			Sellers	
Trader	Order size	Limit price	Limit price	Order size	Trader
Amy	100	70.00	70.25	500	Dana

Table 4.6 Snapshot of the LOB at 10:15

	Buyers			Sellers	
Trader	Order size	Limit price	Limit price	Order size	Trader
Amy	100	70.00	70.25	500	Dana
Elaine	200	70.00			

Table 4.7 Snapshot of the LOB following the trade

	Buyers			Sellers	
Trader	Order size	Limit price	Limit price	Order size	Trader
Amy	100	70.00	70.25	100	Dana
Elaine	200	70.00			

At 10:15, Elaine's buy order for 200 contracts with a limit price of $70.00 will come in. It obviously cannot get matched with the best sell order. In terms of the limit price, it has equal priority with Amy's order. However, Amy's order will be accorded greater priority on the basis of the time priority rule (Table 4.6).

At 10:18, Francis' market buy order for 400 contracts will come in. This kind of an order is assured of execution, provided there are one or more orders on the other side whose cumulative order size is greater than or equal to the size of the incoming order. In this case, since there is an order on the sell side for 500 contracts, the incoming order will be fully filled at a price of $70.25. The situation is now as shown in Table 4.7.

At 10:20, Greg's sell order for 500 contracts, with a limit price of $70.00 will enter. The system will try and match it with Amy's order and a trade will obviously result. However, Greg's order will not be fully filled in the process, since Amy's order is only for 100 contracts. The system will then try and match the remainder of Greg's order

Table 4.8   Snapshot of the LOB following the trade

	Buyers			Sellers	
Trader	Order size	Limit price	Limit price	Order size	Trader
			70.00	200	Greg
			70.25	100	Dana

Table 4.9   Snapshot of the LOB at 10:25

	Buyers			Sellers	
Trader	Order size	Limit price	Limit price	Order size	Trader
			69.90	200	Harry
			70.00	200	Greg
			70.25	100	Dana

Table 4.10   Snapshot of the LOB at 10:30

	Buyers			Sellers	
Trader	Order size	Limit price	Limit price	Order size	Trader
Laura	500	69.75	69.90	200	Harry
			70.00	200	Greg
			70.25	100	Dana

with Elaine's. Once again a trade will result and Elaine's order will be fully filled. However, Greg's order will remain partially unfilled since for the balance of 200 contracts there is no possibility of a match. Consequently, the unfilled portion will continue to stay in the LOB. It will go to the top of the sell side of the LOB since the limit price of $70.00 specified by Greg is lower than the price of $70.25 specified by Dana (Table 4.8).

At 10:25, Harry's sell order with a limit price of $69.90 will enter. Based on the price priority rule it will get precedence over Greg's order (Table 4.9).

At 10:30, Laura's buy order with a limit price of $69.75 will come in. The system will try and match it with Harry's order. Obviously a trade is infeasible. Consequently Laura's order will take its place at the top of the buy side of the LOB (Table 4.10).

QUESTION 106

Is placing a limit order more sensible than placing a market order? After all, it does seem to give the investor more control over the trade?

Yes limit orders allow traders to control the price at which their orders will get executed. A limit buy order will ensure that the buyer will not end up paying more than the limit price specified by him, whereas a limit sell order will ensure that the seller will not end up getting less than the limit price specified by him.

However, when an investor places a limit order there is no guarantee that a suitable match on the other side can be found within a reasonable period of time.

Consider the following LOB at a given point in time (Table 4.11). The last trade price was $70.20.

Assume that Elaine places a buy order for 200 contracts with a limit price of $70.00. It obviously cannot be matched with an existing limit sell order, and consequently will have to take its place in the system (Table 4.12).

Now assume that Steve places a market buy order for 1,500 contracts. It will obviously get executed immediately; 500 contracts will be bought at $70.25, and 1,000 contracts at $70.30. So the last trade price that is reported will be $70.30. The situation is now as shown in Table 4.13.

Once again let us assume that another market buy order is placed immediately for 1,500 contracts, this time by a trader called Ralph. It too will get executed. The last reported trade price will now be $70.40. The situation is now as shown in Table 4.14.

Table 4.11 Snapshot of the LOB at the outset

Buyers			Sellers		
Trader	Order size	Limit price	Limit price	Order size	Trader
Amy	100	70.00	70.25	500	Dana
			70.30	300	Solomon
			70.30	1,700	Sinclair
			70.40	1,500	Denise
			70.50	1,000	Kip
			70.50	1,000	Kara

Table 4.12   Snapshot of the LOB after Elaine's order

	Buyers			Sellers	
Trader	Order size	Limit price	Limit price	Order size	Trader
Amy	100	70.00	70.25	500	Dana
Elaine	200	70.00	70.30	300	Solomon
			70.30	1,700	Sinclair
			70.40	1,500	Denise
			70.50	1,000	Kip
			70.50	1,000	Kara

Table 4.13   Snapshot of the LOB following the trade

	Buyers			Sellers	
Trader	Order size	Limit price	Limit price	Order size	Trader
Amy	100	70.00	70.30	1,000	Sinclair
Elaine	200	70.00	70.40	1,500	Denise
			70.50	1,000	Kip
			70.50	1,000	Kara

Table 4.14   Snapshot of the LOB following the second trade

	Buyers			Sellers	
Trader	Order size	Limit price	Limit price	Order size	Trader
Amy	100	70.00	70.40	1,000	Denise
Elaine	200	70.00	70.50	1,000	Kip
			70.50	1,000	Kara

Seeing the market price jump from $70.20 to $70.40 in a short span of time, other traders desirous of placing buy orders may be induced to place limit orders with prices higher than that of the best order on the buy side. Let us assume that Peter places a buy order for 500 contracts at $70.10, followed by Alex who places a buy order for 1,500 contracts at $70.15. The LOB will then look as follows (Table 4.15).

As you can see, Elaine's order has been pushed back in the queue. There is no way of telling as to when it will get executed, or whether

Table 4.15 Snapshot of the LOB at the end

	Buyers			Sellers	
Trader	Order size	Limit price	Limit price	Order size	Trader
Alex	1,500	70.15	70.40	1,000	Denise
Peter	500	70.10	70.50	1,000	Kip
Amy	100	70.00	70.50	1,000	Kara
Elaine	200	70.00			

it will get executed at all. On the other hand, if Elaine had placed a market order at the outset, it would have been immediately executed at a price of $70.25.

The advantage with a market order therefore is that execution is guaranteed, provided there exist enough limit orders on the other side of the market. The problem, however, is that the trader has no control over the execution price, for the trade will get executed at the limit price of the limit order with which it is matched.

QUESTION 107

What is a "marketable limit order?"

The odds of a limit order being executed on submission would depend on the limit price that is specified by the trader. For a buy order, the higher the limit price, the greater is the chance of early execution. Similarly, for a sell order the lower the limit price the greater is the possibility that it will get executed soon after submission. Limit buy orders with high limit prices and limit sell orders with low limit prices are said to be *aggressively* priced.

In most cases, a limit buy order will be placed at a price that is lower than the best price available in the market, which is the price of the best sell order in the LOB. Similarly, a limit sell order will usually be placed at a price that is higher than the price of the best buy order in the LOB. However, at times, a trader could price his limit order very aggressively.

A marketable limit order by definition is a limit order that can be executed upon submission.

Let us take the case of the following LOB (Table 4.16).

A limit buy order with a limit price of $70.25 or more will be executed as soon as it enters the system. Similarly, a limit sell order with a limit price of $70.00 or less will be executed as soon as it enters the system. Thus the limit price for a marketable limit buy order must be

Table 4.16 Snapshot of an LOB

	Buyers			Sellers	
Trader	Order size	Limit price	Limit price	Order size	Trader
Abbott	500	70.00	70.25	1,300	Patty
Alf	1,000	69.90	70.40	1,200	Lori
Mary	1,500	69.75	70.50	1,500	Kelly

greater than or equal to the best offer that is available. Similarly, the limit price of a marketable limit sell order must be less than or equal to the best bid that is available.

QUESTION 108

A marketable limit order seems to be fairly similar to a market order. Why then would a trader prefer to use such an order instead of a conventional market order?

Both market as well as marketable limit orders embody a desire for quick execution on the part of the trader. However, while in the case of a market order a trader has no control over the execution price, in the case of a marketable limit order he can prescribe a price floor or a price ceiling depending on whether it is a sell or a buy order. The freedom to specify a floor or a ceiling for the price can acquire significance if circumstances were to preclude a marketable limit order from getting executed as planned.

Let us go back to the situation depicted in Table 4.16. Assume that a trader named Ron issues a limit buy order with a limit price of $70.30 for 300 contracts. His expectation at the time of issuing the order is that it will be matched with the best offer on display, which is at $70.25.

However, it may so happen that another market order manages to enter the system before Ron's order. Remember that traders around the country are constantly monitoring the situation, and a split second's delay in order entry can lead to another order or orders acquiring priority.

For instance, let us assume that a large market buy order for 3,000 contracts comes in prior to Ron's order. It will push up the trade price to $70.50. Since Ron has specified a price limit of $70.30, his order will not get executed under the circumstances. Instead, it will go to the top of the buy side as the best bid.

If Ron were to be of the opinion that the execution price is not inconsequential, although the speed of execution is a major factor, then issuing a marketable limit order would make sense. For, had he issued a market order instead, in this case he would have ended up buying 300 contracts at $70.50, an outcome that he may not desire. Thus, the marketable limit order gives the trader control over the execution price. But there is a corresponding cost because a limit order, whether marketable or not, always exposes the trader to execution uncertainty.

QUESTION 109

What is a "stop-loss order," and why is it termed as such?

A stop or a stop-loss order will be placed by a trader who has a position in the market, and would like to cut his losses and quit immediately if conditions were to turn adverse. Such a person may have no desire to close out his position at the time of placing the order. For instance, he may be long in a particular futures contract and may be expecting that the futures price will rise. However, in the event of a sudden unanticipated decline in the market, he may like to ensure that his loss does not exceed an acceptable level. Let us assume that the threshold loss in his opinion corresponds to a price of ρ^*. In such a case he can specify a stop order with an attached trigger price of ρ^*. The stop instruction will prevent the order from getting activated until and unless the trigger is hit or breached. Once the trigger is hit or penetrated, the order will get triggered off and will become a market order.

We will now illustrate a stop-loss sell order.

Assume that the LOB at a point in time looks as shown in Table 4.17.

Victor, a trader based in Pittsburgh, has taken a long position in 800 contracts. He has no desire to offset, for he expects a further rise in the futures price. However, he has in mind a threshold price of $69.60 and if the market were to trade at that level or below, he would like to exit the market immediately. In this case, Victor can place a stop sell order with a trigger price of $69.60.

Assume that a market sell order for 4,000 contracts comes in. It will ensure that Amy's, Arthur's, Alex's, Anthony's, and Jana's orders are fully filled. The last trade price will be $69.25, which is less than the trigger of $69.60 specified by Victor. This will immediately cause Victor's order to get activated and it will enter the system as a market sell order. In this case it will be executed at $68.00.

Table 4.17 Snapshot of an LOB prior to the placement of a stop-sell order

	Buyers			Sellers	
Trader	Order size	Limit price	Limit price	Order size	Trader
Amy	1,200	70.00	70.20	500	Mary
Arthur	1,000	69.85	70.30	1,000	Martin
Alex	500	69.75	70.35	500	Cindy
Anthony	800	69.55	70.40	700	Nigel
Jana	500	69.25	70.50	300	Nancy
Joshua	1,000	68.00	72.00	1000	Neville

The trigger price specified in the case of a stop sell order will always be less than the best price that is available at the time of placing the order, which in Victor's case is $70.00.

Stop-loss orders can also be placed by traders who wish to take long positions in the event of adverse market conditions. For instance, assume that Robby has a short position in 800 contracts. He expects the market to fall further. However, if there were to be a rise in prices and the market were to hit or cross $70.50, then he would like to offset and exit the market immediately.

Let us assume that Robby places a stop buy order with a trigger price of $70.50. Now suppose that a large market buy order for 3,000 contracts enters the system. It will ensure that Mary's, Martin's, Cindy's, Nigel's, and Nancy's orders are completely filled. The last trade price will be $70.50 which corresponds to the trigger specified by Robby. His stop order will immediately get activated and will become a market buy order which will in this case get executed at a price of $72.00.

Once again Robby's intention was to control his losses. However, since he had a short position to start with, the trigger point, in this case $70.50, was greater than the best price available in the market at the time of placing the order, which was $70.20.

Since such orders enable traders to control the potential loss in the event of an adverse market movement they are termed stop-loss orders.

QUESTION 110

What is a "stop-limit" order?

A stop-limit order is also an instruction to hold the order in abeyance until the specified trigger is breached. However, the difference between a stop order and a stop limit order is that the latter, if and when it is activated, will become a limit order. Consequently, such orders require that two threshold prices be specified. The first corresponds to the trigger price which will cause the limit order to be activated. The second is the limit price corresponding to the limit order.

The need for stop-limit orders can be understood by re-examining the illustration used in the previous question. In Victor's case, his sell order got executed eventually at a price of $68.00, even though he had specified a trigger of $69.60. He had no control over the execution price in this case because the stop order became a market order on activation.

If Victor was uneasy about such an eventuality, he could have instead placed a stop-limit order with a trigger price of $69.60 and limit price of, say, $69.25. Had he done so, his order when activated would have become a limit sell order with a limit price of $69.25. He would therefore have been assured of being able to offset at a minimum price of $69.25.

Similarly, when Robby placed a stop buy order it eventually got executed at $72.00 even though the specified trigger was $70.50. To protect himself against the possibility of such an outcome, Robby could have placed a stop-limit order with a trigger price of $70.50 and a limit price of, say, $71.00. Had he done so, his order when activated would have become a limit buy order with a limit price of $71.00. He would then have been assured of being able to offset at a maximum price of $71.00.

QUESTION 111

What is a "market-if-touched" (MIT) order and how is it different from a stop order?

A market-if-touched order is an order that will get activated if the price touches or breaches a pre-specified trigger point. Such an order will become a market order if and when activated. In this respect, it is similar to a stop order.

However, there is a crucial difference between the two types of orders. In the case of a stop-loss sell order, the trigger price will be less than the best available price in the market. For stop-loss buy orders, on the other hand, the trigger will be greater than the best price that is currently available. In the case of an MIT buy order, however, the trigger price will be less than the best price that is currently available. Whereas in the case of an MIT sell order, the trigger price will be more than the best available price.

Thus, while a stop buy order will get activated if the market rises and breaches the trigger, an MIT buy order will get activated if the market falls and hits or goes below the trigger. Similarly, while a stop sell order will get activated if the market falls and breaches the trigger, an MIT sell order will be activated only if the market rises and hits or goes above the trigger.

This would therefore appear to suggest that an MIT order is similar to a limit order. However, there is a crucial difference. On activation, an MIT order will become a market order and will get executed at the best available price. A limit order can only trade at the limit price or better. Thus MIT orders are virtually guaranteed to be executed on activation, but they expose the trader to execution price uncertainty.

Consider the following LOB position (Table 4.18).

Table 4.18 Snapshot of an LOB prior to the placement of an MIT buy order

Buyers			Sellers		
Trader	Order size	Limit price	Limit price	Order size	Trader
Vicky	1,000	70.15	70.25	500	Randy
William	200	70.00	70.25	200	Robert
Liz	600	69.80	70.35	800	Rita
Walter	900	69.75	70.40	700	Steve
Xavier	500	69.60	70.50	800	Tina

Take the case of a trader called Tony who has just placed an MIT buy order for 500 contracts with a trigger price of $70.15. Let us also assume that a market sell order for 500 contracts enters the system immediately after Tony has placed his order.

The last trade price after this market order is fully filled will be $70.15. Under these circumstances, Tony's order will be activated, and will become a market order which in this case will be executed at $70.25.

Had Tony specified a limit order instead of an MIT order, with a limit price of $70.15, his order would continue to remain in the system. He would be assured of a trade price of $70.15, but his order will be subject to execution uncertainty.

QUESTION 112

How long is an order valid for? What are the different validity instructions that a trader can specify?

In his quest to find a suitable match, a trader can specify a validity instruction to indicate the period of time for which he wishes his order to remain valid.

In principle, such instructions can be specified for any kind of order. They are however particularly important for limit orders and stop orders. This is because such orders will not usually trade on submission, and many such orders will stay in the system for long periods of time. In fact, some of these orders may eventually never trade.

We will now consider the various time conditions that can be specified.[2]

Day orders

Such an order is valid only for the duration of the day on which it is submitted. If it remains unexecuted at the end of the day, then the system will automatically cancel it after the close of trading.

Some exchanges in fact permit only day orders. For instance, since 1999 the Stock Exchange of Singapore has been permitting only what are called *good today* limit orders. Every morning, therefore, the system will start with a clean slate with no backlog of orders from the previous day.[3]

Good till canceled orders

Good till canceled orders remain in the system until they are explicitly canceled by the trader. Thus, if they are not executed by the close of trading on a given day, then they will be automatically carried forward to the next business day.

However, an order cannot remain in the system forever. Consequently, the exchange will notify a maximum period of time after which such orders will be automatically canceled if they were to remain unexecuted.

In order to ensure that a trader does not lose track of his unexecuted orders, many brokers will periodically provide their clients with a list of unfilled orders. Sometimes, a broker may automatically cancel such an order at the end of a pre-specified time period, without waiting for an explicit instruction to do so from the client. This is done so as to avoid the administrative costs involved in constantly monitoring stale orders.

Good till days orders

With a good till days order, the trader can specify a period for which he desires the order to remain valid. The implicit instruction is that the order ought to be canceled if it is not executed by then. The length of

---

2. See Harris (2003).
3. See McInish (2000).

the period specified by a trader cannot obviously exceed the maximum length of time for which good till canceled orders can stay in the system. There are various types of such orders, such as good-this-week (GTW) and good-this-month (GTM) orders.

Immediate or cancel orders

An immediate or cancel order has to be executed as soon as it is released into the system, failing which it stands canceled. Sometimes, due to the unavailability of a sizeable order on the other side, only a partial match may be found, in which case a part of the incoming order will be executed and the unfilled portion will be canceled. In some markets, such orders are known as fill-and-kill or good-on-sight orders.

QUESTION 113

What is an open-outcry system of trading?

Until recent years, most derivatives exchanges employed what is called a continuous bilateral oral auction trading mechanism called the open-outcry system.

In such a system, traders are not faceless entities who anonymously submit their orders to the computerized network. Rather, they meet face to face on the floor of the exchange in a central location called the *pit*. The traders who congregate on the floor will cry out their bids and offers in order to attract the attention of others who may be willing to match them. Most traders will also simultaneously keep their ears open for orders being shouted out by others. A trade will take place when a buyer accepts a seller's offer for sale, or when a seller accepts a buyer's bid to buy. If a buyer wishes to accept an offer, he will typically shout out "take it" to indicate his acceptance. A seller who accepts a bid will typically shout out "sold" to signal his acceptance.[4]

When a trader shouts out an order, the others can make out whether he wishes to buy or to sell based on the following convention. Bidders always call out the price first followed by the quantity whereas sellers always call out the quantity first followed by the price. In exchanges like the Chicago Board of Trade (CBOT), traders use an elaborate and well-understood system of hand and finger signals to indicate their intentions, their limit prices, and the quantities which they wish to trade.

---

4. See Harris (2003).

QUESTION 114

What are the order priority rules in open-outcry systems, and how are they enforced in practice?

The first rule that is expected to be followed by all traders is the *open-outcry* rule. That is, a trader who wants other people to respond to his intention to trade must first publicly express his bid or offer by shouting out aloud. Once a person shouts out an order, any trader standing in the pit can respond to it. Often traders take turns in making bids and counter offers, and offers and counter bids, before they ultimately agree upon a price and quantity. The first person who accepts a bid or an offer gets to trade with the trader who has made the corresponding bid or offer.

The primary order precedence rule is based on price priority. That is, a buyer can only accept the lowest offer and a seller can only accept the highest bid. Such a rule is self-enforcing in practice since a buyer will always look for the lowest price while a seller will always search for the highest price.

In order to prevent inferior quotes from adding to the noise and confusion, most open-outcry systems will not allow a trader to bid below the best bid that is currently available, or offer above the best offer that is currently available. Consequently, any trader who wishes to acquire priority must either improve upon the best bid by bidding higher, or improve upon the best offer by offering at a lower price.

In most oral auctions, a *floor time preference* rule is used. That is, priority is given to the trader who was the first to bid or offer at a given price by improving upon the previous bid or offer. As long as this trader is enjoying time preference, no other trader is allowed to bid or offer at the same price. Of course, another trader can always gain priority by bidding higher or offering at a lower price. This rule encourages price competition among traders. For, if a trader is aggressive, the only way that he can get ahead of someone who already has time preference is by improving upon the price.[5]

The time preference rule, unlike the price preference rule, is not self-enforcing. For, from the standpoint of a potential counterparty, it is immaterial as to whose bid or offer he is accepting, as long as he is getting the best possible price. Consequently, a trader who has acquired time preference may have to vocally defend it. That is, if someone else were to bid or offer at the same price, he will have to shout out "That's my bid" or "That's my offer" to ensure that he continues to enjoy priority.

---

5. See Harris (2003).

The difference between the floor time preference rule and the *strict time preference rule* followed by electronic systems is that in an oral auction, once a trade is consummated at a particular price, anyone may bid or offer at that price, and all orders at that price will have equal priority. In contrast the strict time preference criteria ranks orders at a given price strictly in accordance with the time of submission.

It must also be remembered that in an oral auction a bid or an offer is valid only momentarily. A trader who wishes to maintain his priority must shout out his order periodically in order to convey that he continues to be interested in trading.

Once a bid or an offer is accepted by a counterparty, the resulting trade will take place at the price proposed by the trader whose quote was accepted.

QUESTION 115

Is an electronic trading system always preferable to an open-outcry system? What are the pros and cons?

The hallmark of a successful system is its ability to provide liquidity and reduce costs for market participants. Costs in this context can take on two forms. Firstly, there are the direct transactions costs or commissions. Secondly, there are indirect costs like lost revenues due to illiquidity or a lack of market depth.[6]

In an oral-auction system, liquidity is supplied by traders called *locals* who constantly stand ready to buy and sell on their own account. However, the problem is that a local is restricted at any point in time to a single pit. In practice, futures contracts on different assets trade in different pits. A local obviously cannot keep running back and forth between pits. Consequently, he has little choice but to be present at his usual pit even when the trading activity there is considerably reduced.

In contrast, a trader who is using an electronic system can effortlessly switch to a different screen displaying the LOB for a different asset, if he finds that activity in a particular futures contract is slackening. Thus, for relatively inactive contracts, electronic trading is clearly preferable.

In the emerging economies, where derivatives trading is often characterized by low volumes, electronic systems are the preferred modes of trading.

Even in the advanced economies, exchanges are increasingly feeling the need to switch to electronic systems. In the earlier years, derivatives trading was characterized by high volumes in most contracts, because

---

6. See Sankar and Tozzi (1998).

such instruments provided innovative features that were simply not available earlier. Consequently, although the underlying assets were not necessarily sophisticated, traders were nevertheless attracted to such derivative securities. However, as time has passed, the financial instruments that are now emerging tend to be highly specialized and are able to attract the attention of select professional clienteles only. The same is true for derivatives on such financial products. Consequently, derivatives on new products are characterized by relatively lower volumes, thereby encouraging established exchanges to switch over to screen-based systems of trading. Some exchanges like the CBOT and the CME continue to use both types of trading platforms.

Traditional exchanges have also faced declining volumes in recent years due to enhanced competition from newly established exchanges. This is increasingly providing an impetus to them for embracing electronic systems. Electronic systems are also indispensable for cross-border trading, which is likely to increase steadily as the economies of the world integrate. From an operational standpoint, electronic systems can considerably reduce the probability of errors in recording and reporting trades.

Exchanges which are switching over to an electronic trading platform are finding that the operational costs for these systems are lower than the costs for the open-outcry systems which they are replacing. Screen-based trading typically requires less labor, skill, and time. Open-outcry systems entail greater fixed costs due to the need to employ a greater number of personnel. Overhead costs in terms of buildings and back-office facilities also tend to be higher for such systems, as compared to electronic systems.

However, it is not as if the open-outcry system does not have any advantages of its own. Sarkar and Tozzi (1998) argue that highly active contracts are better traded on open-outcry systems. Traders on such exchanges are more accomplished at executing large and complex orders with a minimal impact on prices.

Traders in oral-auction systems also have the advantage of being able to get to know the trading behavior of competitors and counterparties with whom they interact on a regular basis. This kind of knowledge can be invaluable in predicting the response of others, for a trader who is seeking to implement a particular trading strategy. In contrast, in a faceless electronic system, the counterparties remain unidentified.

Finally, in an open-outcry system, order revision is simpler because a quote is valid only for an instant. However, on an electronic system, a trader who seeks to modify or cancel an order issued earlier has to give explicit instructions and hope that the original order does not get executed before it is canceled.

Test your concepts

The answers are provided on page 241.

1. In which of these cases is a buy order placed at a price that is below the best price that is available in the market?
   (a) Stop-loss order
   (b) Limit order
   (c) Market-if-touched order
   (d) (b) and (c).

2. In which of these cases is a sell order placed at a price that is below the best price that is available in the market?
   (a) Stop-loss order
   (b) Limit order
   (c) Market-if-touched order
   (d) (b) and (c).

3. Which of these orders will become a market order if triggered off?
   (a) Stop-loss orders
   (b) Stop-limit orders
   (c) Market-if-touched orders
   (d) (b) and (c).

4. Which of these rules is self-enforcing in an open-outcry system?
   (a) Price priority
   (b) Time priority
   (c) Both (a) and (b)
   (d) Neither (a) nor (b).

5. Open-outcry systems are based on the following order precedence rules:
   (a) Price priority
   (b) Floor time preference
   (c) Strict time preference
   (d) (a) and (b).

6. A limit order that is executable on submission is called:
   (a) A stop-limit order
   (b) A market-if-touched order
   (c) An immediate or cancel order
   (d) None of the above.

7. A trader who has short sold an asset and is worried that the price may abrupty move in an adverse direction is likely to place:
   (a) A stop-sell order
   (b) A stop-buy order
   (c) A stop-limit buy order
   (d) (b) or (c).

8. The limit price for a marketable limit buy order should be:
   (a) Greater than or equal to the best available bid
   (b) Less than or equal to the best available bid
   (c) Less than or equal to the best available ask
   (d) Greater than or equal to the best available ask.

9. Which of these orders gives the trader control over the trade price?
   (a) Limit orders
   (b) Stop-limit orders
   (c) Stop-loss orders
   (d) (a) and (b).

10. A "good today" limit order is:
    (a) A fill or kill order
    (b) A good till canceled order
    (c) A day order
    (d) None of the above.

CHAPTER 5

THE UNDERLYING FINANCIAL ASSETS: KEY CONCEPTS

QUESTION 116

What are equity shares?

Equity shares or shares of common stock of a company are financial claims issued by the firm, which confer ownership rights on the shareholders. Every shareholder is a part owner of the company which has issued the shares. A shareholder's stake in the firm is equal to the fraction of the total share capital of the firm to which he has subscribed.

When a firm makes a profit it will typically pay out a percentage of it in the form of cash to its shareholders. This income that is received from the firm is called a *dividend*. It is not necessary that a firm which desires to pay out dividends in a particular year should have earned a profit in that financial year. A loss-making company may declare dividends out of the profits that it has accumulated from its operations in previous years, or what are known as the *reserves and surplus* of the firm. In practice, a firm will rarely pay out its entire profit for the year as dividends. A part of the profits will be ploughed back into the venture to meet future requirements. The profits that are reinvested in the firm are called *retained earnings*. The earnings that are retained in a particular year will manifest themselves as an increase in the *reserves and surplus* account on the balance sheet of the firm.

The rate of dividends is not fixed and nor is the payment of dividends contractually guaranteed. That is, a shareholder cannot demand a dividend as a matter of right. Dividends can in principle fluctuate substantially from year to year, although firms generally try to keep them at an acceptable level even in years of financial hardship, to avoid sending unwanted distress signals to the market.

Equity shares have no maturity date. Thus, they continue to be in existence as long as the firm itself continues to be in existence. Shareholders have voting rights and have a say in the election of the Board of Directors. If the firm were to declare bankruptcy, then the shareholders would be entitled to the residual value of the assets after the claims of all the other creditors have been settled.

QUESTION 117

We hear of a term called the "ex-dividend date." What does it signify?

In the context of a dividend payment, there are four dates that are important. The first is called the *declaration date*. It is the date on which the decision to pay a dividend is declared by the Directors of the company, and the amount of the dividend is announced. The dividend announcement will mention a second date called the *record date*. Only those shareholders whose names appear as of the record date on the register of shareholders being maintained by the company will be eligible to receive the forthcoming dividend.

A third important date is called the *ex-dividend date*, and is specified by the exchange on which the shares are traded. An investor who purchases shares on or after the ex-dividend date will not be eligible to receive the forthcoming dividend. Quite obviously, the ex-dividend date will be such that transactions prior to that date will be reflected in the register of shareholders on the record date, whereas transactions on or after that date will be reflected in the books only after the record date. Thus, the ex-dividend date will be set a few days before the share transfer book is scheduled to be closed, in order to help the share registrar complete the administrative formalities.

For instance, on the NYSE a T+3 settlement cycle is followed. That is, if a trade occurs on day T, then delivery of shares to the buyer and payment of funds to the seller occurs on day $T+3$. Consequently, anyone who purchases shares two days before the record date or later will not be able to ensure that he is the owner of record as of that date. Hence, on the NYSE the ex-dividend date for an issue is specified as two business days prior to the record date announced by the firm.

Prior to the ex-dividend date the share will be traded *cum-dividend*, which implies that the buyer of the share will receive the coming dividend. On the ex-dividend date the shares begin to trade ex-dividend, which connotes that a potential buyer will no longer be eligible to receive the next dividend if he were to acquire the share.

On the ex-dividend date, the share ought to, in theory, decline by the amount of the dividend. For instance, if the cum-dividend price is $50 per share, and the quantum of the dividend is $2 per share, then from a theoretical standpoint the share should trade at $48 ex-dividend. In practice, the magnitude of the price decline may not equal the size of the dividend, a phenomenon for which various theories have been advanced.

Finally, we have a date called the *distribution date*, which is the date on which the dividends are actually paid or distributed.

QUESTION 118

What is a "stock dividend?"

A stock dividend is a dividend that is distributed in the form of shares of stock rather than in the form of cash. The issue of additional shares without any monetary consideration entails the transfer of funds from the reserves and surplus account to the share capital account. This is known as the *capitalization of reserves*.

From a theoretical standpoint stock dividends do not create any value for an existing shareholder. For instance, assume that a shareholder owns 500 shares of a firm which has issued a total of 500,000 shares. So this individual owns $\frac{1}{1,000}$ th of the firm. If the firm announces a 10% stock dividend, or one additional share for every 10 existing shares, it will have to issue 50,000 shares, of which this investor will receive 50. Thus, after the issue of the additional shares, he will be in possession of 550 shares which is $\frac{1}{1,000}$ th of the total number of shares issued by the firm; that is, 550,000. His stake in the company will therefore remain unaltered.

From the company's point of view, the issue of additional shares does not tantamount to any changes in its asset base or to its earnings capacity. Thus, the share price should theoretically decline after a stock dividend is declared.

Let us go back to our illustration and assume that the share price prior to the stock dividend issue was $55 per share. The ex-dividend price, P, should be such that:

$$500,000 \times 55 = 550,000 \times P$$
$$\Rightarrow P = 50$$

However, the ex-dividend price may not fall to its theoretically predicted value. This is because the market may interpret the stock dividend as a signal of enhanced future profitability from the management. If market participants were to interpret the stock dividend in this manner, then the demand for the shares of the company will rise. Consequently, although the ex-dividend price will in general be lower than the cum-dividend price, it will be higher than what the theoretical calculation would suggest.

Sometimes, a company may declare a stock dividend prior to the payment of a cash dividend. The impact on the share price may be determined as follows.

Let us assume that the company which has 500,000 shares outstanding and whose shares are being traded at $55 each announces a cash dividend of $2 and a stock dividend of 10%. Assume that the cash dividend will also be paid on the additional shares that are to be issued.

The cum-dividend price (cash as well as stock) is obviously $55. The market value of 500,000 shares is therefore:

$$500,000 \times 55 = 27,500,000$$

The market value of 550,000 ex-stock dividend cum-cash dividend shares will also be $27,500,000 since the stock dividend by itself does not add any value. Thus, the theoretical price of ex-stock dividend ex-cash dividend shares will be:

$$\frac{27,500,000 - (2 \times 550,000)}{550,000} = \$48$$

QUESTION 119

What are stock splits and reverse splits?

An $n{:}m$ stock split means that n new shares will be issued to the existing shareholders in lieu of m existing shares. For instance, a 11:10 split means that a holder of 10 existing shares will receive 11 shares. Thus this stock split is exactly analogous to a 10% stock dividend. However, stock dividends entail the capitalization of reserves, as explained earlier, whereas stock splits do not. What happens in such cases is that the par value of existing shares is reduced. Since the number of shares will increase proportionately, the product of the par value and the number of shares outstanding, which is nothing but the issued share capital, will remain unchanged after the split.

The share price after a split will behave in the same way as it would after an equivalent stock dividend. Take the case of our investor who is holding 500 shares worth $55 each. If the company were to announce an 11:10 stock split, he will have 550 shares after the split, which will theoretically be worth $50 each.

Companies generally go in for a split when their share prices become too high, and it is felt that the scrip has become out of reach for small and medium investors. What is high is of course subjective, but in practice it is believed that most managers have a feel for what is the popular price range for their stock. In other words, they are believed to be aware of the price range within which their stock should trade, if it is to attract adequate attention from investors.

A company which perceives its stock price to be too low can go in for a reverse split. A very low stock price can lead to greater transaction costs for traders wishing to take large positions in the stock. Besides, very low share prices can seduce uninformed traders into taking long positions in anticipation of extraordinary profits. For instance, if a share were to be trading at $1, a naive investor may be tempted to buy it, with the hope that a mere $1 rise in the price would translate into a 100% return. This is known as the *penny stock trap*. Such investors fail to realize that a stock that is trading at $1 is priced so low because it is probably what it is worth, and that a gain of the magnitude of 100%, while not impossible, is highly improbable.

The difference between an *n:m* split and an *n:m* reverse split is that in the first case *n* will be greater than *m* whereas in the second case it will be less. For instance, assume that the company announces a 4:5 reverse split instead of an 11:10 split. Thus a holder of 500 shares would have 400 shares after the split. The post reverse split share price would be:

$$P = \frac{500,000 \times 55}{400,000} = \$68.75$$

QUESTION 120

What are pre-emptive rights?

The laws governing companies usually require that existing shareholders be given pre-emptive rights to new shares as and when they are issued.[1] That is, the new shares must first be offered to the existing

---

1. In this case we are talking about shares being issued for a monetary consideration.

shareholders in order to enable them to maintain their proportionate ownership in the company. From the company's standpoint, such a *rights issue* represents a low-cost alternative to the more common underwritten approach for issuing shares to the general public.

Often the rights issue is made at a price that is lower than the prevailing market price of the share. If so, then the right acquires a value of its own. The existing shareholders can in this case either exercise their rights and acquire additional shares, or else sell the rights to someone else.

What is the value of a right? Let us suppose that a company has 500,000 shares outstanding and that shareholders are entitled to purchase one new share for every 10 shares that are currently being held. So in all, 50,000 shares will be issued. Let us assume that the prevailing market price is $50 per share, whereas the existing shareholders are being given the right to acquire additional shares at $39 per share. The market value of the firm prior to the rights issue is:

$$500,000 \times 50 = 25,000,000$$

The post issue theoretical value of the firm will therefore be:

$$25,000,000 + 50,000 \times 39 = 26,950,000$$

The ex-rights price should therefore be:

$$\frac{26,950,000}{550,000} = 49$$

Considering the fact that the shareholder is getting a share worth $49 at $39, the value of the right to acquire a share is $10. Since the shareholder needs ten shares to acquire the right to buy one share, the value of a right is $1.

At first glance it may appear that the existing shareholders are losing, since the ex-rights market price is $49, which is lower than the cum rights price of $50. However, it must be remembered that the shareholders have been given the opportunity to buy new shares at $39, and that this opportunity makes up for the decline in the share price. For instance, if we take the case of a person who owns 50 shares, the value of these shares prior to the issue of rights is $2,500. If he decides to exercise his rights he can acquire five additional shares by paying $39 for each. The value of his shares after the issue is:

$$49 \times 55 = 2,695 = 2,500 + 5 \times 39$$

Thus there is no dilution in terms of value.

If, on the other hand, he decides not to exercise his rights, he can renounce them in favor of another investor. The rights can in this case be sold for $1 per right. The value of his position after renouncing the rights will be:

$$49 \times 50 + 1 \times 50 = 2,500$$

In practice, the ex-rights price may be higher than the theoretically predicted value. This is because the rights issue may be perceived as an information signal by investors. The very fact that the company has chosen to issue additional shares may be construed as a signal of enhanced future profitability. One reason could be that investors believe that the new funds raised in this manner will be used for initiating more profitable projects. Another reason could be that considering the fact that cash dividends are usually maintained at existing levels in the medium term, the shareholders believe that the issue of additional shares is an indicator of greater profitability from the existing ventures of the firm. Both these factors could cause the demand for shares to rise, as a consequence of which the decline in the price will be less than what is predicted according to theory.

QUESTION 121

How are futures contracts adjusted for dividends, stock dividends, stock splits/reverse splits, and rights issues?

We will examine the impact of each of the above corporate actions on an existing futures position. The procedures adopted sometimes differ across exchanges.

Dividends

A dividend declaration will have consequences for a futures contract written on the stock only if the dividend is perceived to be extraordinary.

The adjustment to the futures contract will be made as follows. You should note that in every case, be it an extraordinary dividend or any other relevant corporate action, changes to the futures settlement price and the contract size will only be made at the end of the last day on which the security is traded on a cum basis, that is cum-cash dividend or cum-stock dividend, etc. as the case may be.

In the case of a futures contract, whenever an extraordinary dividend is declared, when the contract is marked to market on the ex-dividend date, the previous day's settlement price will be reduced by the amount of the dividend.

For instance, assume that the futures settlement price on the ex-dividend date is $135, while that on the previous day was $146. Let us assume that each contract is for 100 shares, and that the dividend is $15 per share. For the purpose of marking to market on the ex-dividend date the previous day's settlement price will be taken as $146 − $15 = $131. That is, the dividend will be subtracted from the settlement price. Consequently the profit for a trader who has a long position in one contract will be:

$$(\$135 - \$131) \times 100 = \$400$$

There will be no adjustment made to the contract size.

Stock dividends

Let us assume that a company declares a 40% stock dividend. This means that for every five shares held by an investor, he will be eligible for an additional two shares. The ratio of additional to existing shares may be denoted as 2:5 or in general as A:B.

The adjustment factor is $\dfrac{A + B}{B}$ which is 1.4 in this case.

On the ex-dividend day the contract size will be multiplied by the adjustment factor. For instance, if the futures contracts on a stock have a contract size of 100 shares, the post adjustment contract size will be 140 shares.

For the purpose of marking to market on the ex-dividend date, the settlement price on the previous day will be divided by the adjustment factor. For instance, let us assume that the futures settlement price on the previous day was 133. If so, it will be adjusted to $\dfrac{133}{1.4} = 95$.

So if the settlement price on the ex-dividend date is $100, the profit from marking to market for an investor with a long position in one contract would be:

$$140 \times (100 - 95) = \$700$$

Stock splits/Reverse splits

The adjustment for stock splits and reverse splits is analogous to the system followed for a stock dividend. Assume that a firm undergoes an A:B split or reverse split. The adjustment factor in this case is $\dfrac{A}{B}$. For instance, if a stock undergoes a 3:5 reverse split, the adjustment factor will be 0.60.

The contract size will be multiplied by this factor. And while marking to market on the ex date, the previous day's settlement price will be divided by this factor.

For instance, if the original contract size was 100 shares, it would be adjusted to 60. Let us assume that the previous day's settlement price was $127.50 while the settlement price on the ex-date is $225. Thus the adjusted settlement price will be $\dfrac{127.5}{0.60} = 212.50$.

The profit from marking to market for a person with a long futures position will be:

$$60 \times (225 - 212.50) = \$750$$

Rights issues

Let us assume that a company announces a pre-emptive rights issue where an existing shareholder is entitled to two shares for every five shares that he is holding. The right can be exercised at a price of $38.50 per share. Assume that at the end of the day prior to the expiry of the right, the share price is $42. Consequently, it is profitable to exercise the right. If the rights are exercised the value of the share will drop to:

$$\frac{5 \times 42 + 2 \times 38.50}{7} = 41$$

which is a decline of $1. Consequently, on the next day, the settlement price for the previous day will be reduced by $1 while marking to market. If the right were not to have value on the previous day, no adjustment would be made. In any case, no adjustment would be made to the contract size.

QUESTION 122

&A

What is a stock index?

A stock index is a summary measure of the performance of the market based on the prices, or the market capitalization, of a predefined set of stocks. The index value is intended to serve as a barometer of the performance of the stock market, or of a particular segment of the stock market. Consequently, the stocks constituting the index ought to be chosen so as to be representative of the market or the market segment as the case may be.

QUESTION 123

What is a price weighted index and how is it computed?

A price weighted index is computed by considering only the prices of the component stocks.

At the time of computation of the index, the current prices of all the component stocks will be added up and divided by a number known as the *divisor*. On the base date, or the date on which the index is being computed for the first time, the divisor can be set equal to any arbitrary value. One sensible value is the number of stocks which constitutes the index. Subsequently, whenever there is a relevant corporate action such as a split/reverse split or a stock dividend, the divisor will be adjusted as described later.

So if we are standing at the end of day t, and the closing price of the i th stock on the day is $P_{i,t}$, then the index level I_t is given by:

$$I_t = \sum_{i=1}^{N} \frac{P_{i,t}}{Div_t}$$

where Div_t is the applicable value of the divisor for the day, and N is the number of stocks comprising the index.

Numerical illustration

Let us assume that we are standing on the base date of an index, which has been defined to consist of five stocks. The starting value of the divisor has been chosen to be 5.0. Let the closing prices of these five stocks at the end of the day be as shown in Table 5.1.

Table 5.1 Prices of the constituent stocks on the base date

Stock	Price
3M	80
American Express	55
Coca Cola	45
IBM	80
Merck	35
Total	295

Table 5.2 Prices of the constituent stocks on the following day

Stock	Price
3M	85
American Express	60
Coca Cola	48
IBM	85
Merck	40
Total	318

The end of the day index value will therefore be:

$$\frac{295}{5} = 59.00.$$

Let us suppose that at the end of the following day the prices of the stocks are as shown in Table 5.2.

The value of the index on this day will be $\frac{318}{5} \times 63.60$, and we will conclude that the market has moved up. In this case, it would be the correct deduction for, as can be seen by comparing Tables 5.1 and 5.2, every stock has risen in value.

QUESTION 124

When and how will the divisor be changed?

The divisor has to be adjusted if one or more of the following events were to occur:

- A split or a reverse split in one or more of the constituent stocks.
- A stock dividend on one or more of the constituent stocks.
- A change of composition. That is, a replacement of an existing stock(s) by a new stock(s).

We will illustrate the mechanics of adjustment by considering a scenario where one of the constituent stocks undergoes a split.

Assume that Coca Cola undergoes a 3:1 split at the end of the base date. Let the prices of the constituent stocks at the end of the following day be as shown in Table 5.3.

When we compare Table 5.3 with the previous table we find that all the other stocks have the same value as before, except for Coca Cola

Table 5.3 Prices of the constituent stocks on the following day, assuming a stock split in Coca Cola

Stock	Price
3M	85
American Express	60
Coca Cola	16
IBM	85
Merck	40
Total	286

whose value is one-third of the value it would have been in the absence of the split.

If we were to use a divisor of 5.0 under these circumstances, we will get an index value of $\frac{286}{5} = 57.20$. The conclusion would then be that the market has gone down as compared to the base date. However, this is clearly an erroneous deduction, for every stock, including Coca Cola, has risen in value as compared to the base date. The perceived decline in the index is entirely due to our failure to take the split into account.

If the index is to continue to be an accurate barometer of the market, then clearly an adjustment needs to be made. In practice we would adjust the divisor as follows. First, we would list the theoretical post-split values at the end of the day on which the split is declared (Table 5.4). The split will affect only the price of the stock whose shares have been split. In this case, the theoretical post-split price of Coca Cola will be one-third of its pre-split value of $45.

The new divisor, Div_N, should be such that the pre- and post-split index values for the base date are the same, when the post-split index level is computed using the new divisor. That is, $\frac{265}{Div_N}$ should equal

Table 5.4 Theoretical post-split stock prices

Stock	Price
3M	80
American Express	55
Coca Cola	15
IBM	80
Merck	35
Total	265

59.00. The new divisor is therefore 4.4915. If we use this value of the divisor to compute the index level on the following day, we will get a value of $\dfrac{286}{4.4915} = 63.68$, which is consistent with our earlier observation that the market has risen.

We will continue to use the new divisor until another stock undergoes a split or a reverse split, or if a firm declares a stock dividend. The adjustment procedure for a stock dividend is identical to that for a stock split since the two are mathematically equivalent. So, for instance, if a firm were to declare a stock dividend of 40%, it would be equivalent to a 7:5 split, and consequently would be treated as such.

QUESTION 125

How will the divisor be adjusted if a price weighted index undergoes a change in its composition?

We will illustrate the adjustment procedure in the event of a change in composition, with the help of an example.

Let us assume that at the end of the day following the base date, Merck, which has a prevailing market price of $40, is replaced with General Electric, which has a price of $50. The index level prior to the change is 63.68, as computed earlier. The prices of the stocks contained in the reconstituted index will be as shown in Table 5.5.

The new divisor, Div_N, should be such that:

$$\frac{296}{Div_N} = 63.68 \Rightarrow Div_N = 4.6482$$

Table 5.5 Prices of the component stocks of the reconstituted index

Stock	Price
3M	85
American Express	60
Coca Cola	16
IBM	85
General Electric	50
Total	296

QUESTION 126

Is it true that a higher priced stock carries a greater weight in a price weighted index than a lower priced stock? Why is this considered undesirable?

Yes, it is true that higher priced stocks tend to have a greater impact on price weighted indices than lower priced components of the same index. Let us take the following data (Table 5.6) for our five-stock index on a particular day. Assume that the divisor is 5.0.

The index level is $\dfrac{310}{5} = 62.00$.

Table 5.6 Prices of the constituent stocks on a given day

Stock	Price
3M	85
American Express	60
Coca Cola	45
IBM	90
Merck	30
Total	310

Table 5.7 Prices on the following day: Two different scenarios

	Case A	Case B
Stock	Price	Price
3M	85	85
American Express	60	60
Coca Cola	45	45
IBM	108	90
Merck	30	36
Total	328	316

Consider two possible situations for the following day (Table 5.7). In Case A, IBM's price has gone up by 20%, whereas in Case B, Merck's price has gone up by 20%.

In the first case the index value is 65.60, which represents an increase of 5.81% as compared to the previous day. In the second case the index value is 63.20, which represents an increase of only 1.94% as compared to the previous day. Clearly, a change of 20% in the price of IBM, which is a high-priced stock, has had a greater impact than a similar change in the price of Merck, which is priced considerably lower.

Finance theorists hold the view that the importance accorded to a company ought to be based on its market capitalization and not its share price, where market capitalization is defined as the share price multiplied by the total number of shares outstanding. A model like the capital asset pricing model is consistent with this viewpoint, for it defines the *market portfolio* as a market capitalization weighted portfolio of all assets. Thus, a price weighted index can in a sense be construed as a less than perfect barometer of the stock market.

QUESTION 127

What is a value weighted index and how is it computed in practice?

A value weighted index takes into consideration the market capitalization of a component stock and not merely its price.

Let us assume that we are standing on day t, and let us denote the starting or base date of the index by b. We will use $P_{i,t}$ and $P_{i,b}$ to denote the market prices of the ith stock on days t and b respectively, and $Q_{i,t}$ and $Q_{i,b}$ to denote the number of shares outstanding on those two days.

On the base date, the index can be assigned any value. Let us assume that it was set equal to 100. The level of the index on day t is then defined as:

$$\frac{1}{Div_t} \left(\frac{\sum_{i=1}^{N} P_{i,t}Q_{i,t}}{\sum_{i=1}^{M} P_{i,b}Q_{i,b}} \right) \times 100$$

Div_t represents the value of the divisor on day t. The divisor is assigned a value of 1.0 on the base date. Subsequently it will be adjusted as and when required. However, the circumstances under which it needs to be adjusted are different, as compared to the case of the divisor that is used in connection with a price weighted index. Also note that we have used M to denote the number of component stocks on the base date and N to denote the number of component stocks on day t. In practice, M need not equal N. That is, an index may subsequently be modified to include more or less number of stocks than it had on the base date.

Numerical illustration

We will take the same five stocks as before and use the prices shown in Table 5.8. The difference is that we will now also consider the number of shares issued by each firm.

The total market value is:

$$\sum_{i=1}^{5} P_i Q_i = 467,100,000,000$$

Let us assign the index a value of 100. The corresponding value for the divisor is obviously 1.0.

Let us suppose that on the following day, the prices and number of shares are as depicted in Table 5.9.

The total market value is:

$$\sum_{i=1}^{5} P_i Q_i = 508,650,000,000$$

Table 5.8 Prices, number of shares outstanding, and market capitalization of the components of a value weighted index on the base date

Stock	Price (P)	# of sares (Q)	Market capitalization
3M	85	780,000,000	66,300,000,000
American Express	60	1,250,000,000	75,000,000,000
Coca Cola	45	2,425,000,000	109,125,000,000
IBM	85	1,635,000,000	138,975,000,000
Merck	35	2,220,000,000	77,700,000,000

Table 5.9 Prices, number of shares outstanding, and market capitalization of the components of a value weighted index on the following day

Stock	Price (P)	# of shares (Q)	Market capitalization
3M	90	780,000,000	70,200,000,000
American Express	65	1,250,000,000	81,250,000,000
Coca Cola	50	2,425,000,000	121,250,000,000
IBM	90	1,635,000,000	147,150,000,000
Merck	40	2,220,000,000	88,800,000,000

The value of the index on this day is therefore:

$$\frac{508,650,000,000}{467,100,000,000} \times 100 = 108.8953$$

Our conclusion would therefore be that the market has moved up.

QUESTION 128

Does the divisor have to be adjusted in the event of a split/reverse split or a stock dividend? Why or why not?

There is no need to adjust the divisor if one of the components of the index were to undergo a split or a reverse split or if a firm that is present in the index were to declare a stock dividend. This is because, from a theoretical standpoint, such corporate actions will not have any impact on the market capitalization of the firm.

In the case of a stock split or a stock dividend the share price will decline, whereas in the case of a reverse split the share price will rise. However, in the first two cases the number of shares outstanding will rise whereas in the last case it will decline. The changes in the number of shares outstanding will always be such that there is no impact on the market capitalization. We will now give an illustration of this phenomenon.

Numerical illustration

Assume that 3M has a market price of $90, and that the number of shares outstanding is 780,000,000, and that the firm announces a 20% stock dividend. The share price will immediately decline to $\frac{90 \times 780,000,000}{936,000,000} = \$75$. As can be seen the market capitalization before the stock dividend, which is:

$$90 \times 780,000,000 = 70,200,000,000$$

is the same as the market capitalization after the dividend, which is:

$$75 \times 936,000,000 = 70,200,000,000$$

QUESTION 129

Under what circumstances does the divisor have to be changed in the case of a value weighted index?

The divisor would have to be changed whenever there is a change in the composition of the index. Let us assume that the prices and

Table 5.10 Market capitalization of the component stocks of the reconstituted index

Stock	Price (P)	# of shares (Q)	Market capitalization
3M	90	780,000,000	70,200,000,000
American Express	65	1,250,000,000	81,250,000,000
Coca Cola	50	2,425,000,000	121,250,000,000
IBM	90	1,635,000,000	147,150,000,000
General Electric	50	10,500,000,000	525,000,000,000

number of shares of the companies constituting the index are as shown in Table 5.9, at the end of day t. Assume that Merck, with a price of \$40 and number of shares outstanding equal to 2,220,000,000, is replaced with General Electric, which has a price of \$50 and number of shares outstanding equal to 10,500,000,000. The market capitalization of the component stocks after the change will be as depicted in Table 5.10.

The total market capitalization after the change is 944,850,000,000. The new divisor, Div_N, should be such that:

$$\frac{1}{Div_N} \times \frac{944,850,000,000}{467,100,000,000} \times 100 = 108.8953$$

$$\Rightarrow Div_N = 1.8576$$

QUESTION 130

What is an equally weighted index, and how is it computed?

An equally weighted index is yet another alternative for tracking the performance of a market. Let us assume that we decide to form an index consisting of N stocks. In this case, like in the case of a price weighted index, only the prices of the component stocks are considered.

The value of the index on day t is defined as:

$$I_t = I_{t-1} \times \frac{1}{N} \sum_{i=1}^{N} \frac{P_{i,t}}{P_{i,t-1}}$$

The ratio of the prices $\dfrac{P_{i,t}}{P_{i,t-1}}$ may be expressed as $(1 + r_{i,t})$ where $r_{i,t}$ is the arithmetic rate of return on the i th stock between day t and day $t - 1$. Therefore:

$$\frac{1}{N} \sum_{i=1}^{N} \frac{P_{i,t}}{P_{i,t-1}} = \frac{1}{N} \sum_{i=1}^{N} (1 + r_{i,t})$$

$$= 1 + \frac{1}{N} \sum_{i=1}^{N} r_{i,t} = 1 + \bar{r}_t$$

where $\bar{r}_t$ is the arithmetic average of the returns on all the component stocks between day $t - 1$ and day t. Thus:

$$I_t = I_{t-1} \times (1 + \bar{r}_t)$$

QUESTION 131

Investors talk of holding portfolios that track or mimic an index. How is this accomplished in practice?

It is possible to hold a portfolio that imitates the behavior of a market index. The method of forming such a portfolio would depend on the nature of the index that is being tracked.

To imitate an equally weighted index, one has to put an equal fraction of his wealth in all the assets that constitute the index. So if we start with a capital of $\$W$, and the index consists of N stocks, then we will have to invest an amount of $\dfrac{W}{N}$ in each security.

In order to track a price weighted index one has to hold an identical number of shares of each of the companies that are present in the index.

Finally, forming a portfolio to track a value weighted index is the most complex task. To imitate such an index, the fraction of our wealth that is invested in each asset should be equal to the ratio of the market capitalization of that particular asset to the total market capitalization of all the assets that constitute the index.

QUESTION 132

Once a tracking portfolio is formed, will it continue to track the index under all conditions, or are there circumstances that will warrant adjustment or rebalancing of the portfolio?

In the case of every index, be it equally weighted, price weighted, or value weighted, there will arise circumstances when the tracking portfolio will have to be rebalanced.

Equally weighted portfolios

Equally weighted tracking portfolios need to be rebalanced very frequently. For unless it were to be the case that none of the component stocks undergoes a change in price from one day to the next, an index that is equally weighted on a particular day will no longer be equally weighted on the following day. We will now illustrate as to why an equally weighted portfolio will require rebalancing with the sheer passage of time.

Assume that we have $500,000 and decide to form an equally weighted portfolio consisting of the following four stocks whose prices are shown in Table 5.11.

Since we have $500,000, we will have to invest $125,000 in each stock. So we will buy 2,500 shares of General Electric, 1,250 shares of 3M, 3,125 shares of Merck, and 1,000 shares of IBM. If we assume that the index value is 100, our portfolio is worth 5,000 times the index.

On the next day, assume that the prices of the companies are as shown in Table 5.12.

The amounts invested in the stocks will be $100,000, $156,250, $156,250, and $100,000 respectively. The total portfolio value will be $512,500, of which 19.51% each will be in General Electric and IBM, and 30.49% each will be in 3M and Merck.

Table 5.11 Prices of the stocks constituting an equally weighted index at the time of formation of the portfolio

Stock	Price
General Electric	50
3M	100
Merck	40
IBM	125

Table 5.12 Prices of the stocks constituting an equally weighted index on the following day

Stock	Price
General Electric	40
3M	125
Merck	50
IBM	100

Quite obviously, the portfolio is no longer equally weighted. If we have to reset the weights to 0.25 each, then we will have to rebalance by selling part of our holdings in 3M and Merck, and investing the proceeds in General Electric and IBM.

The total value of the portfolio is $512,500, which means that we would need to have $128,125 in each stock. For this, we would need to buy 703.125 shares of General Electric, and 281.25 shares of IBM. We would need to sell 225 shares of 3M, and 562.50 shares of Merck.

The inflow is $225 \times 125 + 562.50 \times 50 = \$56,250$.

The outflow is $703.125 \times 40 + 281.25 \times 100 = \$56,250$.

Thus we can rebalance at zero net cost. It can be verified that the amount invested in each company is $128,125.

The new index level is $100 \times (1 + \bar{r}_t)$.

$$\bar{r}_t = \frac{(-0.20 + 0.25 + 0.25 + -0.20)}{4} = \frac{0.10}{4} = 0.025$$

Therefore, the new value of the index is 102.50. The total value of the portfolio is $512,500 which is 5,000 times the value of the index. Hence, the portfolio continues to mimic the index.

Price weighted portfolios

A portfolio that is used to track a price weighted index has to be rebalanced whenever there is a split or a reverse split, a stock dividend, or a change in the index composition.

Consider a price weighted index consisting of the four stocks depicted in Table 5.11. Assume that the divisor is equal to 4.0 which would mean that the index level is:

$$\frac{50 + 100 + 40 + 125}{4.0} = 78.75$$

Assume that we form a tracking portfolio by buying 1,000 shares of each of these companies. The value of our tracking portfolio will be:

$$1,000 \times (50 + 100 + 40 + 125) = \$315,000 = 4,000 \times 78.75$$

Thus, our portfolio is worth 4,000 times the index.

Now assume that 3M undergoes a 2:1 split, which means that its post-split theoretical value will be $50. The new divisor, Div_N, should be such that:

$$\frac{50 + 50 + 40 + 125}{Div_N} = 78.75$$

$$\Rightarrow Div_N = 3.3651$$

In order to ensure that our portfolio continues to mimic the index, we need to rebalance in such a way that our portfolio value remains unchanged. Let us denote the number of shares of each stock held before the split by N_0, and the number of shares required after the split by N_N. If the value of our portfolio is to remain unchanged, it should be the case that:

$$N_0 \times Div_o \times I_t = N_N \times Div_N \times I_t$$

$$\Rightarrow N_N = \frac{N_o \times Div_o}{Div_N}$$

In our example, the number of shares of each stock required after the split is:

$$\frac{1,000 \times 4.0}{3.3651} = 1,188.672$$

Assuming that fractional shares can be bought and sold, we will have to buy 188.672 shares of General Electric, Merck, and IBM, and sell 811.328 shares of 3M.[2]

The inflow is $811.328 \times 50 = \$40,566.40$.

The outflow is $188.672 \times (50 + 40 + 125) = \$40,564.48$.

Once again, if we ignore transaction costs, we can rebalance at zero net cost. The difference between the inflow and the outflow is entirely due to rounding errors.

Value weighted portfolios

Assume that there is a value weighted index consisting of four stocks, whose prices and number of shares outstanding are as shown in Table 5.13.

---

2. Remember that we would have 2,000 shares of 3M after the split.

Table 5.13 Components of a value weighted index

Stock	Price (P)	# of shares (Q)	Market capitalization
Alpha	20	100,000	2,000,000
Beta	40	50,000	2,000,000
Gamma	50	100,000	5,000,000
Delta	10	100,000	1,000,000

The total market capitalization is \$10,000,000. Assume that the base period market capitalization is \$16,000,000 and that the current divisor is 1. The index level is therefore 62.50.

Take the case of a person with capital of \$200,000, who wants to create a portfolio to track the index. In order for his portfolio to mimic the index, he must have:

$$\frac{2,000,000}{10,000,000} \times 200,000 = \$40,000 \text{ in Alpha stock,}$$

$$\frac{2,000,000}{10,000,000} \times 200,000 = \$40,000 \text{ in Beta stock,}$$

$$\frac{5,000,000}{10,000,000} \times 200,000 = \$100,000 \text{ in Gamma stock,}$$

$$\text{and } \frac{1,000,000}{10,000,000} \times 200,000 = \$20,000 \text{ in Delta stock.}$$

Consequently, he must buy 2,000 shares of Alpha, 1,000 shares of Beta, 2,000 shares of Gamma and 2,000 shares of Delta. In general, the number of shares of the i th stock is given by:

$$\frac{Q_i}{\sum P_i Q_i} \times W$$

where W is the initial wealth. The total portfolio value in this case is 3,200 times the index value of 62.50.

Now assume that Delta is replaced by Theta, which has a share price of \$35 and has 100,000 shares outstanding. The total market capitalization of the four components of the index will now be \$12,500,000. The divisor will have to be adjusted in such a way that the index level remains unchanged. That is:

$$\frac{1}{Div_N} \times \frac{12,500,000}{16,000,000} \times 100 = 62.50$$

$$\Rightarrow Div_N = 1.25$$

In order for the portfolio to remain value weighted, the investor must have:

$$\frac{2,000,000}{12,500,000} \times 200,000 = \$32,000 \text{ in Alpha stock,}$$

$$\frac{2,000,000}{12,500,000} \times 200,000 = \$32,000 \text{ in Beta stock,}$$

$$\frac{5,000,000}{12,500,000} \times 200,000 = \$80,000 \text{ in Gamma stock,}$$

$$\text{and } \frac{3,500,000}{12,500,000} \times 200,000 = \$56,000 \text{ in Theta stock.}$$

Thus, the investor requires 1,600 shares of Alpha, 800 shares of Beta, 1,600 shares of Gamma and 1,600 shares of Theta. This means that he will have to sell 400 shares of Alpha, 200 shares of Beta, 400 shares of Gamma and 2,000 shares of Delta. He will also have to buy 1,600 shares of Theta.[3]

The inflow $= 400 \times 20 + 200 \times 40 + 400 \times 50 + 2,000 \times 10 = \$56,000$.

The outflow $= 1,600 \times 35 = \$56,000$. Thus, if we ignore transaction costs, then once again we can rebalance at zero net cost. The portfolio value after rebalancing will be \$200,000 which is 3,200 times the index level of 62.50.

QUESTION 133

Which are the famous stock indices in world financial markets, and how are they computed?

The most famous index is undoubtedly the Dow Jones Industrial Average (DJIA), popularly known as the *Dow*. It is a price weighted average of 30 stocks. The list of constituent stocks as of March 16, 2007 is as shown in Table 5.14.

The Nikkei Index, which is a barometer of the Japanese stock market, is also price weighted and includes 225 large Japanese companies.

The Standard & Poor's 500 Index (S&P 500) and the Nasdaq 100 index are both value weighted.

---

3. The number of shares of the i th stock is once again given by:

$$\frac{Q_i}{\sum P_i Q_i} \times W.$$

Table 5.14   Constituents of the Dow Jones Industrial Average

3M	Alcoa	Altria Group
American Express	American International Group	AT&T
Boeing	Caterpillar	Citigroup
Coca-Cola	E.I. DuPont de Nemours	Exxon Mobil
General Electric	General Motors	Hewlett-Packard
Home Depot	Honeywell International	Intel
IBM	Johnson & Johnson	J.P. Morgan Chase
McDonald's	Merck	Microsoft
Pfizer	Procter & Gamble	United Technologies
Verizon Communications	Wal-Mart Stores	Walt Disney

QUESTION 134

What is the meaning of the term "beta," and how is the beta of a stock measured?

The return from a stock is obviously risky. The sources of risk inherent in stock returns may be broadly classified as firm-specific or idiosyncratic on one hand, and market-wide or economy-wide on the other. The terms unsystematic and systematic risk are also used to describe the two sources of risk respectively.

A rational investor will not choose to hold a risky asset in isolation, for all of us are well aware of the adage, *do not put all your eggs in one basket*. Consequently, sensible investors choose to hold what are called well-diversified portfolios of risky securities. In the process, the firm-specific risks of the component stocks get diversified away. If an individual by the course of his actions is able to ensure that he is no longer exposed to risk of a particular kind, he should obviously not receive any compensation for bearing it. Consequently, finance models postulate that idiosyncratic risk is not priced, or in other words does not yield any return for the stock holder.

However, no matter how well diversified a portfolio may be, across assets, across industries, and these days even across countries, there will be a level of risk to which exposure cannot be further reduced. This is termed as market or systematic risk. If exposure to such risk is inevitable, it is obvious that such risk must be priced. Beta is a measure of this risk. The beta of a stock is given by:

$$\beta = \frac{\text{Cov}(r_i, r_m)}{\text{Var}(r_m)}$$

where r_i is the rate of return on asset 'i', r_m is the rate of return on the *market portfolio*, which is a value weighted portfolio of all assets, 'Cov' stands for covariance, and 'Var' stands for the variance. This result was deduced in the process of development of a model called the capital asset pricing model (CAPM).

In order to measure the beta of a stock in practice, the vector of rates of return on the stock has to be regressed on the vector of the rates of return on a large, well-diversified portfolio, like the S&P 500, which is designated as the market portfolio. The slope coefficient from the regression is a measure of the beta of the stock.

QUESTION 135

What are debt securities, and why are they important?

A debt security is a financial claim issued by a borrower to a lender of funds. Unlike an equity share, a debt security does not confer ownership rights on the holder of the instrument. These securities are merely IOUs, which represent a promise to pay interest on the principal amount at periodic intervals, and to repay the principal itself at a pre-specified maturity date.

With the exception of perpetual debt securities which are not common in practice, most debt instruments have a finite life span, and differ from equity shares in this respect. Also, the interest payments that are promised to the lenders at the outset represent contractual obligations on the part of the borrowers. The borrowers are thus required to meet these obligations irrespective of the performance of the firm in a given financial year.

The interest claims of debt holders have to be settled before any residual profits can be distributed by way of dividends to the shareholders. Also, in the event of bankruptcy or liquidation, the proceeds from the sale of assets of the firm must be used to first settle all outstanding interest and principal. Only the residual amount, if any, can be distributed among the shareholders.

Debt securities represent the largest percentage of the total outstanding securities in the global financial markets at any point in time, in terms of value.

Companies issue debt instruments routinely to finance their long-term investments. As discussed earlier, debt securities allow the equity shareholders to obtain financial leverage. They also offer a tax shield to the issuing firm, since the interest on debt is tax deductible unlike the dividends on equity. This facility reduces the effective cost of debt and therefore the overall cost of capital for the issuing corporation, as the following example will illustrate.

Numerical illustration

Consider two firms, A and B (Table 5.15), both of which have reported an operating profit of $100,000 in a financial year. Firm A is entirely equity financed, whereas Firm B has issued debt securities with a principal of $500,000, carrying interest at the rate of 5% per annum. The applicable tax rate is 30%. Let us analyze the profits to which the shareholders are effectively entitled.

Table 5.15 Illustration of a tax shield

Item	Firm A	Firm B
Operating profit	100,000	100,000
Less interest	0	(25,000)
Profit before tax	100,000	75,000
Tax 30%	(30,000)	(22,500)
Profit after tax	70,000	52,500

In terms of the profit after tax, the shareholders of Firm B are entitled to $17,500 less than the shareholders of Firm A, even though the second firm has paid out $25,000 by way of interest. This is because since the interest is tax deductible, the firm has saved 30% of $25,000, or $7,500, by way of taxes. Thus, it has effectively paid only $17,500 by way of interest. The effective rate of interest is therefore:

$$\frac{17,500}{500,000} = 0.035 \equiv 3.5\%$$

The effective cost of debt is therefore less than the stated cost. If we denote the stated interest rate by I, and the tax rate by T, the effective interest rate can be written as $I(1-T)$.

While debt is important for a corporation, in both the public as well as the private sectors of an economy, it is absolutely indispensable for central or federal, state, and local (municipalities) governments when they wish to finance their developmental activities. This is because, such entities obviously cannot issue equity shares.

QUESTION 136

What is the difference between money market instruments and capital market instruments?

Let us first define the money market. The money market is a trading arena for securities with a time to maturity of one year or less at the time of issue. By definition, all money market instruments are debt securities, since equity shares have no maturity date.

The capital market, on the other hand, is a market where assets with a time to maturity of greater than one year at the time of issue are traded. All equity shares are capital market assets. Long-term debt securities are also capital market assets.

In terms of their contribution to the free market system, the two markets perform fundamentally different roles.

A money market provides economic units with the means for adjusting temporary liquidity imbalances. This is because for a business organization it will rarely be the case that cash inflows and cash outflows are perfectly matched at any point in time. Consequently, most firms will either have a cash surplus, which they will seek to invest profitably for a short duration, or a cash deficit, which would have to be financed over a short period.

A capital market on the other hand performs a very different economic function. Its purpose is to channel funds from people who wish to save to those who wish to invest in productive assets, with a view to generating income in the future.

Medium to long-term debt securities which trade in the capital market are known as *notes*, *bonds*, or *debentures*.

QUESTION 137

What is the difference between a Treasury Bond, a Treasury Note, and a Treasury Bill?

In the United States, these terms are used to distinguish between different types of securities issued by the Treasury.

The term Treasury Bond or T-bond refers to a debt instrument with an original time to maturity in excess of 10 years. Treasury Notes or T-notes are similar to T-bonds, except that their terms to maturity at the time of issue are between 1 and 10 years. Treasury Bills or T-bills are money market instruments, unlike T-bonds and T-notes which are capital market instruments, and have maturities of either 3, 6, or 12 months at the time of issue.

The nomenclature for Treasury securities can vary across countries. For instance, the term T-note in Australia is used to refer to a money market security that corresponds to a T-bill in the U.S.

QUESTION 138

What do we mean by coupon paying bonds?

A conventional bond, referred to as a *plain vanilla bond*, pays interest periodically, which is usually every six months.[4] The interest rate expressed as a percentage of the principal amount, or what is called the *face value* of the bond, is called the *coupon rate*. The amount of the coupon can then be calculated as the coupon rate multiplied by the face value. For instance, if a bond has a face value of $1,000 and pays a coupon of 10% per annum on a semi-annual basis, then the quantum of the half-yearly coupon will be:

$$\frac{0.10}{2} \times 1,000 = \$50$$

QUESTION 139

What are zero coupon bonds?

A zero coupon bond does not pay any interest. So, how does the lender benefit by subscribing to such a bond? The answer is simple. In the case of a coupon paying bond, the lender who buys the bond at the time of issue will pay the face value to the borrower. In return, the borrower will pay coupons at regular intervals, and will return the face value at the end. On the other hand, in the case of a zero coupon bond, the price paid at the outset by the lender to acquire the bond will be less than the face value. Subsequently, he will not receive any payments by way of interest, but will receive the face value at maturity. The difference between the face value and the original issue price, therefore, represents the interest.

In the U.S., T-bonds and T-notes are coupon bearing instruments, whereas T-bills are zero coupon securities.

---

4. For every security, the most basic form or version of it is referred to as the *plain vanilla* version.

QUESTION 140

How is a bond valued?

A plain vanilla bond entitles its holder to a series of cash flows. Every six months the bond holder will receive a cash flow equal to the semi-annual coupon. Finally, at maturity he will receive the coupon for the last semi-annual period plus the face value.

In order to value this bond, we need to value this stream of cash flows. However, cash flows arising at different points in time cannot simply be added up. The principle of *time value of money* states that a dollar to be received in the future is worth less than a dollar today, or equivalently a dollar received today is worth more than a dollar to be received in the future. This is because a dollar in hand can always be invested so as to yield more than a dollar in the future. Thus, the future cash flows have to be discounted at the required interest rate in order to derive their *present value*.

The series of semi-annual coupon payments constitutes what is called an *annuity*. An annuity is defined as a series of identical cash flows occuring at equally spaced intervals of time, with the first cash flow occuring one period from now. For an N period annuity paying $1 per period, a required interest rate, or what is called a discount rate, of $r\%$ would imply that the current or the present value of the annuity is:

$$\frac{1}{r}\left[1 - \frac{1}{(1+r)^N}\right] \equiv \text{PVIFA(r,N)}$$

where PVIFA stands for *present value interest factor annuity*.

Similarly, the present value of a single cash flow of $1 arising after N periods can be calculated as:

$$\frac{1}{(1+r)^N} \equiv \text{PVIF(r,N)}$$

where PVIF stands for *present value interest factor*.

Now consider a bond which pays a coupon of $C per annum on a semi-annual basis. Let the number of coupon periods remaining in the life of the bond be N, and assume that the next coupon is due exactly one period from now. Let M represents the principal value or face value of the bond.

The coupon stream is obviously an annuity and each cash flow is $\$\frac{C}{2}$. The present value, using a discount rate of $\frac{y}{2}$ % per period, is:

$$\frac{C}{2} \text{ PVIFA}(\frac{y}{2}, N) = \frac{C}{y} \left[1 - \frac{1}{(1 + \frac{y}{2})^N} \right]$$

The face value which is due at expiration is a one time cash flow. Its present value is:

$$M \times \text{ PVIF}(\frac{y}{2}, N) = \frac{M}{(1 + \frac{y}{2})^N}$$

Thus, the value of the bond is given by:

$$P = \frac{C}{y} \left[1 - \frac{1}{(1 + \frac{y}{2})^N} \right] + \frac{M}{(1 + \frac{y}{2})^N}$$

When a bond is issued, the company will set the coupon rate in such a way that it is almost equal to the discount rate required by investors. Consequently, the value of the bond at the outset will be equal to its principal or face value, and the lenders will pay the face value to acquire the bond from the issuing company. A bond whose price equals its face value is said to trade at *par*.

Subsequently, in the case of a plain vanilla bond, the coupon rate will remain unchanged, which means that the cash flows emanating from the bond will be invariant to changes in market conditions. However, the discount rate used by investors will vary across time. If market conditions were to cause the discount rate to rise, the consequences of discounting a fixed stream of cash flows at a higher rate would be a lower present value or price.

The logic is as follows. If a buyer of a security is entitled to a fixed income stream from it, the only way that he can extract a greater rate of return from it is by paying a lower price for it at the outset. A bond whose price is lower than its face value is said to trade at a *discount*.

On the other hand, if the discount rate were to decline, the value of the bond will exceed its face value. Such bonds are said to be selling at a *premium*. The rationale is that an investor who is prepared to accept a lower rate of return from a fixed stream of cash flows will bid up its price until the actual rate of return from it is equal to his required rate.

The relationship between the discount rate or the required yield, denoted by y, and the annual coupon rate, denoted by c, is what therefore determines whether a bond will sell at par, below par, or above par. The relationship can be summarized as follows:

$$c = y \Rightarrow P = M \equiv \text{Par bond}$$
$$c < y \Rightarrow P < M \equiv \text{Discount bond}$$
$$c > y \Rightarrow P > M \equiv \text{Premium bond}$$

What about zero coupon bonds? A zero coupon bond is very simple to value because it gives rise to only a single cash flow, which is equal to its face value. Thus:

$$P = \frac{M}{(1 + \frac{y}{2})^N} = M \times \text{PVIF}(\frac{y}{2}, N)$$

for a bond maturing after N semi-annual periods. Hence, a zero coupon bond will always sell at a discount from its face value.

Numerical illustration

IBM has issued bonds with a face value of $1,000 maturing after 10 years. The bond pays a coupon of 8% per annum on a semi-annual basis. The required yield in the market is 10% per annum. What should be the fair price of the bond?

Ten years is equivalent to 20 semi-annual periods. The semi-annual coupon is $\dfrac{0.08}{2} \times 1,000 = 40$.

$$P = 40\ \text{PVIF}(5,20) + 1,000\ \text{PVIF}(5,20)$$
$$= 498.4884 + 376.8895 = \$875.3779$$

What would be the price of a 10-year zero coupon bond with a face value of $1,000 if the required yield is 10% per annum?

$$P = 1,000\ \text{PVIF}(5,20) = \$376.8895$$

Notice that we have discounted the cash flow from the zero coupon bond using 5% for 20 periods and not 10% for 10 periods. This is because, in practice, we often like to compare zero coupon bonds with coupon paying bonds, and such comparisons will be meaningful only if the discounting method is common across securities.

QUESTION 141

What is the meaning of the term "yield to maturity?"

The yield to maturity of a bond is the discount rate that makes the present value of the cash flows from the bond equal to its price. The relationship between the price of a bond and its yield is a *chicken and egg story*. That is, we cannot say which one comes first. If an investor has a required yield in mind while buying a bond, he can quote a corresponding price. If the price at which the bond is offered by a counterparty is equal to or less than what he is prepared to pay, then he will obviously buy the bond. Once he has acquired the bond at a particular price, he can work out the corresponding yield that he will be getting.

The yield to maturity corresponds to the concept of an *internal rate of return (IRR)* that a student studies in Capital Budgeting. If we view the bond as an investment, where the price is equal to the initial outflow, and the coupons and face value repayment represent the subsequent inflows, then the yield to maturity is the discount rate that will lead to a *net present value* of zero, or in other words is the IRR. It contains an implicit assumption which is analogous to the assumption contained in an IRR calculation. Namely, that the holder of the bond will continue to hold it until maturity, and that he will reinvest every intermediate cash flow from the time of its receipt until the maturity of the bond, at the yield to maturity itself.

QUESTION 142

What are "callable bonds?"

A callable bond is a bond that permits the issuer to recall it from the market prior to its term to maturity. In other words, it is a bond with an embedded call option that is provided to the issuer.

When is this option likely to be exercised? In a situation where interest rates are declining, it could make sense for an issuer to call back his existing high cost debt and issue fresh bonds with a lower coupon rate. However, this is precisely the scenario in which a bond holder would be reluctant to part with the debt instrument. Thus, callable bonds not only induce cash flow uncertainty for lenders, they also lead to situations where the lenders are forced to part with the bonds despite the fact that it is not in their interest to do so. Thus, such call provisions work in favor of the borrowers and against the lenders. As a consequence, such bonds tend to trade at higher yields as compared to plain vanilla bonds.

QUESTION 143

How is a bond valued in between coupon dates?

When a bond is sought to be valued in between coupon dates, the next coupon date will obviously be a fraction of a coupon period away. The way to value the bond would therefore be to first price it as of the forthcoming coupon date, and to then discount the value so obtained for the fraction of the current coupon period that is remaining. This can be illustrated with the help of an example.

Illustration

Consider a bond with a face value of $\$M$, that has N coupons remaining in its life, and which pays a coupon of $\$ \dfrac{C}{2}$ every semi-annual period. Assume that we are at a time 0, such that the time till the next coupon is N_1 days, and that the current coupon period consists of N_2 days. The cash flows remaining in the life of the bond can then be depicted as shown in Figure 5.1. -1 denotes the previous coupon date.

Figure 5.1 Cash flows from a bond

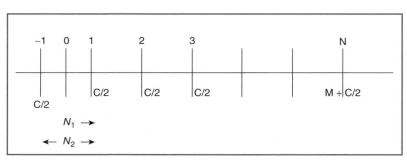

The value of the bond at time 1, which is the next coupon date, would be:

$$\frac{C}{2} + \frac{C}{2} \times \text{PVIFA}(\frac{y}{2}, N-1) + M \times \text{PVIF}(\frac{y}{2}, N-1)$$

Thus, the value of the bond at time t can be expressed as:

$$\frac{1}{(1+\frac{y}{2})^k} \left[\frac{C}{2} + \frac{C}{2} \times \text{PVIFA}(\frac{y}{2}, N-1) + M \times \text{PVIF}(\frac{y}{2}, N-1) \right]$$

where $K = \dfrac{N_1}{N_2}$ is the fraction of the current coupon period that is remaining.

QUESTION 144

What are day-count conventions?

There is no unique way of computing k, or the fraction of the current coupon period that is remaining, when valuing a bond in between coupon payment dates. A day-count convention is a particular method for measuring N_1 and N_2, so as to enable us to compute k. We will discuss three of the more common conventions.

THE ACTUAL-ACTUAL METHOD

This is the convention adopted for valuing Treasury bonds in the U.S. It is also referred to as the *Ack-Ack* method on Wall Street. The best way to illustrate it would be with the help of a numerical example.

Illustration

Assume that a Treasury bond was issued on May 1, 20XX, and that it pays coupons on October 31 and April 30 every year. The scheduled maturity date is April 30, 20(XX + 20), which implies that it is a 20-year bond. We will assume that the face value is $1,000 and that the coupon rate is 12% per annum. Let us also assume that today is August 15, 20XX and that the yield to maturity is 10% per annum.

There are obviously 40 coupons left in the life of the bond. The value of the bond as on the next coupon date, using a YTM of 10%, will be:

$$60 + 60 \times PVIFA(5,39) + 1,000 \times PVIF(5,39)$$

The value of the bond today should therefore be:

$$\frac{1}{(1.05)^k} [60 + 60 \times PVIFA(5, 39) + 1,000 \times PVIF(5, 39)]$$

where $K = \dfrac{N_1}{N_2}$ is as defined earlier.

In the Actual-Actual method, N_1 and N_2 are calculated based on the actual number of days in the corresponding time periods. For the purpose of calculation, the starting date is always excluded, while the ending date is always included. In our case, N_1 and N_2 will be computed as shown in Table 5.16 and 5.17.

Table 5.16 Calculation of N_1

Month	No. of days
August	16
September	30
October	31
N_1	77

Table 5.17 Calculation of N_2

Month	No. of days
May	30
June	30
July	31
August	31
September	30
October	31
N_2	183

So: $k = \dfrac{N_1}{N_2} = \dfrac{77}{183} = 0.4208$

No matter what the starting date and ending dates are, N_2 will always range between 181 and 184.

The value of the bond in this case is therefore:

$$\frac{1}{(1.05)^{0.4208}} [60 + 60 \times PVIFA(5, 39) + 1,000 \times PVIF(5, 39)] = \$ \, 1,205.1714$$

THE 30-360 METHOD

This is the method adopted for corporate bonds in the U.S. While calculating N_1 and N_2 as per this convention, the starting and ending dates are first specified as follows: (yy_1, mm_1, dd_1) and (yy_2, mm_2, dd_2). The corresponding time interval is then calculated as:

$$360(yy_2 - yy_1) + 30(mm_2 - mm_1) + (dd_2 - dd_1)$$

As can be seen, every month is assumed to consist of 30 days, and consequently the year as a whole is assumed to consist of 360 days.

The following additional rules are applicable:

1. If $dd_1 = 31$, then set $dd_1 = 30$.
2. If dd_1 is the last day of February, then set $dd_1 = 30$.
3. If $dd_1 = 30$ or has been set equal to 30, then if $dd_2 = 31$, set $dd_1 = 30$.

Let us go back to our illustration. Assume that the bond has been issued by a U.S. corporation and not by the U.S. Treasury. The starting date is (20XX, 08, 15) and the ending date is (20XX, 10, 31). So:

$$N_1 = 360(20XX - 20XX) + 30(10 - 08) + (31 - 15) = 76$$

N_2 will obviously always be 180. Therefore: $k = \dfrac{76}{180} = 0.4222$.

THE 30-360 EUROPEAN CONVENTION

This is similar to the 30-360 convention, except that the additional rules in this case are slightly different. It is the method that is adopted for government bonds in countries like India.

1. If $dd_1 = 31$, then set $dd_1 = 30$.
2. If $dd_2 = 31$, then set $dd_2 = 30$.

The difference between the 30-360 and 30-360 E methods can easily been seen in the context of our illustration. As per the 30-360 method, $N_1 = 76$. However, as per the 30-360 E method:

$$N_1 = 360(20XX - 20XX) + 30(10 - 08) + (30 - 15) = 75$$

Therefore: $k = \dfrac{75}{180} = 0.4167$.

QUESTION 145

What is the meaning of the term "accrued interest?"

Assume that t_1 and t_2 represent two consecutive coupon payment dates in the life of a bond. Let us denote the sale date of the bond by t^*, such that $t_1 < t^* < t_2$. On t^* the seller will be parting with the right to the entire next coupon, which is due on date t_2, although he would have held the bond for a fraction of the current coupon period. The portion of the next coupon that rightfully belongs to the seller is called the accrued interest and is computed as follows:

$$AI = \frac{C}{2} \times \frac{t^* - t_1}{t_2 - t_1} = \frac{C}{2} \times \frac{N_2 - N_1}{N_2} = \frac{C}{2} \times \left(1 - \frac{N_1}{N_2}\right)$$

where N_1 and N_2 are as defined earlier. The convention that is adopted for calculating the accrued interest for a bond, from the standpoint of computing N_1 and N_2, is identical to the convention that is used to value the bond.

Illustration

In the case of the U.S. Treasury bond which was sold on 15 August 20XX, the accrued interest would be:

$$\frac{120}{2} \times \frac{106}{183} = \$34.7541$$

QUESTION 146

Why do we need to be concerned with accrued interest? Is it the case that the bond valuation equation fails to take the accrued interest into account?

The bond valuation equation values the bond as the present value of all cash flows emanating from it, from the point of sale onwards. This is the technically correct procedure for valuing any financial asset and not just a bond.

The reason why we need to take cognizance of accrued interest is that quoted bond prices are reported net of accrued interest, or are what are called *clean* or *add-interest* prices. Since the convention is to quote prices net of the accrued interest, the buyer obviously needs to compute and factor in the accrued interest in order to determine the total amount payable by him, which is called the *dirty price*.

QUESTION 147

Why is it that bond prices are quoted net of accrued interest?

The rationale behind this market practice may best be illustrated with the help of a numerical example. Consider the 12% Treasury bond maturing on April 30, 20(XX+20). On August 15, 20XX, the price at a YTM of 10% was $1,205.1704. The accrued interest as of this date is:

$$60 \times \frac{106}{183} = 34.7541$$

So the clean price is $1,170.4163.

Assume that eight days hence, the YTM continues to be 10% per annum. The dirty price of the bond will be:

$$\frac{1}{(1.05)^k}[60 + 60 \times \text{PVIFA}(5,39) + 1,000 \times \text{PVIF}(5,39)]$$

$$= \frac{1}{(1.05)^{\frac{69}{183}}}[60 + 60 \times \text{PVIFA}(5,39) + 1,000 \times \text{PVIF}(5,39)]$$

$$= \frac{1}{(1.05)^{0.3770}}[60 + 60 \times \text{PVIFA}(5,39) + 1,000 \times \text{PVIF}(5,39)]$$

$$= 1,207.7496$$

The difference in the dirty prices as computed at the beginning and end of this eight-day interval is:

$$1,207.7496 - 1,205.1704 = \$2.5792$$

The accrued interest on the second date is:

$$60 \times \frac{114}{183} = 37.3770$$

The change in the accrued interest during the period is therefore:

$$37.3770 - 34.7541 = 2.6229$$

Thus, the difference in the dirty prices is almost entirely due to the increase in the accrued interest.

A bond analyst, who is tracking the market, will be concerned about the changes in the required market yield. Consequently, he needs to be able to focus on yield-induced price changes. If the price were to be contaminated with accrued interest, the effects of yield-induced changes cannot be easily deduced. Hence, the market convention is to report prices net of accrued interest. Any observed price changes in the very short run will therefore be entirely yield induced.

QUESTION 148

Is it true that the accrued interest can sometimes be negative? What would this mean?

During a coupon period, in some bond markets there arises a point in time called the *ex-dividend date*, which is a misnomer, considering the fact that bonds do not pay dividends. However, the implications are the same as in the case of equity shares. An investor who sells the bond on or after the ex-dividend date will be entitled to receive the forthcoming coupon. Consequently, on the ex-dividend date, the bond price will decline by the present value of this coupon, since the potential buyer will no longer be entitled to it.

However, consider the situation from the buyer's perspective. Even though he is buying the bond after the ex-dividend date, he is entitled to the accrued interest for the period from the date of purchase until the next coupon date. In this case, however, the accrued interest will have to be paid by the seller since he will be receiving the entire coupon amount. This facet is captured by calculating and subtracting the accrued interest from the clean price in order to arrive at the dirty price. In other words, the deduction of the present value of the forthcoming coupon on the ex-dividend date has the effect of causing the dirty price to go below the clean price. This leads to the accrued interest being negative from the standpoint of the seller.

Illustration

Consider the 12% Treasury bond maturing on 30 April 20(XX+20). Assume that 15 October 20XX is the ex-dividend date. So the price of the bond on that date will be:

$$\frac{1}{(1.05)^k}[60 \times PVIFA(5,39) + 1,000 \times PVIF(5,39)]$$

$$= \frac{1}{(1.05)^{\frac{16}{183}}}[60 \times PVIFA(5,39) + 1,000 \times PVIF(5,39)]$$

$$= \frac{1}{(1.05)^{0.0874}}[60 \times PVIFA(5,39) + 1,000 \times PVIF(5,39)]$$

$$= 1,165.1911$$

An instant before going ex-dividend, the cum-dividend dirty price would have been:

$$= \frac{1}{(1.05)^{0.0874}} [60 + 60 \times \text{PVIFA}(5,39) + 1,000 \times \text{PVIF}(5,39)]$$

$$= 1.224.9358$$

The cum-dividend clean price is:

$$1,224.9358 - 60 \times \frac{167}{183} = 1,170.1817$$

As can be seen, the cum-dividend clean price is greater than the ex-dividend dirty price by an amount of $4.9906. This is the concept of a negative accrued interest. The amount is approximately equal to the accrued interest for the remaining 16 days in the coupon period, which is:

$$\frac{16}{183} \times 60 = \$5.2459$$

QUESTION 149

What is the meaning of the term "duration?" How is the duration of a bond calculated?

It has been observed that long-term bonds are more susceptible to changes in the YTM than shorter term bonds. Let us take the case of two bonds with a face value of $1,000 each. We will assume that both pay a coupon of 10% per annum on a semi-annual basis, and that the YTM is 10% per annum in both cases. However, bond A has a time to maturity of 5 years, while bond B has a time to maturity of 10 years. Both the bonds will obviously sell at par since the coupon rate is equal to the YTM.

Now assume that the YTM increases to 12% per annum. The price of bond A will decline to $926.3991, whereas that of bond B will decline to $885.3009. Thus the price of bond A will decline by 7.36%, whereas that of bond B will decline by 11.47%. Thus, it does indeed appear that long-term bonds are impacted more by interest rate changes.

Why should this be the case? The present value of a cash value is given by:

$$\frac{CF}{(1+r)^t}$$

The larger the value of t, the greater is the impact of a change in the discount rate, r, on the corresponding cash flows. A 10-year bond has a considerable amount of its cash flows coming in at later points in time as compared to a 5-year bond. Hence, it is not really surprising that its price, which is nothing but the sum of the present values of the cash flows emanating from it, is more vulnerable to changes in the interest rate.

However, there is another interesting feature that merits an explanation. Consider a 5-year zero coupon bond with a face value of $1,000. When the YTM is 10%, its price is:

$$\frac{1,000}{(1.05)^{10}} = 613.9133$$

whereas when the YTM is 12%, its price is:

$$\frac{1,000}{(1.06)^{10}} = 558.3948$$

The corresponding decline in price is 9.0434%.

While it is understandable that a long-term bond ought to be more vulnerable to interest rate changes, it does seem surprising that a 5-year zero coupon bond should be more price sensitive than a 5-year bond that pays a coupon of 10%. What could be the reason?

A coupon paying bond is a series of cash flows arising at six-monthly intervals. In other words, it is a portfolio of zero coupon bonds. When we look at its time to maturity we are merely taking cognizance of the last of the cash flows. If the bond itself is a portfolio of zero coupon components, its effective time to maturity ought to be construed as an average of the times to maturity of the component zero coupon bonds.

On the other hand, a 5-year zero coupon bond will give rise to a single cash flow after 5 years. Hence its stated time to maturity is the same as its effective time to maturity. When perceived in this manner, it is not surprising that a zero coupon bond is more price sensitive, for after all it does have a greater effective time to maturity.

The term "duration" refers to a measure of the effective term to maturity of a plain vanilla bond. It is obtained by weighing the term to maturity of each component cash flow by the fraction of the total present value of the bond that is contributed by that particular cash flow. A numerical illustration ought to be useful.

Illustration

Consider the 5-year 10% coupon paying bond with a face value of $1,000. If the YTM is 10% per annum, what should be the duration?

Table 5.18 Computing the duration

Time = t	Cash flow = CF_t	Present value of cash flow $= \dfrac{CF_t}{(1+\frac{y}{2})^t}$	Weight of cash flow $W_t = \dfrac{CF_t}{P_0(1+\frac{y}{2})^t}$	Weighted time $w_t \times t$
1	50	47.6190	0.04762	0.04762
2	50	45.3515	0.04535	0.09070
3	50	43.1919	0.04319	0.12957
4	50	41.1351	0.04114	0.16456
5	50	39.1763	0.03918	0.19590
6	50	37.3108	0.03731	0.22386
7	50	35.5341	0.03553	0.24871
8	50	33.8420	0.03384	0.27072
9	50	32.2304	0.03223	0.29007
10	1,050	644.6089	0.64461	6.4461
	Total	1,000	1.00	8.1078

The weighted average of the times to maturity of each of the component cash flows is 8.1078 semi-annual periods or 4.0539 years. On the other hand, the 5-year zero coupon bond has a single cash flow and hence its weighted average time to maturity is the same as its stated time to maturity of 5 years. Consequently, it is not surprising that the 5-year zero coupon bond is more price sensitive than the 5-year coupon paying bond.

QUESTION 150

What is the relationship between the duration of a bond and its price sensitivity?

The relationship between the duration of a bond and the rate of change of its percentage change in price with respect to a yield change may be expressed as:

$$\frac{\frac{dp}{P}}{dy} = -\frac{D}{(1+\frac{y}{2})}$$

where D is the duration of the bond expressed in annual terms.

$$\frac{D}{(1+\frac{y}{2})}$$

is called the modified duration of the bond, D_m. Thus the rate of change of the percentage change in price of a bond with respect to the yield is equal to its modified duration. Thus, it is the duration of a bond, and not its stated time to maturity, which accurately captures the relationship between a change in the yield and its corresponding impact on the price of the bond.

 QUESTION 151

Unlike in the case of bonds, T-bill prices are quoted in terms of yields. What do these yields signify and how do we deduce the corresponding prices for the bills?

T-bills are zero coupon instruments and are always quoted at a discount from their face values. The quoted yield on a T-bill is an indicator of the applicable discount from the face value, based on the prevailing market conditions. Consequently, it is known as a *yield on a discount basis*. The conversion of a quoted yield into the corresponding price for a T-bill may best be illustrated with the help of an example.

Numerical illustration

Consider a T-bill with a face value of $1,000,000 and 108 days to maturity. Let the quoted yield be 8%.

The corresponding price can be computed as follows.

The discount from the face value for 108 days is:

$$1,000,000 \times 0.08 \times \frac{108}{360} = \$24,000$$

The applicable price is therefore:

$$1,000,000 - 24,000 = \$976,000$$

 QUESTION 152

Is it true that an investor who buys a T-bill at a particular yield will always get a rate of return that is greater than the quoted yield if he were to hold the bill until maturity?

Yes, this inference is correct. The quoted yield is an annualized percentage of the face value. For instance, if the applicable dollar discount is 24,000 as in the above case, the quoted yield "d" is given by:

$$\frac{24,000}{1,000,000} \times \frac{360}{108} = 0.08$$

However, when we calculate the rate of return it is always measured as an annualized percentage of the investment which is made. In this case, the rate of return will be:

$$\frac{24,000}{976,000} \times \frac{360}{108} = 0.0820$$

Since the investment in the case of a zero coupon instrument such as a T-bill will always be less than its face value, the corresponding rate of return for an investor who buys and holds the bill until maturity will always be greater than the quoted yield.

QUESTION 153

What is the difference between an "on-the-run" security and an "off-the-run" security? Is it true that on-the-run bills are always more liquid than off-the-run bills?

Let us take the case of 13-week T-bills that are issued once a week by the U.S. Treasury. The most recently issued 13-week bills will be referred to as on-the-run bills. However, there may be another security, such as a T-note issued earlier, that also has 13 weeks to maturity. Such securities would be referred to as off-the-run instruments.

Off-the-run securities tend to be less liquid than on-the-run securities for the following reason. For some time after they are issued, Treasury securities tend to be actively traded. However, subsequently most instruments pass into the hands of investors who choose to hold them until the date of maturity. Consequently, off-the-run instruments tend to be less liquid in practice than on-the-run instruments.

QUESTION 154

What is a Eurodollar?

A eurocurrency deposit is a freely traded currency deposited in a bank outside its country of origin. Eurodollar deposits are therefore U.S. dollar-denominated deposits placed with banks outside the United States. Similarly, Euroyen are Japanese yen deposited with banks outside Japan. The term 'Euro' is therefore used to refer to the fact that such deposits are maintained outside the country to which the currency belongs. It so happened that in the earlier years, banks that were accepting such deposits were primarily located in Europe. Today a Eurodollar deposit can be opened in virtually any part of the globe. There are active eurocurrency markets in Singapore, Hong Kong and Tokyo, which are referred to as the Asian Dollar markets.

QUESTION 155

One of the reasons that has been advanced to explain the rapid growth of such markets is that such deposits are not subject to reserve requirements. What are reserves and what implications do they have for commercial banks?

In most countries banks are required by law to hold a certain percentage of deposits raised by them in the form of an account with the central bank of the country and/or approved government securities.

From the standpoint of a bank, the larger the reserve requirement the smaller is the amount available for commercial lending. This has direct implications for the profitability of a bank since reserves yield less than market rates of return. Consequently, the higher the reserve ratio the lower will be the rate of interest paid by the bank to its depositors and the higher will be the rate charged by it to its borrowers.

Numerical illustration

Assume that banks are required by law to maintain 10% reserves yielding nil returns and that a bank raises $100 by way of deposits at a rate of interest of 9% per annum. Thus, the bank is effectively raising $90 by way of loanable funds on which it is paying an amount of $9 by way of interest. Thus, the effective rate of interest for the bank is 10% per annum and not 9%.

QUESTION 156

The absence of regulatory reserves obviously enabled Eurobanks to raise funds at attractive rates of interest and offer loans at competitive rates. What were the other factors that lead to the rapid growth of the eurocurrency market?

By the end of World War II, the U.S. dollar was the primary vehicle currency for international trade, displacing the British pound, which had held centre stage until then. Consequently most countries sought to accumulate dollar balances to finance their global trading activities. The satellites of the U.S.S.R., or the Warsaw Pact countries, also required access to dollar-denominated funds. However, since the Cold War was on, these countries were reluctant to hold balances with banks based in the U.S. They were more comfortable keeping such balances with banks in Europe. As trade grew, European banks soon discovered that there was a ready demand for such funds by parties located outside the U.S. Thus, the eurocurrency market got a huge impetus.

There were two other factors that led to a boom in eurobanking. The U.S. government imposed high reserve requirements on deposits placed with U.S. banks and imposed a ceiling on interest rates payable on such deposits by enacting a legislation termed as Regulation Q. Thus banks in the U.S. were unable to offer attractive rates to depositors and were at the same time constrained to charge high rates from their borrowers. The net result was a shift in business to the euromarket.

In 1973 there was an Arab–Israeli war. Soon afterwards, the Arab nations began to realize the full worth of their oil reserves as a means of influencing global policies. The net result was that crude oil prices became highly volatile and most oil nations were flush with dollar balances from oil sales, the so-called Petrodollars. Eurobanks were able to offer relatively higher rates on dollar deposits and were at the same time in a position to make loans at competitive rates. This ability to efficiently recycle these Petrodollars gave a major impetus to the growth of the eurocurrency market.

QUESTION 157

What are Federal Funds?

U.S. banks are required by law to maintain reserves with one of the district member banks of the Federal Reserve system. The reserve requirement is based on a bank's average deposits over a two-week period. At any point in time a bank will either have a surplus with the Federal Reserve or else it will have a deficit. Banks do not like to maintain surplus reserves since they do not earn interest. Banks with surpluses can lend these to those with deficits. These funds which are transferred from one account in the Federal Reserve system to another are referred to as Federal Funds, or Fed Funds in short. The Fed Funds rate is a key benchmark from the standpoint of the short-term interest rate structure in the U.S.

QUESTION 158

What do we mean by a foreign exchange rate?

Every asset, whether physical or financial, has a value in terms of the unit of currency of a country. A foreign country's currency is no exception. It too has a value in terms of the currency of the home country. The value of one unit of the foreign currency in terms of units of the home currency is called the foreign exchange rate or simply the exchange rate.

QUESTION 159

What is the difference between "direct quotes" and "indirect quotes?"

Let us take the case of equity shares of a company. We can express the value of the shares as a number of dollars per share or equivalently as the number of shares per dollar. Quite obviously, the second convention does not contribute anything meaningful by way of expositional clarity and is therefore seldom if ever used.

However, when we have two currencies that are involved, we can meaningfully quote the exchange rate as the number of units of the domestic currency per unit of the foreign currency, or equivalently as the number of units of the foreign currency per unit of the domestic currency.

In the indirect system of quotation, the exchange rate is expressed as the number of units of the foreign currency per unit of the domestic currency. For instance, a quote of USD 2.25/INR 100 would constitute an indirect quote in India.

On the contrary, as per the direct system of quotation the exchange rate is expressed as the number of units of the domestic currency per unit of the foreign currency. For instance, a quote of INR 44/USD would represent a direct quote in India.

QUESTION 160

What are European terms and American terms, with reference to exchange rates?

When an exchange rate is quoted as a number of units of a currency per US dollar it is referred to as a quote in European terms. For instance, a quote of GBP 0.55/USD would be a quote as per the European convention. However, a quote that expresses the value of a currency in terms of the number of US dollars is said to be a quote in American terms. For instance, a quote of USD 1.85/GBP would be a quote as per the American convention.

Test your concepts

The answers are provided on page 241.

1. A T-bill with 90 days to maturity is quoting at a yield of 7.5%. If an investor buys and holds this bill to maturity, he will:
   (a) Earn a return of 7.5%
   (b) Earn a return of less than 7.5%
   (c) Earn a return of more than 7.5%
   (d) Earn a return that depends on the reinvestment rate.

2. A bank is quoting an interest rate of 6% per annum on a three-month deposit. The reserve ratio is 10%. Reserves earn interest at the rate of 2% per annum. The insurance premium on deposits is 10 basis points. Consider a deposit of $100. The effective cost of the deposit for the bank is:
   (a) 6.10%
   (b) 6.77%
   (c) 6.54%
   (d) 6.00%.

Use this information for the next two questions.

A bond with a face value of $1,000 and 10 years to maturity, paying coupons at the rate of 6% per annum on a semi-annual basis, on April 15 and October 15 every year, has been issued on April 15, 2003. Assume that today is March 8, 2004.

3. Assuming that the bond has been issued by the U.S. Treasury, the accrued interest as of today is:
   (a) $23.442
   (b) $23.607
   (c) $23.769
   (d) $23.832.

4. Assuming that the bond has been issued by General Motors, the accrued interest as of today is:
   (a) $23.442
   (b) $23.607
   (c) $23.769
   (d) $23.832.

5. Consider a bond with a face value of $1,000. Assume that it has 10 years left to maturity and that every year it pays a coupon of $100. If the price of the bond is $1,000, then:
   (a) The YTM is > 10%
   (b) The YTM is < 10%
   (c) The YTM is = 10%
   (d) Unable to specify.

6. A zero coupon bond will:
   (a) Always sell at par
   (b) Always sell at a premium
   (c) Always sell at a discount
   (d) May sell at a premium or a discount.

7. If the reserve requirement that is imposed on bank deposits were to be increased:
   (a) The interest rate on deposits will go up
   (b) The interest rate on deposits will go down
   (c) The rate charged on loans will go up
   (d) Both (b) and (c).

8. Assume that an exchange is following a T+5 settlement cycle. The ex-dividend date for a stock will be:
   (a) Five days before its record date
   (b) Four days before its record date
   (c) Five days after its record date
   (d) Four days after its record date.

9. Which of these corporate actions leads to the capitalization of reserves:
   (a) Stock splits
   (b) Reverse splits
   (c) Stock dividends
   (d) Cash dividends.

10. A company has 100,000 shares outstanding and announces a 2:5 rights issue. The current stock price is $100 and the proposed issue price is $75. The value of the right to acquire a share is:
    (a) $25.0000
    (b) $92.8571
    (c) $17.8571
    (d) $7.1429

CHAPTER 6

PRODUCTS AND EXCHANGES

 QUESTION 161

Which are the major derivatives exchanges in the world?

Some of the leading derivatives exchanges in the world are the following. Their contact details are given in Appendix A.

Asia and Oceania

- Australian Securities Exchange
- Central Japan Commodity Exchange
- Dalian Commodity Exchange
- Hong Kong Exchange
- Korea Exchange
- National Stock Exchange of India
- Singapore Exchange
- Bombay Stock Exchange Limited, Mumbai
- The Tokyo Commodity Exchange
- Taiwan Futures Exchange
- Tokyo Financial Exchange

Europe and U.K.

- EUREX
- Euronext.liffe
- The London Metal Exchange
- OMX The Nordic Exchange

Africa and The Middle East

- South African Futures Exchange
- The Tel Aviv Stock Exchange

North America

- American Stock Exchange
- Chicago Board Options Exchange
- Chicago Board of Trade
- Chicago Mercantile Exchange
- International Securities Exchange
- Mercado Mexicano de Derivados (Mexican Derivatives Exchange)
- New York Mercantile Exchange
- Philadelphia Stock Exchange

South America

- Bolsa de Mercadorias & Futuros (BM & F) – Brazilian Mercantile and Futures Exchange
- BOVESPA

QUESTION 162

How active are the major international derivatives exchanges in terms of trading volumes?

In terms of volumes during the year 2006, the top 20 derivatives exchanges in the world were as shown in Table 6.1.

Table 6.1   Top 20 derivatives exchanges worldwide

Exchange	Volume
Korea Exchange	2,474,593,261
EUREX	1,526,751,902
Chicago Mercantile Exchange	1,403,264,034
Chicago Board of Trade	805,884,413
Euronext.Liffe	730,303,126
Chicago Board Options Exchange	674,735,348
International Securities Exchange	591,961,518

(continued)

Table 6.1 (continued)

Exchange	Volume
BOVESPA	287,518,574
Bolsa de Mercadorias & Futuros	283,570,241
New York Mercantile Exchange	276,152,326
Mexican Derivatives Exchange	275,217,670
Philadelphia Exchange	273,093,003
American Stock Exchange	197,045,745
NYSE Arca (Pacific Exchange)	196,586,356
National Stock Exchange of India	194,488,403
OMX Group	123,167,736
Dalian Commodity Exchange	117,681,038
Taiwan Futures Exchange	114,603,379
JSE Securities Exchange South Africa	105,047,524
Boston Options Exchange	94,390,602

Source: FIA Annual Volume Survey: Volume Growth Accelerates by Galen Burghardt *Futures Industry Magazine*, March-April, 2007 Reproduced with permission

QUESTION 163

Which are the major exchange-traded derivatives contracts in the world, in terms of trading volumes?

In terms of volumes as measured in millions of contracts traded during the year 2006, the top 20 derivatives contracts in the world were as shown in Table 6.2.

Table 6.2 Top 20 derivatives contracts worldwide

Contract	Exchange	Sector	Volume
KOSPI 200 Options	Korea Exchange	Equity	2,414.42
Eurodollar Futures	CME	Interest	502.08
Euro-BUND Futures	EUREX	Interest	319.89
Eurodollar Options	CME	Interest	268.96
TIIE 28 Futures	Mexican Derivatives Exchange	Interest	264.16
E-mini S&P 500 Futures	CME	Equity	257.93
10-year T-Note Futures	CBOT	Interest	255.57
DJ Euro STOXX 50 Futures	EUREX	Equity	213.51
Euribor Futures	Euronext	Interest	202.09
Euro-Bobl Futures	EUREX	Interest	167.31
Euro-Schatz Futures	EUREX	Interest	165.32
1-Day Interbank Deposit Futures	BM&F	Interest	161.65
DJ Euro STOXX 50 Options	EUREX	Equity	150.05
5-year T-Note Futures	CBOT	Interest	124.87

(continued)

Table 6.2   (continued)

Contract	Exchange	Sector	Volume
S&P 500 Index Options	CBOE	Equity	104.31
Taiex Options	Taiwan Futures Exchange	Equity	96.93
30-year T-bond Futures	CBOT	Interest	93.75
Sterling Futures	Euronext	Interest	83.00
E-mini NASDAQ 100 Futures	CME	Equity	79.94
TA-25 Index Options	Tel Aviv	Equity	75.49

Source: FIA Annual Volume Survey: Volume Growth Accelerates by Galen Burghardt *Futures Industry Magazine*, March-April, 2007 Reproduced with permission

QUESTION 164

Is Chicago the nerve center of the global futures market?

Traditionally, Chicago has been the most important location for derivatives trading. Three of the leading exchanges are located in the city. These are:

1. Chicago Board Options Exchange.
2. Chicago Board of Trade.
3. Chicago Mercantile Exchange.

Of late, however, the dominance of the Chicago-based exchanges has eroded to an extent. New, state-of-the-art electronic trading exchanges such as Eurex, based in Frankfurt, have made substantial inroads into the global derivatives market. These exchanges, along with the exchanges in emerging markets, have acquired substantial market share in recent years. However the importance of Chicago-based exchanges can be gauged from the fact that eight out of the 20 most actively traded derivatives contracts in the world are traded in Chicago.

QUESTION 165

What are the specifications of the foreign exchange futures contracts that are traded on the Chicago Mercantile Exchange (CME)?

The CME trades futures contracts on the following currencies (Table 6.3). The contract details are as shown in Table 6.4. The basic unit of a price is a point. The point description denotes the U.S. dollar equivalent

Table 6.3 FOREX futures on the CME: the underlying currencies

Australian Dollar	Brazilian Real
British Pound	Canadian Dollar
Chinese Renminbi	Czech Koruna
Euro	Hungarian Forint
Israeli Shekel	Japanese Yen
Korean Won	Mexican Peso
New Zealand Dollar	Norwegian Krone
Polish Zloty	Russian Ruble
South African Rand	Swedish Krona
Swiss Franc	

Table 6.4 FOREX futures contract details

Currency	Contract size	Symbol	Point description	Tick size
Australian Dollar	100,000	AUD	$0.0001	$10.00
Brazilian Real	100,000	BRL	$0.0001	$5.00
British Pound	62,500	GBP	$0.0001	$6.25
Canadian Dollar	100,000	CAD	$0.0001	$10.00
Chinese Renminbi	1,000,000	CNY	$0.00001	$10.00
Czech Koruna	4,000,000	CZK	$0.000001	$8.00
Euro	125,000	EUR	$0.0001	$12.50
Hungarian Forint	30,000,000	HUF	$0.0000001	$6.00
Israeli Shekel	1,000,000	ILS	$0.0001	$10
Japanese Yen	12,500,000	JPY	$0.000001	$12.50
Korean Won	125,000,000	KRW	$0.0000001	$12.50
Mexican Peso	500,000	MXN	$0.00001	$12.50
New Zealand Dollar	100,000	NZD	$0.0001	$10.00
Norwegian Krone	2,000,000	NOK	$0.00001	$20
Polish Zloty	500,000	PLN	$0.00001	$10.00
Russian Ruble	2,500,000	RUB	$0.00001	$25
South African Rand	500,000	ZAR	$0.00001	$12.50
Swedish Krona	2,000,000	SEK	$0.00001	$20
Swiss Franc	125,000	CHF	$0.0001	$12.50

of one point, whereas the tick size connotes the minimum observable fluctuation in the value of a contract.

At any point in time six contract months are listed from the March quarterly cycle for all currencies except the Brazilian Real, the Chinese Renminbi, the Korean Won, the Mexican Peso, the Russian Ruble, and the South African Rand. For instance, assuming that today is December 26, 2006, which is the fourth Tuesday of December, the following contracts will be available:

March-07; June-07; September-07, December-07, March-08, and June-08.

Contracts expire on the second business day prior to the third Wednesday of the month. In this case the December-06 contract would have expired on 18 December.

For the Brazilian Real the 12 nearest calendar months are available at any point in time. For the Chinese Renminbi, the Korean Won, the Mexican Peso and the South African Rand, the 13 nearest calendar months, plus the next two months from the March cycle, are listed at any point in time. For the Russian Ruble the four nearest months from the March cycle are listed at any point in time.

Thus on January 2, 2007, the availability of contract months for these currencies would be as follows:

Brazilian Real – January 2007 to December 2007
Chinese Renminbi – January 2007 – January 2008, March 2008, June 2008
Korean Won – January 2007 – January 2008, March 2008, June 2008
Mexican Peso – January 2007 to January 2008, March 2008, June 2008
South African Rand – January 2007 to January 2008, March 2008, June 2008
Russian Ruble – March 2007, June 2007, September 2007, and December 2007

The Brazilian Real, the Chinese Renminbi, the Korean Won, and Russian Ruble futures contracts are cash settled. All other contracts are settled by physical delivery.

QUESTION 166

What are E-Mini foreign exchange futures contracts?

The CME offers contracts on certain assets with a smaller contract size. These contracts, called E-Mini contracts, are currently available for the Euro and the Japanese Yen, in the case of foreign currency futures. The contract size is 62,500 Euros for the futures contract on the Euro and 6,250,000 yen for the contract on the Japanese Yen. The tick size is $6.25 for both contracts. Contracts are available for the two nearest months from the March cycle. For instance, on December 26, 2006, we would find the March-07 and June-07 contracts being traded. All contracts are settled by physical delivery.

QUESTION 167

What are cross-rate futures contracts? What are the specifications for such contracts on the CME?

The FOREX futures contracts that we discussed involved the exchange rates of foreign currencies with respect to the U.S. dollar. The CME also trades futures contracts based on the exchange rates of two foreign or non-American currencies with respect to each other. These are known as cross-rate futures contracts. The contract specifications are as shown in Table 6.5.

Table 6.5 Cross-rate contract details

Cross rate	Contract size	Point description	Tick size
Australian Dollar/ Canadian Dollar	200,000 AUD	0.0001 CAD/AUD	20.00 CAD
Australian Dollar/ Japanese Yen	200,000 AUD	0.01 JPY/AUD	2,000 JPY
Australian Dollar/ New Zealand Dollar	200,000 AUD	0.0001 NZD/AUD	20.00 NZD
British Pound/ Japanese Yen	125,000 GBP	0.01 JPY/GBP	1,250.00 JPY
British Pound/ Swiss Franc	125,000 GBP	0.0001 CHF/GBP	12.50 CHF
Canadian Dollar/ Japanese Yen	200,000 CAD	0.01 JPY/CAD	2,000 JPY
Chinese Renminbi/ Euro	1,000,000 CNY	0.00001 EUR/CNY	10.00 EUR
Chinese Renminbi/ Japanese Yen	1,000,000 CNY	0.001 JPY/CNY	1,000 JPY
Euro/ Australian Dollar	125,000 EUR	0.0001 AUD/EUR	12.50 AUD
Euro/ British Pound	125,000 EUR	0.0001 GBP/EUR	6.25 GBP
Euro/ Canadian Dollar	125,000 EUR	0.0001 CAD/EUR	12.50 CAD
Euro/ Czech Koruna	4,000,000 CZK	0.000001 EUR/CZK	8.00 EUR
Euro/ Hungarian Forint	30,000,000 HUF	0.0000001 EUR/HUF	6.00 EUR
Euro/ Japanese Yen	125,000 EUR	0.01 JPY/EUR	1,250.00 JPY

(continued)

Table 6.5 (continued)

Cross rate	Contract size	Point description	Tick size
Euro/ Norwegian Krone	125,000 EUR	0.001 NOK/EUR	62.50 NOK
Euro/ Polish Zloty	500,000 PLN	0.00001 EUR/PLN	10.00 EUR
Euro/ Swedish Krona	125,000 EUR	0.001 SEK/EUR	62.50 SEK
Euro/ Swiss Franc	125,000 EUR	0.0001 CHF/EUR	12.50 CHF
Swiss Franc/ Japanese Yen	250,000 CHF	0.01 JPY/CHF	1,250.00 JPY

All contracts, with the exception of the Chinese Renminbi contracts, are settled by physical delivery. At any point in time, six contract months are listed from the March quarterly cycle.

The Chinese Renminbi contracts are cash settled. At any point in time, the 13 nearest calendar months plus the next two months from the March cycle are listed.

QUESTION 168

What are the specifications of the major stock index futures contracts that are traded on the CME?

The CME trades futures contracts on a number of indices. Details of some of the prominent contracts are summarized in Table 6.6.

The relationship between *point description*, *currency equivalent*, and *tick size* can be illustrated as follows.

Take the case of the E-Mini S&P 500 futures contract. One point is equivalent to 0.01 units in terms of the index. Since each index unit is worth $50, each point is worth $0.50. The minimum observable change in the futures price is 25 points or $12.50 per contract.

In the case of the Nikkei 225 Yen denominated contract, each point is one index unit, which is worth 500 JPY. The minimum observable price change is 5 points or 2,500 JPY.

The expiration dates differ from contract to contract. The E-Mini S&P and the E-Mini NASDAQ 100 contracts normally expire on the third Friday of the contract month. The Nikkei 225 contracts, both dollar

Table 6.6 Specifications of futures contracts on major indices

Contract	Index	Multiple	Point description	Currency equivalent	Tick size
E-Mini S&P 500	S&P 500	$50	0.01 Index units	$0.50	$12.50
E-Mini NASDAQ 100	NASDAQ-100	$20	0.01 Index units	$0.20	$5.00
S&P 500	S&P 500	$250	0.01 Index units	$2.50	$25.00
NASDAQ 100	NASDAQ 100	$100	0.01 Index units	$1.00	$25.00
Nikkei 225	Nikkei 225	500 JPY	1 Index unit	500 JPY	2,500 JPY
Nikkei 225	Nikkei 225	$5	1 Index unit	$5.00	$25.00

Table 6.7 Available expiration months in general

Contract	Available months
E-Mini S&P 500	2 months from the March quarterly cycle
E-Mini NASDAQ 100	2 months from the March quarterly cycle
S&P 500	8 months from the March quarterly cycle
NASDAQ 100	3 months from the March quarterly cycle
Nikkei 225 (Yen)	5 months from the March quarterly cycle and 3 serial months
Nikkei 225 (Dollar)	4 months from the March quarterly cycle

Table 6.8 Available expiration months on 26 December 2006

Contract	Available months
E-Mini S&P 500	March-07 and June-07
E-Mini NASDAQ 100	March-07 and June-07
S&P 500	March-07; June-07, Sep-07; Dec-07; March-08; June-08; Sep-08; and Dec-08
NASDAQ 100	March-07; June-07; Sep-07
Nikkei 225 (Yen)	March-07; June-07; Sep-07; Dec-07; March-08; and Jan-07; Feb-07; and April-07
Nikkei 225 (Dollar)	March-07; June-07; Sep-07; and Dec-07

denominated as well as yen denominated, expire on the business day preceding the second Friday of the contract month. The S&P 500 and the NASDAQ 100 contracts expire on the business day prior to the third Friday of the expiration month. All the contracts are cash settled.

The number of contracts that will be available at any point in time is as described in Table 6.7.

Assume that today is December 26, 2006, which is the fourth Tuesday of December. The December contracts would have all expired. The expiration months shown in Table 6.8 will be available for the various products.

QUESTION 169

What are the specifications of the major interest rate futures contracts that are traded on the CME?

Some of the major interest rate futures contracts offered by the CME are the following:

- Eurodollar Futures
- LIBOR Futures
- Euroyen Futures
- 13-Week U.S. T-bill Futures.

Eurodollar futures

The underlying asset is a time deposit with a principal amount of $1 MM and three months to maturity. The futures price is quoted as an index number which is equivalent to an implicit interest rate. For instance, a quoted price of 92 would imply an interest rate of:

$$100.00 - 92.00 = 8.00\%$$

The contract value corresponding to a futures price of F may be calculated as:

$$1,000,000 - 1,000,000 \times \frac{(100.00 - F)}{100.00} \times \frac{90}{360}$$

Thus the contract value corresponding to a quoted price of 92 is:

$$1,000,000 - 1,000,000 \times \frac{(100.00 - 92.00)}{100.00} \times \frac{90}{360}$$
$$= 1,000,000 - 20,000 = 980,000$$

The contracts expire at 11:00 a.m. London Time, on the second London bank business day before the third Wednesday of the contract month. At any point in time, 40 contract months from the March quarterly cycle, as well as the four nearest serial months, will be listed.

So on December 26, 2006, the available contract months will be:

March, June, September, and December of 2007–2016, and January 2007, February 2007, April 2007, and May 2007. All contracts are cash settled.

LIBOR futures

The underlying asset is a time deposit with a principal amount of $3 MM and one month to maturity. The quoted futures price is in terms of an index number which is equivalent to an implicit interest rate. The contract value corresponding to a quoted futures price of 94 is:

$$3,000,000 - 3,000,000 \times \frac{(100.00 - 94.00)}{100.00} \times \frac{30}{360}$$
$$= 3,000,000 - 15,000 = 2,985,000$$

The contracts expire at 11:00 a.m. London Time, on the second London bank business day before the third Wednesday of the contract month. At any point in time, contracts for the next 12 consecutive months will be listed. So on December 26, 2006, the available contract months will be January to December 2007. The contracts are cash settled.

Euroyen futures

The underlying asset is a time deposit with a principal amount of 100 MM JPY, and three months to maturity. The quoted futures price is in terms of an index number which is equivalent to an implicit interest rate. The contract value corresponding to a quoted futures price of 94 is:

$$100,000,000 - 100,000,000 \times \frac{(100.00 - 94.00)}{100.00} \times \frac{90}{360}$$
$$= 100,000,000 - 1,500,000 = 98,500,000$$

The contracts expire at the close of the trading session immediately preceding the last trading day for the 3-month Euroyen futures contract on the Singapore Exchange. The last trading day on the Singapore Exchange is the second business day immediately preceding the last Wednesday of the contract month. At any point in time, 20 contracts will be listed from the March quarterly cycle. Thus on December 26, 2006, the available months will be March, June, September, and December of 2007–2011. The contracts are cash settled.

91-Day T-bill futures

The underlying asset is a 13-week (91-day) T-bill with a face value of $1 MM. The quoted futures price is in terms of an index number which is equivalent to an implicit discount yield. The contract value corresponding to a quoted futures price of 96 is:

$$1,000,000 - 1,000,000 \times \frac{(100.00 - 96.00)}{100.00} \times \frac{90}{360}$$
$$= 1,000,000 - 10,000 = 990,000$$

The contracts expire at 12:00 p.m. Chicago time on the business day of the weekly 91-day T-bill auction in the week of the third Wednesday of the contract month. At any point in time, four months from the March cycle plus two serial months will be listed. Thus on 26 December 2006, the available months will be January 2007, February 2007, March 2007, June 2007, September 2007, and December 2007. The contracts are cash settled.

QUESTION 170

What are the specifications of the stock index futures contracts that are traded on the CBOT?

The CBOT offers futures contracts on the Dow Jones Industrial Average. The contract size is 10 times the value of the index. Contracts expire on the third Friday of the contract month, and are cash settled. Prices are quoted in terms of index points, where each point is equivalent to $10. At any point in time, the four nearest months from the March quarterly cycle are listed for trading, plus two additional December months. That is, on January 2, 2007, the following months would be listed:

March-07, June-07, Sep-07, Dec-07, Dec-08, and Dec-09

There is also a mini-sized Dow futures contract. The contract size in this case is $5 times the index level. Contracts expire on the third Friday of the contract month, and are cash settled. Prices are quoted in terms of index points, where each point is equivalent to $5. At any point in time, the four nearest months from the March quarterly cycle are listed for trading.

The CBOT has now introduced a big Dow futures contract. The contract size is $25 times the index level. Contracts expire on the third Friday of the contract month, and are cash settled. Prices are quoted in terms of index points, where each point is equivalent to $25. At any point in time, the four nearest months from the March quarterly cycle are listed for trading.

QUESTION 171

What are the salient features of the long-term interest rate futures contracts that are traded on the Chicago Board of Trade?

The CBOT trades futures contracts on the following products:

- 2-year T-notes
- 5-year T-notes
- 10-year T-notes
- 30-year T-bonds.

Let us examine the details of each of these contracts.

2-year T-note futures

The underlying asset is a T-note with a face value of $200,000. Multiple grades are allowable for delivery. The deliverable grades must have an original maturity of not more than 5 years and 3 months, and an actual maturity of not less than 1 year and 9 months from the first day of the delivery month, and not more than 2 years from the last day of the delivery month. The actual futures price is subject to a multiplicative adjustment factor called the *conversion factor*. Prices are quoted in terms of points and one quarter of $\frac{1}{32}$ of a point.

A point is $1 for a face value of $100. Thus a quote of 91-165 denotes a price of $91 + \frac{16.5}{32}$ for a bond with a face value of 100. Thus the corresponding price for a note with a face value of $200,000 will be:

$$200,000 \times \frac{91.515625}{100} = \$183,031.25$$

The available contract months are March, June, September and December.

5-year T-note futures

The underlying asset is a T-note with a face value of $100,000. Multiple grades are allowable for delivery. The deliverable grades must have an original maturity of not more than 5 years and 3 months, and an actual maturity of not less than 4 years and 2 months from the first day of the delivery month. The actual futures price is subject to a conversion factor. Prices are quoted in terms of points and one half of $\frac{1}{32}$ of a point. Thus a quote of 90-165 denotes a price of:

$$100,000 \times \frac{90.515625}{100} = \$90,515.625$$

for a note with a face value of $100,000. The available contract months are March, June, September and December.

10-year T-note futures

The underlying asset is a T-note with a face value of $100,000. Multiple grades are allowable for delivery. The deliverable grades must have an actual maturity of not less than 6 years and 6 months from the first day of the delivery month, and not more than 10 years from that date. The actual futures price is subject to a conversion factor. Prices are quoted in terms of points and one half of $\frac{1}{32}$ of a point. The available contract months are March, June, September and December.

30-year T-bond futures

The underlying asset is a T-bond with a face value of $100,000. Multiple grades are allowable for delivery. The deliverable grades must, if they are callable in nature, not be callable for at least 15 years from the first day of the delivery month, and if they are not callable in nature, must have a maturity of at least 15 years from the first day of the delivery month. The actual futures price is subject to a conversion factor. Prices are quoted in terms of points and $\frac{1}{32}$ of a point. The available contract months are March, June, September and December.

All the above contracts are subject to delivery settlement.

QUESTION 172

What are mini-sized T-bond and T-note futures?

There are two mini-sized interest rate contracts available on T-notes and T-bonds at the CBOT. The first is a 10-year T-note futures contract where the underlying asset is a T-note with a face value of $50,000. Multiple grades are allowable for delivery. The deliverable grades must have an actual maturity of not less than 6 years and 6 months from the first day of the delivery month, and not more than 10 years from that date. The actual futures price is subject to a conversion factor. Prices are quoted in terms of points and one half of $\frac{1}{32}$ of a point. The available contract months are March, June, September and December.

The second mini-sized contract is on 30-year T-bonds. The underlying asset is a bond with a face value of $50,000. Multiple grades are allowable for delivery. The deliverable grades must, if they are callable in nature, not be callable for at least 15 years from the first day of the delivery month, and if they are not callable in nature, must have a maturity of at least 15 years from the first day of the delivery month. The actual futures price is subject to a conversion factor. Prices are quoted in terms of points and one half of $\frac{1}{32}$ of a point. The available contract months are March, June, September and December.

Both the mini contracts are delivery settled.

QUESTION 173

What are the specifications of the FED Funds futures contracts on the CBOT?

The underlying asset is Federal Funds with a value of $5 million dollars. Prices are quoted as 100.00 minus the Fed Funds overnight rate. At any point in time contracts for the next 24 calendar months will be available. The last trading day is the last business day of the delivery month. Contracts are cash settled.

QUESTION 174

Why are short-term interest rate futures prices quoted in terms of an index and not directly in terms of interest rates?

The futures prices for short-term interest rate contracts are expressed as an index. That is, the quoted price is expressed as 100 minus an implicit rate of interest.

There are two reasons for this. Firstly, a short position in interest rate futures would indicate a desire to borrow whereas a long position would embody a desire to lend. Thus the bid corresponds to the borrowing rate whereas the ask corresponds to the lending rate. Hence a futures price quote in terms of interest rates would lead to the bid being higher than the ask. However, an index expressed as 100 minus the interest rate would ensure that the price for a short position is lower than the price for a long position.

Secondly, from the perspective of a short, a rise in the interest rate should lead to a profit if he were to offset his futures position. On the contrary, from the point of view of a long, a fall in interest rates should lead to a profit at the time of offsetting. This can be demonstrated as follows.

Take the case of a person who is going short in a eurodollar futures contract at a rate of 8% per annum. Thus he is prepared to pay an interest of:

$$1,000,000 \times 0.08 \times \frac{90}{360} = \$20,000$$

on a principal amount of $1,000,000.

Assume that the rate a month later is 10%. If he were to offset by going long, he would be effectively agreeing to lend at an interest of:

$$1,000,000 \times 0.10 \times \frac{90}{360} = \$25,000$$

In the process he would make a profit of $5,000.

Thus rising interest rates will lead to profits for the short whereas declining rates would lead to profits for the long. If we were to express the futures price in terms of the rate of interest, shorts would benefit from rising futures prices, whereas longs would stand to gain from declining futures prices. In all the other markets we have seen that declining futures prices lead to profits for the shorts, whereas rising futures prices signify profits for the longs. In order to be consistent with this treatment of profits and losses, the futures prices for short-term interest rate products are expressed as an index. If the index rises, the longs will gain, wheres if it falls, the shorts will gain.

QUESTION 175

Why are bond prices quoted as per $100 of face value?

Bond prices are always quoted per $100 of face value. The rationale is the following. Consider two bonds, one with a face value of $1,000 and the other with a face value of $2,000. If the prices of the two bonds are equal and are quoted as, say, $1,400, the implications would be very different for the two bonds. A quote of $1,400 would imply that the $1,000 face value bond is trading at a significant premium, whereas the implication would be that the $2,000 face value bond is trading at a considerable discount.

However, if prices were to be quoted as per $100 of face value, a price exceeding $100.00 would signify a premium bond, whereas a price of less than $100.00 would connote a discount bond. In the U.S. prices are quoted in terms of 32nds of a dollar. Thus a price of $94-08 would imply a price of:

$$94 + \frac{8}{32} = \$94.25$$

per $100 of face value. A price of $94–08+ would signify a price of:

$$94 + \frac{8}{32} + \frac{1}{64} = \$94.265625$$

per $100 of face value.

QUESTION 176

What is the conversion factor, and how is it computed for T-note and T-bond contracts?

As per the specifications for T-note and T-bond futures contracts, a wide variety of bonds with different coupons and maturity dates will be eligible for delivery. The choice as to which bond to deliver will be made by the short and obviously the price received by him will depend on the bond that he chooses to deliver.

Now logically, if the short delivers a more valuable bond he should receive more than what he would were he to deliver a less valuable bond. To facilitate comparisons between bonds, the exchange specifies a conversion factor for each bond that is eligible for delivery. The conversion factor is nothing but a multiplicative adjustment factor, considering the fact that multiple bonds are eligible for delivery.

The conversion factor for a given bond is the value of the bond per $1 of face value, as calculated on the first day of the delivery month, using an annual YTM of 6% with semi-annual compounding.[1] For the

---

1. It was 8% until March, 2000.

purpose of calculation, the life of the bond is rounded off down to the nearest multiple of three months. If, after rounding off, the life of the bond is an integer multiple of semi-annual periods, then the first coupon is assumed to be paid after six months. If, however, after rounding off, the life of the bond is not equal to an integer multiple of semi-annual periods, then the first coupon is assumed to be paid after three months and the accrued interest is subtracted.[2]

The invoice price for the T-bond contract, which is the price received by the short, is calculated as follows:

$$\text{Invoice price} = \text{Invoice principal amount} + \text{Accrued interest}$$
$$= CF_i \times F \times 100{,}000 + AI_i$$

where CF_i is the conversion factor of bond i,[3] F is the quoted futures price per dollar of face value[4] and AI_i is the accrued interest.

We will now illustrate as to how to calculate the conversion factor using suitable examples.

Example I

Let us assume that we are short in a June futures contract and that today is June 1, 2001. Consider a 7% T-bond that matures on July 15, 2029.

On June 1, this bond has 28 years and $1\frac{1}{2}$ months to maturity. When we round off down to the nearest multiple of three months, we get a figure of 28 years.

The first coupon is assumed to be paid after six months. The conversion factor may therefore be calculated as follows:

$$CF = \frac{\frac{7}{2}\text{PVIFA}(3,56) + 100\text{PVIF}(3,56)}{100}$$
$$= \frac{94.3791 + 19.1036}{100}$$
$$= 1.1348$$

---

2. These principles will become clear when you go through the examples given below.
3. Do not confuse it with the symbol for cash flows used in the discussion on duration. The potential for confusion is unfortunate but unavoidable.
4. T-bond futures prices are quoted in the same way as the cash market prices; that is, they are clean prices.

Example II

Instead of the July 2029 bond, consider another bond that is maturing on September 15, 2029. On June 1, 2001, this bond has 28 years and $3\frac{1}{2}$ months to maturity. The life of the bond when we round off down to the nearest multiple of three months is 28 years and 3 months.

In this case, we assume that the first coupon is paid after three months. The CF can be calculated in three steps as shown below.

1. First find the price of the bond three months from today, using a yield of 6% per annum.

$$P = \frac{7}{2} + \frac{7}{2}PVIFA(3,56) + 100PVIF(3,56)$$
$$= 3.5 + 94.3791 + 19.1036$$
$$= \$116.9827$$

2. Discount the price gotten above for another three months.

$$\frac{116.9827}{(1.03)^{\frac{1}{2}}} = \$115.2665$$

3. Subtract the accrued interest for three months, from the price obtained in the second step.

$$AI = \frac{7}{2} \times \frac{1}{2} = 1.75$$
$$CF = \frac{115.2665 - 1.75}{100} = 1.1352$$

Illustration of an invoice price calculation for a T-bond

Let us assume that on June 15, 2001 we announce our intention to deliver the 7% bond maturing on September 15, 2029, under the June futures contract. The actual delivery will take place two business days later; that is, on June 17. How do we calculate the invoice price?

The first step is to calculate the accrued interest.

The last coupon would have been paid on March 15, 2001 and the next will be due on September 15, 2001. Between the two coupon dates there are 184 days. Between the last coupon date and the delivery date, there are 94 days. The accrued interest for a T-bond with a face value of $100,000 is:

$$AI = \frac{0.07}{2} \times \frac{94}{184} \times 100,000 = \$1,788.0435$$

The futures settlement price on June 15[5] is assumed to be 95-12. This corresponds to a decimal futures price per dollar of face value of:

$$\frac{95 + \frac{12}{32}}{100} = 0.95375$$

The conversion factor has already been calculated to be 1.1352.

$$\text{Invoice price} = 0.95375 \times 1.1352 \times 100,000 + 1,788.0435$$
$$= \$110,057.7435$$

QUESTION 177

Why do we need to adopt two different procedures for computing the conversion factor?

The conversion factor is used to multiply the quoted futures price, which is a clean price. Hence, the factor should not be contaminated with accrued interest. In Example I, the bond has a life that is an integer multiple of semi-annual periods after rounding off. Hence, there is no question of accrued interest. However, in Example II, accrued interest for three months is present in the value we get in the second step. Therefore, we have to subtract this interest in order to arrive at the conversion factor.

---

5. Notice that the settlement price is based on the day the intention to deliver is declared, whereas accrued interest is calculated as of the delivery day. This is because once the intention to deliver is declared, marking to market will cease and hence the futures price payable by the long is the settlement price as of that day. However, since the long receives the bond only on the delivery day, accrued interest must be computed until that day.

QUESTION 178

What is the significance of the lot size in the context of stock index futures?

Index futures prices are always quoted in index points. To calculate the value of a futures contract in terms of the domestic currency, the futures price has to be multiplied by the lot size specified by the exchange.

The multiple for contracts on the S&P 500 is 250. So in the context of the S&P 500 futures contracts, the profit for an investor who takes a long position at a futures price of 1175 and then offsets his contract at 1200 would be calculated as:

$$\pi = 250 \times (1{,}200 - 1{,}175) = \$6{,}250$$

The multiple for futures contracts on the NASDAQ 100 index is 100, while that for contracts on the Nikkei 225 is $5. Contracts with a smaller lot size called E-Mini contracts are available on both the S&P 500 as well as the NASDAQ 100. The multiple is $50 in the case of contracts on the S&P 500, while in the case of the NASDAQ 100 it is $20.

The CBOT offers futures contracts on the Dow Jones Industrial Average. The multiple is $10 for regular contracts, and $5 for mini sized contracts.

QUESTION 179

What are futures options? Why do they lead to cash inflows for the option holder, in the event of exercise?

A futures option is an option that is written on a futures contract. Since a futures contract by itself is a derivative security, a futures option is a derivative of a derivative.

These options work as follows. Take the case of a call option that has been written on a futures contract on euros. Each futures contract is for 125,000 euros, and the option has an exercise price of $1.15. Assume that the last settlement price for the futures contract was $1.20.

If the call were to be exercised, a long position in a futures contract would be set up for the option holder. The futures position would obviously be set up at the prevailing futures price. However, the exercise of the option entitles the long to have a futures position established at the exercise price of the option. In practice, this is achieved by paying the option holder the difference between the previous settlement price of the futures contract and the exercise price of the option, which constitutes an inflow due to marking to market. Thus the option holder will receive a cash inflow equal to this difference. In this case the cash flow would be:

$$125,000 \times (1.20 - 1.15) = \$6,250$$

He may choose to keep an open position in the futures contract or else close out his position at the prevailing futures price.

At the same time, a short futures position would be established for the seller of the option. He will, in this case, have a cash outflow of $6,250. He too could either keep an open position in the futures contract, or else offset it at the prevailing futures price.

In the case of a put option on a futures contract, a short position in a futures contract would be set up for the option holder, were he to choose to exercise. In accordance with the logic used earlier, he would in addition receive a cash inflow equal to the difference between the exercise price and the previous settlement price.

For instance, assume that the investor had a put option on euros with an exercise price of $1.25. Assume that the last settlement price was $1.15. Upon exercise of the option, the investor would receive a cash inflow of:

$$125,000 \times (1.25 - 1.15) = \$12,500$$

When the put option is exercised a long position in the futures contract would be set up for the option writer. He will incur a cash outflow of $12,500. Both the option holder as well as the writer are free to keep their futures positions open, or else close them out.

QUESTION 180

Why would an investor prefer an option on a futures contract to an option on an underlying asset?

Options on futures contracts tend to be very popular in those cases where the delivery of the underlying asset is cumbersome. An example would be the case of options on agricultural commodities or livestock. In such cases, many investors may prefer an option on a futures contract, since the underlying asset is a derivative and not a physical asset. The advantage of taking delivery of a futures contract is that the investor need not deliver or take delivery of the underlying asset at all. For, he can simply offset the futures position after it has been established.

Futures contracts and futures options tend to trade in adjacent pits on open-outcry exchanges. This proximity is cited as a cause for greater market efficiency.

CHAPTER 7

TRADING STRATEGIES

QUESTION 181

What are the different types of trading strategies that can be implemented using futures contracts?

Futures contracts may be used with one of the following objectives in mind:

- hedging
- speculating
- arbitrage
- quasi-arbitrage

We have examined hedging, speculating, and arbitrage in adequate detail earlier. We will now illustrate a quasi-arbitrage strategy in detail.

The fundamental relationship of equivalency between a spot and a futures position is that:

$$Spot - Futures = Synthetic\ T\text{-}bill$$

That is, a long position in the spot asset, and a short position in a futures contract, is equivalent to an artificial or synthetic risk-less investment. Thus if we have two of the three assets in their natural form, a synthetic version of the third asset can be created. The creation of the synthetic version of an asset by using the above relationship is termed as quasi-arbitrage.

Example

Rachel Kahn, a high net worth investor based in Cincinatti, is planning to invest in a risk-less asset for six months. One option is to directly invest in T-bills. The ask price for a six-month T-bill with a face value of $100,000, is $96,000. The brokerage fee for a $100 investment in T-bills is 10 cents. So for each T-bill that she buys, Rachel has to pay a commission of $96. Thus the strategy of investing in T-bills will yield a return of:

$$\frac{100,000 - (96,000 + 96)}{(96,000 + 96)} \equiv 4.0626\%$$

Now let us consider another option that Rachel can explore. Assume that IBM shares are available at a price of $100.25 per share. Futures contracts on IBM stock with six months to expiration are available for $105. The brokerage fees payable in the market are as follows. For every share that is bought or sold in the spot market, a 15 cents commission is payable. And while transacting in the futures market, a fee of 5 cents is payable per share.

In Rachel's case, instead of investing in T-bills, she can go long in the spot market and take a short position in the futures market, thereby creating an investment in a synthetic T-bill. Her transaction costs are 15 cents for every share that she buys and 5 cents for every futures contract that she goes short in. Consequently, her rate of return is:

$$\frac{105 - (100.25 + 0.20)}{(100.25 + 0.20)} \equiv 4.5296\%$$

Thus, her rate of return if she follows this strategy will be higher than what she would get if she were to invest in T-bills. Hence, a person like Rachel who is looking for a risk-free investment would rather engage in a cash and carry strategy to buy synthetic T-bills. This is why it is called quasi-arbitrage.

QUESTION 182

How does one implement a hedging strategy using stock index futures contracts?

It can be shown that the number of futures contracts required to set up a minimum variance hedge for a stock portfolio is given by:

$$h = \beta_P \frac{P_t}{I_t}$$

where β_P is the beta of the portfolio whose value is sought to be hedged, P_t is the current value of the portfolio, and I_t is the current value of the index in dollars.

Take the case of a portfolio manager who is handling a portfolio which is currently worth 10 MM dollars and is worried that the market is going to fall. If he decides to hedge, he needs to hedge in such a way that he will make a profit on the futures contract if the market were to fall. So, obviously, he needs to go short in index futures.

Assume that the current value of the index is 250 and that each index point is worth $250. The value of the index in dollar terms is therefore:

$$250 \times 250 = \$62,500$$

As per the no-arbitrage condition, the futures price is given by:

$$F_t = I_t \left[1 + r \times \frac{(T-t)}{360} \right] - D_T$$

where I_t is the current index level, $(T-t)$ is the time till expiration of the futures contract, and D_T is the future value of the dividends paid by the component stocks between t and T, as calculated at T. D_T is measured in terms of index units.

Consider a futures contract with 72 days to expiration, which we will assume coincides with the hedging horizon of the manager. If the future value of dividends in index units is assumed to be 10, and the risk-less rate of interest is taken as 10%, then the current no-arbitrage futures price is given by:

$$250 \left[1 + 0.10 \times \frac{72}{360} \right] - 10 = 245$$

We will assume that the beta of the portfolio relative to the index is 1.25. The number of futures contracts required for a risk-minimizing hedge is therefore:

$$1.25 \times \frac{10,000,000}{62,500} = 200 \text{ contracts}$$

We will examine the performance of the hedge in two different terminal scenarios.

The index rises in value

Let the index value at expiration be 260. The value of our portfolio can be calculated as follows:

$$\text{The return on the index} = \frac{260 - 250}{250} \equiv 4\%.$$

$$\text{The dividend yield} = \frac{10 \times 250}{250 \times 250} \equiv 4\%.$$

Thus, the total return on the market $= 4\% + 4\% = 8\%$.

$$\text{The risk-less rate for 72 days} = \frac{0.10 \times 72}{360} \equiv 2\%.$$

Therefore, the rate of return on our portfolio is:

$$2 + 1.25(8 - 2) = 9.5\%$$

Our portfolio is hence worth $10(1 + 0.095)$ MM $= \$10.95$ MM.
The profit/loss from the futures market is:

$$(245 - 260) \times 250 \times 200 = \$(750,000)$$

Thus, the net value of our holdings is $10.95 - 0.75 = \$10.2$ MM.

As we can see, our hedged portfolio has earned a 2% rate of return. How can we explain this? The futures contract has helped remove all the inherent market risk. Therefore, it is obvious that our portfolio will earn the risk-less rate of return, which is 2% for 72 days.

The index declines in value

Let the index value at expiration be 220: If so, then:

$$\text{The return on the index} = \frac{220 - 250}{250} \equiv -12\%.$$

$$\text{The dividend yield} = \frac{10 \times 250}{250 \times 250} \equiv 4\%.$$

The total return on the market $= -12\% + 4\% = -8\%$.

$$\text{The risk-less rate for 72 days} = \frac{0.10 \times 72}{360} \equiv 2\%.$$

Therefore, the rate of return on our portfolio is:

$$2 + 1.25(-8 - 2) = -10.5\%$$

Our portfolio is hence worth $10(1 - 0.105)$ MM = \$8.95 MM.

The profit/loss from the futures market is:

$$(245 - 220) \times 250 \times 200 = \$1,250,000$$

Thus, the net value of our holdings = $8.95 + 1.25 = \$10.2$ MM.

Once again, the rate of return on the hedged portfolio is 2%.

In practice, however, our hedge may not perform perfectly. Firstly, dividends and interest rates may change over the life of the hedge. Secondly, the return on the index over 72 days may not be perfectly correlated with the return on our portfolio.

QUESTION 183

How does one use index futures to change the beta of a portfolio?

It can be shown that the number of futures contracts required to change the beta of a portfolio from β^* to β_T is given by:

$$N = (\beta_T - \beta^*)\frac{P_t}{I_t}$$

where P_t is the value of the portfolio, and I_t is the value of the index in dollars.

If we want to increase the beta, N will be greater than zero, and we should go long in the required number of futures contracts, whereas if we want to decrease the beta, we should go short.

Example

An investor is holding a portfolio that is worth \$300,000,000. The current beta is 0.85. The investor is bullish about the market and wants to increase the beta to 1.20. The S&P 500 index is currently at 800 and the index multiplier is 250.

The number of futures contracts required is given by:

$$N = (1.20 - 0.85)\frac{300,000,000}{800 \times 250} = 525$$

Quite obviously the investor needs to go long.

QUESTION 184

What is "program trading?"

Program trading is nothing but cash and carry and reverse cash and carry arbitrage using stock index futures. If the futures contract is overpriced the arbitrageur will go short in futures contracts and buy the stocks underlying the index, in the same proportions as they are contained in the index. On the contrary, if the contract were to be underpriced, the arbitrageur would short sell the stocks contained in the index, and go long in futures contracts.

Since index arbitrage requires the taking of a long or a short position in all the stocks constituting the index on a simultaneous basis, a computer-based system is obviously required to initiate this kind of arbitrage. It is because of the use of computer programs to facilitate such arbitrage activities that index arbitrage has come to be referred to as program trading.

QUESTION 185

How is program trading implemented in practice?

We will illustrate our arguments using a numerical example.

Consider a hypothetical price weighted index based on five stocks, the prices of which are as shown in Table 7.1.

If we assume that the divisor is equal to 5, the index value is 66.00.

Assume that today is July 1, 20XX and that there is a futures contract based on the above index, that expires on September 21, 20XX; that is, 82 days later. We will also assume that 3M will pay a dividend of $10

Table 7.1 Prices of the constituents of the stock index

Stock	Price
3M	90
American Express	60
Coca Cola	45
IBM	90
Merck	45
Total	330

on July 21, that IBM will pay a dividend of $15 on August 10 and that American Express will pay a dividend of $10 on September 1. The borrowing/lending rate for all investors will be taken to be 10% per annum.

Let us first compute the future value of the dividends. On July 21 a dividend of $10 will be received. This can be reinvested till September 21 to yield:

$$10 \times \left(1 + 0.10 \times \frac{62}{360}\right) = 10.1722$$

Similarly, the future values of the other two dividends, as of 21 September, are 15.175 and 10.0556.

To preclude arbitrage opportunities, the futures price, in dollar terms, should be a value F such that:

$$F + 15.175 + 10.1722 + 10.0556 = 66.00 \times 5 \times \left[1 + 0.10 \times \frac{82}{360}\right] = 337.5166$$

$$\Rightarrow F = \$302.1138$$

However, the convention is to express the futures price in terms of index units and not in dollar terms. Thus the futures price should be:

$$\frac{302.1138}{5} = 60.4228$$

If F were not equal to this value, there will be arbitrage opportunities.

Cash and carry index arbitrage

Let us assume that F = 62.

Consider the following strategy. Borrow $330 to buy the five stocks which constitute the index and go short in one futures contract. When the dividends are received periodically, reinvest them till the expiration of the futures contract at the lending rate. At expiration, the futures price will be set equal to the spot index value at that point in time, since *index futures contracts are always cash settled*. Therefore, at the time of expiration, the shares should be sold at the prevailing market prices.

Table 7.2 Stock prices at expiration

Stock	Price
3M	95
American Express	65
Coca Cola	50
IBM	95
Merck	45
Total	350

Assume that the spot prices of the shares at the time of expiration are as shown in Table 7.2.

The corresponding index value is 70.

The profit/loss from the futures market is $62 - 70 = (8)$ index units, which is equivalent to $8 \times 5 = \$(40)$.

The cash inflow when the stocks are sold is \$350. The payoffs from the reinvested dividends is:

$$10.1722 + 15.175 + 10.0556 = \$35.4028$$

The net cash flow at expiration is therefore:

$$350 + 35.4028 - 337.5166 - 40 = \$7.8862$$

\$7.8862 is equivalent to $\dfrac{7.8862}{5} = 1.5772$ index units, which is the difference between the quoted futures price of 62 and the no-arbitrage price of 60.4228. It is important to note that the profit will always be equal to the difference between the quoted price and the no-arbitrage price and will be independent of the actual stock prices prevailing at expiration. This is because we have made the assumption that the arbitrageur will be able to sell the shares in the market at the same prices as those used to compute the index value at expiration.

Reverse cash and carry index arbitrage

Consider the same information as in the above example, but assume that the futures price is 59.50.

A potential arbitrageur will now do the following. He will short sell all the five stocks which constitute the index and invest the proceeds at the lending rate of 10%. Simultaneously, he will go long in a futures contract. When the dividends are due, he will borrow the requisite amounts and pay the person(s) who have lent him the shares. At expiration, he will acquire the shares at the prevailing spot prices and return them. He will also be required to repay the amounts borrowed for the dividend payments with interest and will be entitled to the profit/loss from the futures market. The amount that he had originally lent out after selling the shares short will now be returned to him with interest.

Therefore, the net cash flow at expiration will be:

$$-350 - 35.4028 + 337.5166 + 5(70 - 59.50) = \$4.6138$$

which is equivalent to 0.9228 index units, which is the difference between the futures price of 59.50 and the no-arbitrage price of 60.4228. Once again, the profit will be independent of the stock prices prevailing at expiration.

QUESTION 186

What is stock picking?

Stock picking refers to the art of finding stocks that are underpriced or overpriced. Consider the following representation of the rate of return on stock i.

$$r_i = r + \beta_i (r_m - r) + \varepsilon_i + \alpha_i$$

ε_i is the unsystematic error, that is, the return due to unsystematic risk, which is expected to have a value of zero. The term $\beta_i(r_m - r)$ is the excess return due to market risk. α_i is what we call an *abnormal return*, which is due to mispricing of the stock. If the stock is correctly priced, then α_i will be zero. If $\alpha_i > 0$, then it implies that the stock is underpriced, whereas if $\alpha_i < 0$, it implies that the stock is overpriced.

A stock picker is a person who believes that a stock is underpriced or overpriced and seeks to take advantage of it. However, if he takes a position in the stock without hedging against movements in the market as a whole, there is a risk that even if he were to realize the abnormal return that he expects, the general market movement may be such that he would make an overall loss. Index derivatives allow the stock picker to capture the "alpha" while diversifying away the "beta." This can best be illustrated with the help of an example.

Example

A stock picker believes that Coca Cola is underpriced and that he will get a positive abnormal return if he buys it. Assume that the risk-less rate is 2% and that the beta of Coca Cola is 1.5.

Let us assume that his hunch turns out to be correct and that α_i does turn out to be 0.5%. However, it so happens that $r_m = -5\%$, that is, the market goes down. If we assume that $\varepsilon_i = 0$ then:

$$r_i = 2 + 1.5(-5 - 2) + 0.5 = -8\%$$

Thus although he *backed the right horse*, he has ended up with a negative rate of return. This situation could have been avoided, had he hedged using stock index futures.

Let us assume that he invests $1,000,000 in the stock and goes short in S&P index futures when the index level is 250 and the futures price is at 245. The dividend yield is 4%. The appropriate number of futures contracts is given by:

$$h = \beta_P \times \frac{P_t}{I_t}$$

$$= 1.5 \times \frac{1,000,000}{250 \times 250} = 24$$

If the dividend yield is taken to be 4%, a return of −5% on the market corresponds to a decline of 9% in the index level. Thus the corresponding index value is 227.50.

The rate of return on the stock in such a scenario is −8%, which means that the terminal stock value is $1,000,000(1 − 0.08) = \$920,000$.

The profit/loss from the futures position is:

$$24 \times 250(245 - 227.5) = \$105,000$$

The value of the stock plus the futures profit/loss is:

$$920,000 + 105,000 = \$1,025,000$$

The overall rate of return is therefore 2.5%. This value of 2.5% corresponds to the risk-less rate of 2%, plus the abnormal return of 0.5%. In technical terms, we say that index derivatives allow the stock picker to capture the "alpha," while diversifying away the "beta."

Thus, if you believe that the stock is underpriced but want to hedge yourself against market risk, you should buy the stock and go short in stock index futures. Similarly, if you believe that the stock is overpriced, short sell the stock and go long in stock index futures.

QUESTION 187

What is "portfolio insurance?"

We have seen earlier that an investor can move from an actual spot position to a synthetic T-bill position by going short in futures contracts. The end result is the creation of a risk-free investment, which gives the risk-less rate of return.

In practice, a portfolio manager may convert a fraction of his risky portfolio into equivalent synthetic T-bills using futures contracts and continue to hold the balance in the form of the risky portfolio. Now, in principle, the value of this risky component can at worst go to zero. The risk-less equivalent will continue to earn the risk-free rate of return. Hence, such a strategy puts a floor on the value of the overall portfolio. The portfolio may end up earning more, but cannot earn less.

Such a risk-management strategy is called *portfolio insurance.* In practice, fund managers will constantly watch the market and sell and buy futures contracts in order to move from equities to synthetic debt and vice versa. At any point in time, the greater the level of insurance required, the more will be the number of futures contracts which have to be sold. The technique of constantly switching from one asset position to another is called *dynamic hedging.*

QUESTION 188

Does trading in stock index futures lead to enhanced volatility in the stock market?

Trading in stock index futures has attracted its share of criticism. Many policy makers have suggested that trading in index futures increases the volatility of the market as a whole. More specifically, it has been argued that program trading and portfolio insurance make markets more volatile.

Program trading entails the initiation of cash and carry and reverse cash and carry strategies by arbitrageurs. Let us take the case of cash and carry arbitrage. An arbitrageur who engages in this strategy will go long in the index and short in the futures. On the expiration date of the contract, he will issue a market on close order as explained earlier, in order to offload his shares. Offloading of large volumes of shares is likely to have an impact on the market only if there is a large supply demand imbalance. A priori, we have no reason to presume that such an event will occur, because in the course of trading over the life of the futures contract there would have been traders entering into cash and carry strategies, as well as those entering into reverse cash and carry positions. Consequently there is little reason to presuppose that program trading will increase stock market volatility.

What about portfolio insurance? If stock markets fall, portfolio managers will seek to insure a larger fraction of their portfolio. This will entail taking short positions in futures contracts. Such widespread selling can depress futures prices, thereby inducing a further drop in stock prices, since the two are inextricably linked, thereby exacerbating the problem.

The evidence as to whether trading in index futures has coincided with an increase in market volatility is not very compelling.[1] But even assuming that index futures are responsible for enhanced volatility, the question remains as to whether volatility per se is bad? As Kolb argues, volatility is a manifestation of the arrival of fresh information into the market. As new information is received, buyers and sellers will reassess their perceptions of the values of different assets and the observed prices will then adjust to reflect these changes. This process of adjustment gives rise to volatility. In free market economics, accurate prices are considered to be imperative for the correct allocation of resources. From that standpoint, volatility can be construed as evidence of a market that is informationally efficient. Thus volatility, per se, need not be undesirable. Of course, it must be mentioned that volatility arising due to factors unrelated to the arrival of pertinent information is not always desirable.

QUESTION 189

How can a client lock in a borrowing rate in U.S. dollars using Eurodollar futures?

Let us assume that today is July 1, 20XX. General Electric requires 1 million dollars on September 19 for a period of 90 days, for which it will pay the LIBOR that prevails on that day. The company is worried

---

1. See Kolb (2000).

that rates may rise before September 19, which is the last day of trading for the September futures contract. The current September futures price is 91 and the current 90-day LIBOR is 8.85%.

The first question that we should ask ourselves is as to whether the company should go in for a long hedge or a short hedge. If the rates rise, the hedge should lead to a profit in the futures market. That is, if the index falls, the company should gain. So obviously GE requires a short hedge.

Hence the maxim is that borrowers require short hedges, while lenders require long hedges.

Assume that GE goes short in one September futures contract. Let us consider two different scenarios on September 19.

Case A: LIBOR = 8%

The interest payable on the loan of 1 MM is:

$$0.08 \times 1,000,000 \times \frac{90}{360}$$
$$= \$20,000$$

Gain/loss from the futures market is:

$$1,000,000 \times \frac{(F_0 - F_1)}{100} \times \frac{90}{360}$$
$$= 1,000,000 \times \frac{(91 - 92)}{100} \times \frac{90}{360}$$
$$= (2,500)$$

Therefore, the effective interest paid is:

$$20,000 + 2,500 = \$22,500$$

Case B: LIBOR = 10%

The interest payable is:

$$0.10 \times 1,000,000 \times \frac{90}{360}$$
$$= \$25,000$$

Profit/loss from the futures position is:

$$1,000,000 \times \frac{(91 - 90)}{100} \times \frac{90}{360}$$
$$= \$2,500$$

Thus, the effective interest paid is:

$$25,000 - 2,500 = \$22,500$$

Hence, irrespective of what happens on 19 September, the company will end up paying $22,500 as interest. This amount corresponds to a rate of:

$$\frac{22,500}{1,000,000} \times \frac{360}{90} \equiv 9\%$$

which is the rate implicit in the initial futures price of 91.

Thus hedging with ED futures allows you to lock in the rate implicit in the current futures price.[2]

Notice another feature. Since the ED futures contract is cash settled, the profit/loss from the futures position is paid/received on 19 September, whereas the interest on the loan of 1 MM is payable only 90 days hence. Thus if this profit were to be reinvested or the loss were to be financed, the effective interest paid on the loan would be higher than 9% in case A and lower than 9% in case B. While studying ED futures contracts, we will ignore such interest on profits/losses.

QUESTION 190

How can a client lock in a lending rate in U.S. dollars using Eurodollar futures?

Once again assume that today is July 1, 20XX. YES Bank plans to lend 1 million dollars on September 19 for a period of 90 days, for which it will receive the LIBOR that prevails on that day. The bank is worried that rates may fall before September 19, which is the last day of

---

2. Note, it does not ensure that you are able to lock in the LIBOR prevailing at the inception of the hedge, which in this case happens to be 8.85%.

trading for the September futures contract. The current September futures price is 91.50 and the current 90-day LIBOR is 8.85%.

Since the bank is lending it obviously requires a long hedge. Assume that it goes long in one September futures contract. Let us consider two different scenarios on September 19.

Case A: LIBOR = 8%

The interest receivable on the loan of 1 MM is:

$$0.08 \times 1,000,000 \times \frac{90}{360}$$
$$= \$20,000$$

Gain/loss from the futures market is:

$$1,000,000 \times \frac{(F_1 - F_0)}{100} \times \frac{90}{360}$$
$$= 1,000,000 \times \frac{(92 - 91.50)}{100} \times \frac{90}{360}$$
$$= \$1,250$$

Therefore, the effective interest received is:

$$20,000 + 1,250 = \$21,250$$

Case B: LIBOR = 10%

The interest receivable is:

$$0.10 \times 1,000,000 \times \frac{90}{360}$$
$$= \$25,000$$

Profit/loss from the futures position is:

$$1,000,000 \times \frac{(90 - 91.50)}{100} \times \frac{90}{360}$$
$$= \$(3,750)$$

Thus, the effective interest received is:

$$25,000 - 3,750 = \$21,250$$

Hence, irrespective of what happens on 19 September, the bank will end up receiving $21,250 as interest. This amount corresponds to a rate of:

$$\frac{21,250}{1,000,000} \times \frac{360}{90} \equiv 8.5\%$$

which is the rate implicit in the initial futures price of 91.50.

QUESTION 191

How does one hedge the rate on a loan which is not for an exact period of 90 days, with the help of Eurodollar futures?

We can use ED futures to lock in rates for an N day loan, where N is fairly close to 90. This can be done if the interest rate for the N day loan moves closely with the interest rate for a 90-day loan. The appropriate hedge ratio can be derived as follows.

Let us assume that, $d_N = \alpha + d_{90} + e$, where d_N is the annualized rate for an N day loan and d_{90} is the annualized rate for a 90-day loan. If we assume that $e = 0$, then:

$$\Delta d_N = \Delta d_{90}$$

Consider an N day loan for Q million dollars. The change in the interest received/paid due to an interest rate change is:

$$Q \times 1,000,000 \times \frac{\Delta d_N}{100} \times \frac{N}{360}$$

The profit/loss per futures contract used for hedging is:

$$1,000,000 \times \frac{\Delta d_{90}}{100} \times \frac{90}{360}$$

We need to choose the number of futures contracts, Qf, in such a way that:

$$Q \times 1,000,000 \times \frac{\Delta d_N}{100} \times \frac{N}{360} = Q_f \times 1,000,000 \times \frac{\Delta d_{90}}{100} \times \frac{90}{360}$$

By assumption, $\Delta d_N = \Delta d_{90}$.
Therefore:

$$Q \times N = Q_f \times 90$$
$$\Rightarrow \frac{Q_f}{Q} = \text{the hedge ratio} = \frac{N}{90}$$

We will illustrate as to how this hedge will work, with the help of the following example.

Example

Assume that we are standing on July 1, 20XX and that we will have 10 MM to lend from September 19 to January 5; that is, for a period of 108 days. The September futures contract expires on September 19 and the current price is 91.75. The rate that we will receive when the loan is made is assumed to be the LIBOR prevailing at that point in time, plus 100 b.p.[1]

Since we need to hedge a lending rate, we need to go long in ED futures.

$$Q_f = 10 \times \frac{108}{90} = 12$$

Let us see how this hedge will perform in practice.

Case A: LIBOR = 8%

The actual interest received is:

$$0.09 \times 10,000,000 \times \frac{108}{360} = \$270,000$$

Profit/loss from the futures position is:

$$12 \times 1,000,000 \times \frac{(92 - 91.75)}{100} \times \frac{90}{360}$$
$$= \$7,500$$

The effective interest received = $277,500.

---

[1] 1 b.p.stands for basis point where one basis point is one hundredth of one percent.

Case B: LIBOR = 8.5%

The actual interest received is:

$$0.095 \times 10,000,000 \times \frac{108}{360} = \$285,000$$

Profit/loss from the futures position is:

$$12 \times 1,000,000 \times \frac{(91.5 - 91.75)}{100} \times \frac{90}{360}$$
$$= \$(7,500)$$

The effective interest received = \$277,500.

Thus, irrespective of what happens on September 19, we are assured of an interest amount of \$277,500. This corresponds to an interest i such that:

$$10,000,000 \left[1 + i \times \frac{108}{360}\right] = 10,277,500$$

i is therefore equal to 9.25%, which corresponds to the rate of 8.25% implicit in the initial futures price, plus the 100 b.p. premium that the lender is getting over LIBOR.

QUESTION 192

Is it true that a series of futures contracts can be used by a bank to convert a floating rate source of funds to a fixed-rate loan to be offered to a borrower?

It is indeed possible to use a series of Eurodollar futures contracts to offer a fixed-rate loan to a client, in a situation where the lender is borrowing at a floating rate of interest. We will illustrate the concept with the help of an example.

Silverline Technologies Limited, a software company based in Mauritius, wants a loan for 100 million U.S. dollars for a period of one year from June 15, 20XX. Let us assume that it approaches Barclays Bank for a fixed-rate loan.

Barclays Bank is in a position to raise money at LIBOR + 100 b.p., for periods of three months at a time. The question is, how should it quote a fixed rate of interest to Silverline?

We will assume that the 90-day LIBOR on June 15 is 6.8% and that September, December and March contracts are available at 93.1, 92.8 and 92.6 respectively. For ease of exposition, we will assume that the dates on which Barclays Bank will roll over its three-month borrowings, namely September 15, December 15 and March 15, are the same as the dates on which the futures contracts for those months expire.

Consider a strategy of going short in 100 September, December and March futures contracts.

For the first quarter, the interest expense for the bank is:

$$100,000,000 \times 0.078 \times \frac{90}{360} = \$1,950,000$$

The short position in September contracts will lock in a rate of 7.9% for a period of 90 days from September to December. This corresponds to an interest expense of:

$$100,000,000 \times 0.079 \times \frac{90}{360} = \$1,975,000$$

Similarly a short position in 100 December contracts will lock in:

$$100,000,000 \times 0.082 \times \frac{90}{360} = \$2,050,000$$

for the 90-day period from December to March.

Finally, the 100 March contracts will lock in:

$$100,000,000 \times 0.084 \times \frac{90}{360} = \$2,100,000$$

for the last quarter.

Thus the total interest payable by the bank for the one-year period is:

$$1,950,000 + 1,975,000 + 2,050,000 + 2,100,000 = \$8,075,000$$

This corresponds to an interest rate of 8.075% for the year.

Barclays Bank can now quote a fixed rate for a one-year loan to Silverline, based on this effective cost of funding, after factoring in hedging costs and a suitable profit margin.

QUESTION 193

What are strip hedges and stack hedges?

In the above example, it was assumed that Barclays Bank would use 100 futures contracts for each of the expiration months; that is, September, December and March. Such a hedge, where the same number of contracts for each maturity are used at the outset, is called a *strip hedge*.

In practice, when the maturity of a contract is very far away, the market may be very illiquid and may be subject to large bid–ask spreads. For instance, in the above example, when the hedge is initiated in June, it is conceivable that the March futures may be illiquid. If so, rather than starting with an equal number of September, December and March contracts, the firm may initially start with an unequal number of September and December contracts and subsequently take a position in the March contracts. Such a hedge, where the number of contracts for each maturity is not equal, is called a *stack hedge*. We will illustrate it with the help of an example.

Example of a stack hedge

Let us assume that the March futures contracts are perceived to be illiquid when the hedge is initiated on June 15. The bank may therefore decide to hedge using 100 September contracts and 200 December contracts. The September contracts will lock in a rate for September. Out of the 200 December contracts, 100 are intended to lock in a rate for December. The remaining 100 December contracts are meant for hedging the March exposure. On September 15, the bank may decide to go short in March futures, if we assume that the March contracts have begun to be actively traded by then. If so, out of the 200 December contracts, 100 will be offset by going long in December futures and a short position will be taken in 100 March contracts.

QUESTION 194

Which would be better from the lender's perspective, a stack hedge or a strip hedge?

The performance of the stack hedge vis a vis the strip hedge would depend on the movement of interest rates between June and September.

Case A: The stack hedge is equivalent to the strip

Consider the case where the December futures price moves from 92.8 to 92.5 between June and September, while the March futures price moves from 92.6 to 92.3.

When the 100 extra December contracts are liquidated in September, the profit from the position will be:

$$100,000,000 \times \left(\frac{92.8 - 92.5}{100} \right) \times \frac{90}{360}$$

$$= \$75,000$$

The 100 March contracts which the bank will enter into at 92.3 will lock in an interest expense of:

$$100,000,000 \times 0.087 \times \frac{90}{360} = \$2,175,000$$

The effective interest expense for the last quarter is therefore:

$$2,175,000 - 75,000 = \$2,100,000$$

which is the same as that in the case of the strip hedge.

In other words, if the implicit yield for a three-month Eurodollar loan to be made in December, as contained in the December futures price, changes by the same magnitude as the yield for a three-month ED loan to be made in March, as contained in the March futures price, then the strip and stack hedges will be equivalent. In interest rate parlance, we say that there has been a *parallel shift* in the *yield curve*.

Case B: The strip outperforms

If the increase in the December yield is less than the increase in the March yield, then the strip hedge will outperform the stack.

Let us assume that the December futures price moves to 92.5, while the March futures price moves from 92.6 to 92.1.

The profit gotten by offsetting the extra December contracts will be the same, namely \$75,000. But the interest expense for the last quarter is now:

$$100,000,000 \times 0.089 \times \frac{90}{360} = \$2,225,000$$

The effective interest is:

$$2,225,000 - 75,000 = \$2,150,000$$

which is greater than the amount of 2,100,000 that was locked in by the strip hedge.

The same would be true if the decrease in the December yield were to be more than the decrease in the March yield. For instance, assume that the December futures price moves to 93.1, whereas the March futures price moves to 92.8.

The profit from the December position will be:

$$100,000,000 \times \left(\frac{92.8 - 93.1}{100} \right) \times \frac{90}{360}$$
$$= \$(75,000)$$

The interest expense for the last quarter will be:

$$100,000,000 \times 0.082 \times \frac{90}{360} = \$2,050,000$$

The effective interest is:

$$2,050,000 + 75,000 = \$2,125,000$$

which is greater than the amount of 2,100,000 that was locked in by the strip hedge.

Case C: The stack outperforms

If the increase in the yield for the nearby month is more than in the yield for the distant month, then the stack hedge will outperform the strip.

Let us assume that the December futures price moves from 92.80 to 92.50, while the March futures price moves from 92.6 to 92.5.

The effective interest rate for the last quarter is:

$$100,000,000 \times 0.085 \times \frac{90}{360} - 75,000$$
$$= 2,125,000 - 75,000$$
$$= \$2,050,000$$

The same would be true if the decrease in the December yield were to be less than the decrease in the March yield. For instance, assume that the December futures price moves to 93.1, whereas the March futures price moves to 93.3.

The profit from the December position will be:

$$100,000,000 \times \left(\frac{92.8 - 93.1}{100} \right) \times \frac{90}{360}$$
$$= \$(75,000)$$

The interest expense for the last quarter will be:

$$100,000,000 \times 0.077 \times \frac{90}{360} = \$1,925,000$$

The effective interest is:

$$1,925,000 + 75,000 = \$2,000,000$$

which is less than the amount of 2,100,000 that was locked in by the strip hedge.

QUESTION 195

What is the TED spread?

A Treasury Bill–Eurodollar spread or TED spread refers to the strategy of holding opposite positions in T-bill and ED futures contracts expiring in the same month.

A person who is long in T-bill futures and short in ED futures is said to be *long the TED spread*, whereas a person who is short in T-bill futures and long in ED futures is said to be *short the TED spread*.

The TED spread = T-bill futures price – ED futures price
= (100 – Implied T-bill rate) – (100 – Implied ED rate)
= Implied ED rate – Implied T-bill rate

If a speculator expects the yield spread between T-bills and Eurodollar deposits to widen, then he will go long the TED spread. If the spread does indeed widen, then he will make a profit, as the following example demonstrates.

Example I

Let us assume that on June 15, the December T-bill futures contract is priced at 91.7, while the ED futures contract is priced at 91.3:

The TED spread = 91.7 − 91.3 = 0.4 ≡ 40 b.p.

Let us assume that on 15 August the T-bill futures are priced at 91.5, while the ED futures are priced at 91.

The TED spread = 91.5 − 91 ≡ 50 b.p.

Profit from the T-bill futures is:

$$1{,}000{,}000 \times \frac{(91.5 - 91.7)}{100} \times \frac{90}{360}$$
$$= \$(500)$$

Profit from the ED futures is:

$$1{,}000{,}000 \times \frac{(91.3 - 91)}{100} \times \frac{90}{360}$$
$$= \$750$$

The effective profit = 750 − 500 = $250.

This amount of 250 represents a widening of 10 b.p. in the TED spread.

$$1{,}000{,}000 \times \frac{\Delta\delta}{100} \times \frac{90}{360} = 250$$
$$\Rightarrow \Delta\delta = 0.10.$$

On the other hand, if the speculator expects the TED spread to narrow, he would go short the TED spread.

Example II

Let us assume that on August 15, the T-bill futures are priced at 91.5, whereas the ED futures are priced at 91.2.

The TED spread = 91.5 − 91.2 = 0.3 ≡ 30 b.p.

For a person who is short the TED spread, the profit from the T-bill futures position is:

$$1{,}000{,}000 \times \frac{(91.7 - 91.5)}{100} \times \frac{90}{360}$$
$$= \$500$$

And the profit from the ED futures is:

$$1,000,000 \times \frac{(91.2 - 91.3)}{100} \times \frac{90}{360}$$

$$= \$(250)$$

The effective profit = 500 − 250 = $250, which represents a narrowing of 10 b.p. in the spread.

QUESTION 196

How is the duration of a bond important for hedging the value of a bond?

It can be shown that the hedge ratio for a bond portfolio with a duration of D_h is given by:

$$CF_{CTD} \times \frac{D_h \times P_h \times (1 + \frac{y_{CTD}}{2})}{D_{CTD} \times P_{CTD} \times (1 + \frac{y_h}{2})}$$

where P_h and P_{CTD} are the prices of the portfolio and the cheapest to deliver bond respectively; D_h and D_{CTD} are their respective durations; CF_{CTD} is the conversion factor of the cheapest to deliver bond; and y_h and y_{CTD} are the YTMs of the portfolio and the cheapest to deliver bond respectively.

The required number of futures contracts is:

$$\frac{\text{Face value of spot exposure}}{\text{Face value of the bond underlying the futures contract}} \times h$$

Example

Assume that today is August 7 2001. September futures contracts expire on September 30. The cheapest to deliver bond has been determined to be a 7% coupon bond maturing on October 15, 2028. Its quoted price is 79-26, which corresponds to a YTM of 9% per annum, and the conversion factor is 1.1329. The quoted futures price is 70-16.

Consider a portfolio manager who is holding 10,000 IBM bonds maturing on August 7, 2026. The face value is $100, the coupon rate is 12% per annum and the YTM is 10% per annum. The manager plans to sell the bonds on September 30 and wants to protect himself against an increase in the yield, using T-bond futures contracts.

The duration of the CTD bond on August 7 is 10.6866 years. The dirty price is 81.9724. The price of the IBM bonds is $118.2559 and the corresponding duration is 9.3570 years.

The hedge ratio is therefore:

$$1.1329 \times \frac{(9.3570 \times 118.2559 \times 1.045)}{(10.6866 \times 81.9724 \times 1.05)} = 1.4242$$

Let us assume that the YTM of the IBM bonds on September 30 is 11% per annum, and that the YTM of the CTD bond is 10%. The price of the IBM bond will therefore be 110.1837 and the futures price will be 63.6747. If the yield had remained at 10%, the dirty price of IBM would have been $119.9615.

The loss from the spot market is:

$$10,000 \times (110.1837 - 119.9615) = \$(97,778)$$

The profit from the futures market is:

$$10,000 \times 1.4242 \times (70.50 - 63.6747) = \$97,205.9226$$

The net profit = 97,205.9226 − 97,778 = $(572.0774)

The percentage of the loss in the spot market that is covered by the futures market = $\dfrac{97,205.9226}{97,778} \equiv 99.41\%.$

QUESTION 197

How can T-bond futures contracts be used to change the duration of a portfolio of bonds?

Consider a portfolio which currently has a duration of D_h. Let D_T denote the target duration, or in other words the duration that we wish to achieve. Let D_{CTD} be the current duration of the cheapest to deliver bond. It can be shown that:

$$h = \frac{(D_T - D_h) \times P_h \times (1 + \frac{y_{CTD}}{2})}{D_{CTD} \times P_{CTD} \times (1 + \frac{y_h}{2})} \times CF_{CTD}$$

The required number of futures contracts is:

$$\frac{\text{Face value of spot exposure}}{\text{Face value of the bond underlying the futures contract}} \times h$$

Obviously to increase the duration we would need to go long in futures contracts, that is $h > 0$, whereas to decrease the duration we would need to go short in futures, that is $h < 0$.

We will illustrate the principles with the help of an example.

Example

Consider a bond with a face value of $100,000 and a current price of $90,000. The YTM is 12% per annum and the duration is 12.5 years. The CTD bond has a dirty price of $85 per $100 of face value. It has a YTM of 10% per annum, the conversion factor is 1.125, and a duration of 10 years.

Assume that we are holding 10,000 bonds. If we want to decrease the duration of our portfolio from 12.5 to 8 years, how many futures contracts do we require?

$$h = \frac{(8 - 12.50) \times 90,000 \times (1 + 0.05)}{10 \times 85,000 \times (1 + 0.06)} \times 1.125$$

$$= -0.5310$$

For 10,000 bonds, we would need to go short in 5,310 futures contracts.

QUESTION 198

What is "covered interest arbitrage?"

Cash and carry and reverse cash and carry arbitrage strategies using foreign exchange forward/futures contracts are known as covered interest arbitrage strategies. The following examples will illustrate the mechanics.

Cash and carry covered interest arbitrage

Consider the following information. The spot rate for Singapore dollars is $0.5275 and the three-month outright forward rate is $0.5575.

The rate of interest applicable for a three-month loan in Singapore is 7.5% on an annualized basis, while the rate for the same period in the U.S. is 4.5% on an annualized basis.

Let us consider the following strategy. Borrow $0.5275 and buy one Singapore dollar in the spot market. This can be immediately invested in Singapore to yield:

$$\left(1 + \frac{0.075}{4}\right) = \text{SGD } 1.01875$$

after three months. Simultaneously, at the outset, go short in a forward contract to sell SGD 1.01875.

After three months, when your deposit in Singapore matures, you can sell the proceeds under the forward contract and will receive $0.5575 \times 1.01875 = \$0.5680$. Out of this you can use

$0.5275 \times \left(1 + \frac{0.045}{4}\right) = \$0.5334$, to pay off your loan in the U.S. The

balance, $0.5680 - 0.5334 = \$0.0346$, is a pure arbitrage profit.

Covered interest reverse cash and carry arbitrage

Let us assume that all the other variables have the same values as in the above example, except the forward rate, which we will assume is $0.5025. The cash and carry strategy will not yield profits as you can verify, but the following strategy will pay off.

Borrow one Singapore dollar and convert it into U.S. dollars. You will get $0.5275. Lend this money out at 4.5%. After three months you are assured a sum of $0.5334. At the outset, go long in a forward

contract to buy $\left(1 + \frac{0.075}{4}\right) = 1.01875$ Singapore dollars after three

months. This will cost you $0.5025 \times 1.01875 = \$0.5119$. At the end of three months, you can take delivery under the forward contract and pay off your loan in Singapore. The balance, of $\$0.5334 - \$0.5119 = \$0.0215$, is a pure arbitrage profit.

If we denote the spot rate as S, the forward rate as F, the domestic interest rate as i_d and the foreign interest rate as i_f, then[3] the no-arbitrage condition can be expressed as:

$$S(1 + i_d) = F(1 + i_f)$$

$$\Rightarrow F = S \times \frac{(1 + i_d)}{(1 + i_f)}$$

---

3. In this case, the U.S. interest rate is the domestic rate and the Singapore interest rate is the foreign rate.

The kind of arbitrage that we have illustrated above is called *covered interest arbitrage* and the relationship:

$$\frac{F}{S} = \frac{(1 + i_d)}{(1 + i_f)}$$

is called the *interest rate parity* equation.

$$\frac{F}{S} = \frac{(1 + i_d)}{(1 + i_f)} \Rightarrow \frac{(F - S)}{S} = \frac{(i_d - i_f)}{(1 + i_f)}$$

In practice, this is often approximated as:

$$\frac{(F - S)}{S} = (i_d - i_f)$$

because $1 + i_f \cong 1$, if i_f is very small.

In practice, however, there could be deviations from the interest rate parity relationship, which would-be arbitrageurs are unable to exploit. The reasons could be many. Firstly, in real life, buying and selling foreign exchange either in the spot or the forward markets entails the payment of transaction costs. Secondly, not all countries permit the free flow of capital across borders. Thus, if governments impose exchange control, one may observe deviations from interest rate parity that cannot be arbitraged away. In practice, even a perception that exchange rate controls may be imposed in a country in the future can be adequate to preclude investors from attempting to arbitrage away perceived deviations. Finally, in the real world, investors have to pay taxes on income and profits, which vary from country to country. Thus, an investor's ability to make arbitrage profits on a post-tax basis could depend on his tax status.

QUESTION 199

How can foreign exchange futures contracts be used to hedge an export transaction?

Assume that today is June 21, 20XX. Eli Lilly has exported a consignment of anti-depression drugs to a company in Zurich and is scheduled to receive 25MM Swiss francs, after two months. The company is worried that the dollar will appreciate by then and therefore decides to hedge using September futures contracts. Since the company will be selling the Swiss francs on receipt, it requires a short hedge[4]. Since each Swiss franc futures contract is for 125,000 CHF, 200 contracts are required. We will assume that the price of the September contract on June 21 is 0.5150 USD/CHF.

On August 20, assume that the following prices prevail in the market. Spot: 0.4985 USD/CHF
September futures: 0.5025 USD/CHF.
If Eli Lilly had not hedged, it would have received:

$$25,000,000 \times 0.4985 = USD\ 12,462,500$$

On the other hand, since it has hedged using the futures contracts, the payoff would be as follows. The profit/loss from the futures market is:

$$200 \times 125,000 \times (0.5150 - 0.5025) = USD\ 312,500$$

Therefore, the total proceeds are:

$$12,462,500 + 312,500 = USD\ 12,775,000$$

The effective exchange rate is:

$$\frac{12,775,000}{25,000,000} = 0.5110\ USD/CHF$$

QUESTION 200

How can foreign exchange futures contracts be used to hedge an import transaction?

American Airlines has ordered spare parts for its aircraft from Rolls Royce, U.K. The total cost is GBP 4MM and the payment is due one month from today. Let us assume that we are standing on August 1, 20XX. The company is worried that the dollar will depreciate, which means that the cost in dollars will go up. Since it will be buying British pounds, the appropriate hedge, if it decides to hedge, is a long hedge.

The following prices (Table 7.3) are observable on 1 August.

Let us assume that the following rates (Table 7.4) prevail on September 1.

If the company does not hedge, then it would have to purchase 4MM GBP at 1.4220, leading to a total outflow of USD 5,688,000.

---

4. The logic is that if the dollar appreciates, the dollar price of Swiss francs will fall and consequently the short hedger will gain.

Table 7.3   Prices on August 1

	Bid	Ask
Spot	1.4025	1.4075
Sep futures	1.4120	1.4190

Table 7.4   Prices on September 1

	Bid	Ask
Spot	1.4150	1.4220
Sep futures	1.4250	1.4335

However, if it had hedged, its effective cost can be calculated as follows. The appropriate number of futures contracts required is:

$$\frac{4,000,000}{62,500} = 64$$

The profit/loss from the futures market is:

$$62,500 \times 64 \times (1.4250 - 1.4190) = USD\ 24,000$$

The effective cost = 5,688,000 − 24,000 = USD 5,664,000 and the effective exchange rate is:

$$\frac{5,664,000}{4,000,000} = 1.4160\ USD/GBP$$

Test your concepts

The answers are provided on page 241.

1. The TED spread will always be:
   (a) Greater than zero
   (b) Less than zero
   (c) Equal to zero
   (d) Cannot say.

2. A hedge which uses a different number of futures contracts for each maturity that is being hedged is called:
   (a) A rolling hedge
   (b) A stack hedge
   (c) A strip hedge
   (d) None of the above.

3. If there is a parallel shift in the yield curve, the following statement will be true:
   (a) The strip hedge will outperform the stack
   (b) The stack hedge will outperform the strip
   (c) The performance of the two will be equal
   (d) Cannot say.

4. A party which has exported goods and expects to be paid in foreign exchange will need to take:
   (a) A short position in forward contracts
   (b) A short position in futures contracts
   (c) A long position in futures contracts
   (d) (a) or (b).

5. A party which has exported goods and expects to be paid in domestic currency will need to take:
   (a) A short position in forward contracts
   (b) A short position in futures contracts
   (c) A long position in futures contracts
   (d) None of the above.

6. Portfolio insurance imposes:
   (a) A floor on the rate of return from the portfolio
   (b) A ceiling on the rate of return from the portfolio
   (c) Both a floor as well as a ceiling on the rate of return from the portfolio
   (d) Neither a floor nor a ceiling on the rate of return from a portfolio.

7. If a stock is underpriced:
   (a) The excess return will be positive
   (b) The abnormal return will be positive
   (c) The abnormal return will be negative
   (d) None of the above.

8. Program trading is a term used for:
   (a) Cash and carry index arbitrage
   (b) Reverse cash and carry index arbitrage
   (c) Both (a) and (b)
   (d) (Neither (a) nor (b).

9. Which of these is true from the standpoint of locking in an interest rate using futures contracts?
   (a) Borrowers require short hedges
   (b) Lenders require long hedges
   (c) Both (a) and (b)
   (d) None of the above.

10. If the domestic interest rate is equal to the foreign interest rate, then in the case of a forward contract on a foreign currency:
    (a) The forward rate will be equal to the spot rate
    (b) The forward rate will be greater than the spot rate
    (c) The forward rate will be less than the spot rate
    (d) Cannot say.

SOLUTIONS TO TEST YOUR CONCEPTS

Q. No.	Ch. 1	Ch. 2	Ch. 3	Ch. 4	Ch. 5	Ch. 7
1	d	d	d	d	c	a
2	a	c	d	a	c	b
3	d	d	b	d	c	c
4	d	c	d	a	d	d
5	b	a	b	d	c	d
6	d	c	d	d	c	a
7	d	b	c	d	d	b
8	c	d	b	d	b	c
9	d	d	c	d	c	c
10	d	b	c	c	c	a

APPENDIX A

MAJOR DERIVATIVE EXCHANGES

ASIA AND OCEANIA

- **Central Japan Commodity Exchange**

  Address

  3-2-15, Nishiki, Naka-ku
  Nagoya, Aichi 460-0003
  Japan
  Phone: 52-951-2172
  website: www.c-com.or.jp

- **Dalian Commodity Exchange**

  Address

  No. 18 Huizhan Road
  Dalian – 116023
  China
  Phone: 086-411-84808888
  website: www.dce.com.cn

- **Hong Kong Exchange**

  Address

  12/F One International Finance Center, 1 Harbor View Street,
  Central
  Hong Kong
  Phone: 2522-1122
  website: www.hkex.com.hk

- **Korea Exchange**

  Address

  600-015 50, Jungang-dong 5-Ga, Joong-gu
  Busan
  South Korea
  Phone: 82-51-662-2000
  website: www.krx.co.kr

- **National Stock Exchange of India**

  Address

  Exchange Plaza
  Plot No. C/1, G Block
  Bandra-Kurla Complex
  Bandra (E)
  Mumbai – 400051
  India
  Phone: 22-26598100
  website: www.nse-india.com

- **Singapore Exchange**

  Address

  2 Shenton Way
  #19-00 SGX Center 1
  Singapore 068804
  Phone: 6236-8888
  website: www.sgx.com

- **Australian Securities Exchange**

  Address

  Exchange Center
  20 Bridge Street
  Sydney, NSW 2000
  Australia
  Phone: 2-9338-0000
  website: www.asx.com.au

- **Bombay Stock Exchange Limited, Mumbai**

  Address

  Phiroze Jeejeebhoy Towers
  Dalal Street
  Mumbai – 400001
  India
  Phone: 22-22721233
  website: www.bseindia.com

- **The Tokyo Commodity Exchange**

  Address

  10-7 Nihonbashi Horidomecho 1-Chome, Chuo-ku
  Tokyo 103-0012
  Japan
  Phone: 3-3664-0089
  website: www.tocom.or.jp

- **Taiwan Futures Exchange**

  Address

  14th Floor
  100 Roosevelt Road
  Sec. 2 Taipei 100
  Taiwan
  Phone: 02-2369-5678
  website: www.taifex.com.tw

- **Tokyo Financial Exchange**

  Address

  Ichiban-cho Tokyu Building
  21 Ichiban-cho, Chiyoda-ku
  Tokyo 102-0082
  Japan
  Phone: 3-3514-2400
  website: www.tfx.co.jp

EUROPE & U.K

- **EUREX**

  Address

  Eurex Frankfurt AG
  Neue Börsenstrasse 1
  60487 Frankfurt/Main
  Germany
  Phone: 69-211-11700
  website: www.eurexchange.com

- **Euronext.liffe**

  London Address

  Cannon Bridge House
  1 Cousin Lane
  London EC4R 3XX
  U.K.
  Phone: 20-7623-0444
  website: www.euronext.com

  Paris Address

  39 rue Cambon
  75039 Paris Cedex 1
  France
  Phone: 1-4927-1000

- **The London Metal Exchange**

  Address

  56 Leadenhall Street
  London EC3A 2DX
  U.K.
  Phone: 20-7264-5555
  website: www.lme.co.uk

- **OMX The Nordic Exchange**

  Address

  SE-105 78
  Stockholm
  Sweden
  Phone: 8-405-6000
  website: www.omxgroup.com/nordicexchange

AFRICA AND THE MIDDLE EAST

- **South African Futures Exchange**

  Address

  One Exchange Square
  Gwen Lane, Sandown, 2196
  Johannesberg
  R.S.A.
  Phone: 011-520-7000
  website: www.safex.co.za

- **The Tel Aviv Stock Exchange**

  Address

  54 Ahad Ha'am Street
  Tel Aviv
  Israel
  Phone: 3-5677411
  website: www.tase.co.il

NORTH AMERICA

- **American Stock Exchange**

  Address

  86 Trinity Place
  New York, NY 10006
  U.S.A.
  Phone: 212-306-1000
  website: www.amex.com

- **Chicago Board Options Exchange**

  Address

  400 South LaSalle Street
  Chicago, Illinois 60605
  U.S.A.
  Phone: 1-877-THE-CBOE
  website: www.cboe.com

- **Chicago Board of Trade**

  Address

  141 West Jackson Boulevard
  Chicago, Illinois 60604-2994
  U.S.A.
  Phone: 312-435-3500
  website: www.cbot.com

- **Chicago Mercantile Exchange**

  Address

  20 South Wacker Drive
  Chicago, Illinois 60606
  U.S.A.
  Phone: 312-930-1000
  website: www.cme.com

- **International Securities Exchange**

  Address

  60 Broad Street
  New York, NY 10004
  U.S.A.
  Phone: 212-943-2400
  website: www.iseoptions.com

- **Mercado Mexicano de Derivados
  (Mexican Derivatives Exchange)**

  Address

  Paseo de la Reforma 255, Piso de Remates
  Col. Cuauhtemoc
  Mexico D.F 06500
  Phone: 5255-5726-6600
  website: www.mexder.com.mx

- New York Mercantile Exchange

  Address

  World Financial Center
  One North End Avenue
  New York, NY 10282-1101
  U.S.A.
  Phone: 212-299-2000
  website: www.nymex.com

- Philadelphia Stock Exchange

  Address

  1900 Market Street
  Philadelphia, PA 19103
  U.S.A.
  Phone: 215-496-5000
  website: www.phlx.com

SOUTH AMERICA

- Bolsa de Mercadorias & Futuros (BM & F) –
  Brazilian Mercantile & Futures Exchange

  Address

  Praca Antonio Prado, 48
  Cep: 01010-901-Sao Paulo-SP
  Brazil
  Phone: 11-3119-2000
  website: www.bmf.com.br

- BOVESPA

  Address

  Rue XV de Novembro, 275
  01013-001-Sao Paulo-SP
  P.O. Box 3456
  Brazil
  Phone: 5511-3233-2000
  website: www.bovespa.com.br

REFERENCES

CHAPTER 1

1. Edwards, F.R. and C.W. Ma, *Futures and Options*, McGraw Hill Inc., 1992.
2. Harris, L., *Trading and Exchanges: Market Microstructure for Practitioners*, Oxford University Press, 2003.
3. Linsmeier, T.J. and N.D. Pearson, "Value at Risk", *Financial Analysts Journal* (March/April 2000).
4. Lofton, T., *Getting Started in Futures*, John Wiley, 1993.
5. Resnick, B.G, *The Globalization of World Financial Markets*, In P.L. Cooley (ed.), *Advances in Business Financial Management*, The Dryden Press, 1996.

Websites

- www.bba.org.uk

CHAPTER 2

1. Hull, J., *Fundamentals of Futures and Options Markets*, Prentice Hall, 2004.
2. Siegel, D.R. and D.F. Siegel, *The Futures Markets*, Irwin, 1994.

CHAPTER 3

1. Koontz, S.R. and W.D. Purcell, *Agricultural Futures and Options*: *Principles and Strategies*, Prentice Hall, 1999.

CHAPTER 4

1. Harris, L., *Trading and Exchanges*, Oxford University Press, 2003.
2. McInish, T.H., *Capital Markets: A Global Perspective*, Blackwell, 2000.
3. Sarkar A., and Tozzi M., "Electronic Trading on Futures Exchanges," *Derivatives Quarterly* (1998).

CHAPTER 6

1. Burghardt, G. "FIA Annual Volume Survey: Volume Growth Accelerates." Futures Industry Magazine, March-April 2007.

Websites

- www.cbot.com
- www.cme.com
- www.futuresindustry.org

CHAPTER 7

1. Kolb, R.W., *Futures, Options, & Swaps*, Blackwell Publishers, 2000.
2. Parameswaran, S., *Futures Markets; Theory and Practice*, Tata McGraw-Hill, 2003.
3. Siegel, D.R. and D.F., Siegel *Futures Markets*, The Dryden Press, 1990.

INDEX

Clean price 171–173, 200, 202
Clearing margin 12, 37
Clearing member 27
Clearinghouse 10–13, 15, 18–20, 27, 34, 36, 38
Commitment contracts 2
Consumption asset 59, 61
Contango 67, 68, 74–79, 95, 109
Contingent contracts 3
Convenience asset 60, 66
Convenience value 59–61, 66, 77, 79
Conversion factor 195–197, 199, 200, 202, 231, 233
Coupon rate 161, 163–165, 167, 173, 231
Covered interest arbitrage 233, 235
Covering the short position 50
Cross hedging 94
Cross-rate futures 189
Cum-dividend 134–136, 173
Currency equivalent of a point 190
Currency swaps 7

D

Day order 112, 126, 132
Declaration date 134
Deep-discount brokers 43
Delivery adjusted spot price 32, 33
Delivery price 63, 64
Direct quotes 180
Dirty price 170–173, 232, 233
Discount bonds 169, 199
Discount brokers 43
Distribution date 135
Dividend risk 68
Divisor 143–150, 153–155, 212
Dow Jones Industrial Average 156, 157, 194, 203
Downtick 54
Duration 126, 160, 173–175, 200, 231–233

E

Edwards and Ma 19
E-mini contracts 188, 203
Equally weighted index 150–153
Eurodollar futures 185, 192, 198, 218, 220, 222, 224
Eurodollars
European options 4
European terms 180
Euroyen futures 192–193
Exchange for physicals (EFP) 37
Ex-dividend date 134, 140, 172, 182
Exercise price 4–5, 22–26, 28, 43, 84–87, 106, 203–204
Expiration date 4, 10, 30, 64, 92–95, 98–100, 109, 190, 217

F

Federal funds 179, 197
Federal Reserve 42, 179
Financing risk 68, 79
Floor time preference 128, 129, 131
Foreign exchange futures 186, 188, 235, 236
Forward price 47, 63–65
Full carry 66, 68, 78, 79
Full service brokers 43
Futures Commission Merchant (FCM) 27
Futures options 203, 205

G

Gambling 103
Good-on-sight orders 127
Good-till-canceled order 126, 127, 132
Good-till-days order 126
Good-this-month orders 127
Good-this-week orders 127
Gross margining 19